Les
Parfums
de
Rosine

La rose de Rosine

Parfum de Rosine

PAUL POIRET

FASHION IS A FEAST

PAUL POIRET FASHION IS A FEAST

Edited by
**MARIE-SOPHIE CARRON
DE LA CARRIERE**

Musée des Arts Décoratifs

T&H

In 1986, the Union Centrale des Arts Décoratifs, the ancestor of our Musée des Arts décoratifs, together with the Union Française des Arts du Costume, founded a fashion museum called the Musée des Arts de la Mode, whose first exhibition at the Pavillon de Marsan, 'Moments de mode', with photography by David Seidner, went on to become a landmark. In the same year, the curator responsible for this event, Yvonne Deslandres, published a monograph on Paul Poiret, with a cover featuring a close-up photograph of the rose from the iconic *Joséphine* gown. In it, she wrote: 'Few clothes designers have earned a rightful place in the history of costume, as opposed to the history of fashion. Paul Poiret, the unwitting inventor of twentieth-century woman, deserves this honour because of his abundant gifts, the high quality of his work and the generosity with which he lavished his many innovations on his contemporaries, not only in his own field but in every creative sphere.' What could be more natural, then, to devote an exhibition to him at the Musée des Arts décoratifs?

Like an artist of the Renaissance, Paul Poiret placed no boundaries on his knowledge, his fields of expression or his innovations. So much so, in fact, that Elsa Schiaparelli, celebrated by our institution in 2022, called him 'the Leonardo of fashion'. He was undeniably a couturier, but he was also an interior designer, a perfumer, a party host, an entrepreneur, a gourmet and a painter. To that list, Léon-Paul Fargue would add bird-tamer and talented teller of the tales of La Fontaine. Although an innovator, Poiret was nonetheless part of a long chain of designers that the Musée intends to celebrate and promote, in accordance with its founding mission that remains an ongoing driving force. To break away from the S-shaped silhouette that dominated in the late 19th century and free women from the tyranny of the corset, he took inspiration from the lightweight gowns of the Directory and Empire periods: in this way, he made contemporary fashion seem young and new while drawing on sources that were over a hundred years old. A century later, other designers looked back on him in their turn, taking inspiration, paying homage, creating new twists on his work, ranging from famous figures like Jean Paul Gaultier and John Galliano, to up-and-coming names like Alphonse Maitrepierre. In these pages, Christian Lacroix, whom I would like to thank for his extraordinary portrait of Paul Poiret, pays him a personal and emotional tribute, telling of his surprise, as a child, on finding a Poiret outfit in a frieze illustrating the history of fashion – a tunic decorated with stylized flowers and edged with fur, over a long pleated skirt.

The lively and imaginative design of this catalogue, created by the talented Anette Lenz and echoing her graphics for the exhibition, throws a contemporary light on Poiret's art. It emphasizes the details of the clothes, brings the vintage photography to life, and sets off the informative historical essays. We hope that the exhibition and this book will fill visitors and readers with admiration and surprise, as well as joy and inspiration.

Lionel Sauvage *President, Les Arts Décoratifs*

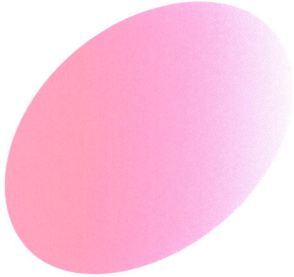

'Poiret came and shook everything up.' Was Christian Dior thinking of Boileau's *L'Art poétique* when he wrote these words? 'Then came Malherbe, and in France became the first / To allow a clear cadence to be felt in verse.' Poiret's cadence is the polar opposite of that of the illustrious poet, yet like him, he set the rhythm of a new modernity. It matched the flowing dances of Isadora Duncan, softened the female silhouette, sometimes adorning women with a feathered turban, other times with a long coat falling like a chapan. Such flights of fancy inspired many superlatives. Poiret was called 'magnificent', 'flamboyant', a 'sultan', a 'pasha', a 'maharaja'... The Americans crowned him the 'King of Fashion'. But fashion was only one facet of his enchantments. He thought of himself as 'an artist, not a couturier'.

Fascinated as a child by the illuminated fountains at the 1889 Universal Exhibition in Paris, Poiret seemed to wander through life in a state of childlike exhilaration. This state gave him all kinds of freedom and allowed him to pursue any whim. In every creative field, he went where his imagination took him, working with an innate sense of form and format. 'Poiret entertains himself and entertains Paris,' said Maurice Sachs, himself entertained. Poiret transformed fashion, making it fun and free, and asked Paul Iribe and Georges Lepape to celebrate it in their illustrations. His models paraded through his home at 107 Faubourg Saint-Honoré, and followed him faithfully as far as Russia and the USA. Young women with no artistic training were allowed to give their spontaneity free rein at the school he founded to revitalize the art of decoration. A painter himself, Poiret knew and collected Derain, Van Dongen, Dunoyer de Segonzac and Dufy, whose decorative creations adorned both his clothes and his interiors. An aesthete with highly developed senses, he was the first couturier to create perfumes, played the violin, and excelled at gastronomy to the point of belonging to a famous gourmet association, the Club des Cent, before being forced out by an angry dispute. Mischievous and out of pocket, he went on to form the rival Club des Purs Cent. As its president, he published a book, *107 recettes ou curiosités culinaires* ('107 recipes or culinary curiosities'), which opened with 'the salad of the new poor man', perhaps a witty homage to Boni de Castellane. No one ever knew which would win out in Poiret, the prodigy or the profligate. Parties became another object for his imagination, his whimsy and his extravagance. They included the Feast of Bacchus, the Festival of Kings, the Parakeets Ball and best known of all, the legendary Thousand and Second Night.

Anette Lenz, art director of the exhibition and its catalogue, has chosen bold colours and graphics to celebrate Poiret without resorting to pastiche. Along with Marie-Sophie Carron de la Carrière, who curated the exhibition with the invaluable assistance of Marie-Pierre Ribère and Astrid Novembre, the conservation, restoration and display teams played a key role in getting the garments ready to be photographed and exhibited.

The collections of the Union Française des Arts du Costume, combined with those of the Musée des Arts décoratifs, lend themselves well to this joyful celebration. Outfits donated to the collection by Denise Boulet-Poiret in the 1960s stand alongside more recent acquisitions such as the beautiful *Reine reflets* gown, generously acquired for the museum by Krystyna Campbell-Pretty in 2024. Fashion illustrations by Victor Lhuer for Poiret, rediscovered in the archives in 2018, echo the recently unearthed registered photographs of designs, and the donations from the son of Agnès Jallat, a former Martine School girl, in 2019 and 2023.

This richness has been matched by the generosity of lenders to whom we owe a great debt of gratitude, including Agnès Mulon, Claude Bernès, Sabine Rang des Adrets, the Fondation Azzedine Alaïa, the Fundación Museo de la Moda, the Bibliothèque nationale de France, the Centre Pompidou–Musée National d'Art Moderne, The Metropolitan Museum of Art, the Mobilier National, the Musée de Grenoble, the Musée d'Orsay, and the Palais Galliera–Musée de la Mode de la Ville de Paris.

'I wanted to find excuses to keep my friends close to me': that was Poiret's reason for organizing so many parties. It's also a good reason to stage exhibitions. The Friends of the Musée des Arts Décoratifs, GRoW @ Annenberg, Krystyna Campbell-Pretty and her family, Hubert and Mireille Goldschmidt, as well as Christine and Steve Schwarzman are among these faithful friends, whom we are happy to keep, to gather, and to thank.

This exhibition is to be savored like a celebration. May it carry you away on a long and sumptuous 'Thousand and Third Night.'

Bénédicte Gady *Interim Director, Musée des Arts décoratifs*

List of authors

Marie-Sophie Carron
de la Carrière
*Chief curator of heritage
Musée des Arts décoratifs,
department of fashion and
textiles, head of collections
from 1800 to 1946*

Mary E. Davis
*Fashion historian, critic and
professor at Yale University*

Sophie Fontanel
Journalist and writer

Christian Lacroix
Couturier and designer

Marion Neveu
*Assistant curator
Musée des Arts décoratifs,
department of graphics arts,
wallpaper collection*

Astrid Novembre (A. N.)
*Exhibitions assistant
Musée des Arts décoratifs*

Christine Peltre
*Professeur emeritus of
contemporary art history at
the University of Strasbourg*

Cécile Pichon-Bonin
*Research fellow at CNRS,
LIR3S*

Éric Pujalet-Plaà
*Assistant curator
Musée des Arts décoratifs,
department of Fashion and
Textiles, collections from 1947
to the present*

Colombe Pringle
*Journalist, granddaughter of
Nicole Groult (Paul Poiret's
sister)*

Sébastien Quéquet
*Assistant curator
Musée des Arts décoratifs,
department of graphics arts,
photography collections*

Hélène Renaudin (H. R.)
*Assistant curator
Musée des Arts décoratifs,
department of Fashion and
Textiles, pre-1800 collections*

Marie-Pierre Ribère (M.-P. R.)
*Assistant curator
Musée des Arts décoratifs,
department of Fashion and
Textiles, collections from 1800
to 1946*

Olivier Saillard
*Fashion historian and director
of the Fondation Azzedine Alaïa*

The world according to Paul Poiret
Marie-Sophie Carron de la Carrière
18

Who are you, Paul Poiret?

Marie-Sophie Carron de la Carrière
26

An Oriental soul
Christine Peltre
28

Legal records of Paul Poiret's designs
Sébastien Quéquet
37

Poiret in America
Mary E. Davis
40

The 'Leonardo of fashion', Poiret by Schiaparelli
Marie-Sophie Carron de la Carrière
49

A family of artists
Paul Poiret and his sisters
Colombe Pringle
52

'She can have everything'
Denise Poiret and fashion
Sophie Fontanel
58

The Poiret style

69 *1811* evening gown
73 *Joséphine* evening gown
77 *Ispahan* coat
81 *Mosaïque* evening gown
85 *Lavallière* evening gown
89 Evening coat
93 Evening gown
97 *Flammes* shawl and culotte-dress
101 *Mélodie* dress
105 *Bretonne* dress
109 Jacket
113 Summer dress
117 *Martinique* dress
121 *Ballon* travel coat
125 *La Source* coat
129 *Marrakech* evening gown

Poiret the Magnificient
Christian Lacroix
130

The Poiret lifestyle

Marie-Sophie Carron de la Carrière
142

The Martine School
Artistic creation and educational innovation
Cécile Pichon-Bonin
144

The wallpapers of the Martine School
Marion Neveu
155

The couturier's last master strokes
Paul Poiret in the 1930s
Marie-Pierre Ribère
158

When fashion meets fragrance
Marie-Sophie Carron de la Carrière
167

From couture to gastronomy
Marie-Sophie Carron de la Carrière
171

Couturier and art collector
Marie-Sophie Carron de la Carrière
174

From Poiret to Dior
Éric Pujalet-Plaà
189

Paul Poiret in the collections of the Fondation Azzedine Alaïa
Olivier Saillard
195

After Paul Poiret
Éric Pujalet-Plaà and Marie-Pierre Ribère
200

Reference

Chronology
Marie-Sophie Carron de la Carrière and Astrid Novembre
220

Complete catalogue of works by Paul Poiret in the collection of the Musée des Arts décoratifs
228

Exhibited works
236

Bibliography
247

Index
248

Marie-Sophie Carron de la Carrière

The world according to Paul Poiret

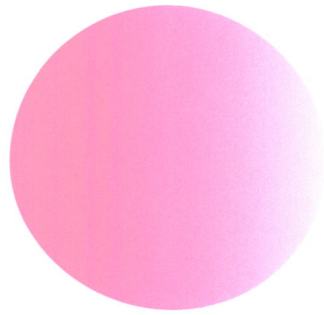

1
See the exhibition 'Couturier superstar', Paris: Musée de la Mode et du Textile, 2002.

2
Al. Terego, 'Les opinions de Monsieur Pétrone', *La Grande Revue*, May 1909, p. 147.

3
Henry Muller, afterword in Paul Poiret, *En habillant l'époque*, Paris: Grasset, 1930, reissued 2022, p. 267.

4
After the Paul Poiret brand passed through the hands of a series of different owners, the Luxembourgish company Luvanis acquired it in 2014, selling the rights the following year to the South Korean luxury group Shinsegae International. After an unsuccessful attempt to revive the fashion label in 2018, the Poiret brand launched a line of cosmetics.

5
Lucien François, *Comment un nom devient une griffe*, Paris: Gallimard, 1961, p. 22.

6
In Paris, at the Musée Jacquemart-André and the Palais Galliera; in New York, at the FIT and the Metropolitan Museum of Art; in Moscow, at the Kremlin Museum; in Tokyo, at the Fashion Foundation.

7
In 2005 (Piasa) and 2008 (Beaussant Lefèvre).

8
André Doderet, 'Ce que nous devons à Paul Poiret', *Vogue*, 1 January 1931.

9
Elsa Schiaparelli, *Shocking Life*, Paris: Denoël, 1954, p. 54.

Dubbed the great reformer of fashion by Christian Dior, Paul Poiret was celebrated among fashion designers as early as the 1950s. The retrospective of this major figure in 20th-century fashion at the Musée des Arts décoratifs in Paris consciously draws on the brilliant curator Guillaume Garnier's remarkable exhibition of the designer's work at the Palais Galliera in 1986, titled 'Paul Poiret and Nicole Groult: Masters of Art Deco Fashion'. However, that exhibition took place in a very different context. Above all, the mid-1980s was the era of famous fashion designers who were idolized, who became media superstars:[1] the 'great, majestic designer, emperor of all fashion', reigning supreme over his fashion house, was no longer an ordinary supplier who used the servants' stairs at his clients' houses.[2] It was also the era when major luxury groups began to be formed, acquiring historic labels from the 1990s onwards and looking to designers to relaunch them. Paul Poiret's label was slowly forgotten, as it was not revived by any charismatic, creative character – someone who would have known how to 'bring it to life, put their own stamp on it and inject a little magic into it through their taste, their research and their magnificent imagination'.[3]

An inventory of memory

Despite being active across a number of areas, the company founded by Paul Poiret in 1903 went bankrupt during the financial crisis of 1929 and eventually folded in 1933.[4] The global celebrity enjoyed by the designer turned out to be fleeting. Seventeen years after his death in 1944, the man who had been dubbed 'the Sun King of high fashion', already toppled from his throne during his lifetime, was spoken of as a figure belonging to a distant past: 'Nothing remains of the name Poiret apart from memory.'[5]

It was thanks to a number of museum exhibitions held between 1974 and 2011 that the name of Paul Poiret was once again inscribed in the pantheon of designers in the great fashion capitals of the world, both in the West and in Asia.[6] Each exhibition was testament to the interest that this Parisian designer, so often attracting extravagant epithets ('the Magnificent', 'the King of Fashion'), sparked around the world. In collaboration with the designer's family, two major auctions were held in Paris in the 2000s.[7] Shining a light on the wardrobe of Denise Poiret, his wife, they played their part in bringing these carefully preserved pieces of family heritage to the wider art market.

The union of fashion and art

Like a modern artistic director, Poiret discovered and collected new talents, whom he invited to collaborate on his creative projects. Foreshadowing the Art Deco movement, as defined in 1925, he embraced all the applied arts, bringing together the different disciplines, and created a new style that covered both clothing and interiors, combining all the component parts under a single label. A sensitive, knowledgeable and sensual artist, he used his gifts in a variety of contexts, from couture and stage costumes to decorative arts – furniture, textile printing, wallpaper, carpets, lighting – to interior design and perfume, as well as painting and music, teaching – through the school that he founded – and gastronomy, the only art form that, in his view, engaged all the senses. Eager to shine a light on all his diverse undertakings, he invented new forms of marketing and advertising, entrusting young artists (CAT. 198, P. 26) to create them, and held memorable costume parties. When his fashion house closed down, the press compared him to 'the great artisans of the Renaissance', writing, 'Paul Poiret was interested in all the art forms related to the one to which he dedicated himself'.[8] In her memoirs published in 1954, ten years after Poiret's death, Elsa Schiaparelli went as far as calling him a 'genius' of multiple disciplines. The designer dubbed him 'the Leonardo of fashion', likening him to that ideal Renaissance man, whose curious mind embraced all areas of knowledge.[9]

CAT.158 André Derain, *Portrait of Paul Poiret*, 1915, oil on canvas.
Grenoble, Musée de Grenoble

10
Poiret, *En habillant l'époque*,
p. 59.

The support and collaboration of modern independent women

In order to put into practice his ideas for reforming and diversifying fashion, throughout his life Paul Poiret relied on a number of women, both when opening his fashion house and, later, to model his designs and spread the word about them. His mother, Louise Poiret, to whom he dedicated the book *En habillant l'époque*, lent him money to set up his fashion house in 1903: 'My mother saw in my eyes the fire of enthusiasm that leads to success; and she lent me fifty thousand francs.'[10] Earlier, it was the designer Mme Chéruit who bought some fashion sketches from the young Poiret, aged nineteen, to encourage him in his vocation. Later, he could count on the loyal patronage of actresses, such as Andrée Spinelly, who were true ambassadors for his brand both in town and on stage, and dancers, such as Nyota Inyoka, who were seeking costumes that would allow them complete freedom of movement.

However, the muse and inspiration for the designer's creative projects was none other than his wife, Denise, née Boulet. She wore her husband's designs on all occasions and was the heroine of the unforgettable parties held by the couple. Although she stepped out from her husband's shadow after their divorce in 1928, she later became a dedicated guardian of his work and, in the 1960s, donated a number of pieces from her personal wardrobe to the Union française des arts du costume, a collection managed by the Musée des Arts décoratifs. Her generosity in ensuring that Poiret's works would be remembered by posterity has therefore played an important part in realizing this monographic exhibition.

A designer but also a loving father to his five children, including three daughters, Poiret named some of his businesses after them: his interior design business (Martine), his perfume business (Rosine) and even his packaging workshop (Colin). The oldest of four siblings, he had close emotional ties to his three sisters – Germaine Bongard, Jeanne Boivin and Nicole Groult – as could be seen in the exhibition at the Palais Galliera, which brought together these four creative talents, with each sibling making a name for themselves in the worlds of fashion and jewelry design.

Finally, in 1927, when fleeing his company's financial troubles, it was with his friend Colette, one of the greatest writers of the 20th century, that Poiret briefly found consolation, realizing his long-held desire to act on stage.

From the turn of the 20th century to the late 1920s, against the backdrop of a world war and an economic crisis, these women who surrounded Poiret were representatives of a changing world, where women were gaining financial independence and breaking free from traditional expectations.

'My influence'

Paul Poiret undoubtedly laid the groundwork for a number of 20th-century fashion designers. Elsa Schiaparelli, Christian Dior and Azzedine Alaïa were the first to pay tribute to this trailblazer who, like a mentor figure, influenced many generations of contemporary designers inspired by his Orientalist cuts, his 'exotic' motifs drawn from world folklore and his use of recycled materials.

As well as clothes, the exhibition at the Musée des Arts décoratifs explores the man's extraordinary journey and colourful life, and invites viewers to share his groundbreaking visions of fashion, as being true reflections of his approach to life. Drawing on museum's rich collections, the exhibition places the couturier's designs in the context of the cultural flourishing in Paris in the first quarter of the 20th century. The name of Paul Poiret, a unique and multifaceted man with a talent for happiness and a zest for life, is reborn through this retrospective.

WHO
ARE
YOU
PAUL
POIRET?

He could turn his hand to everything:
he was a pattern maker, cutter, watercolourist,
decorator, perfumier, poet, art critic, actor,
a wonderful reciter of La Fontaine's fables,
a creator of upholstery trimmings, a ceramicist,
a bird charmer, a businessman,
a hotel manager, a wine merchant,
a theatre director, a saddler and a fortune teller
as much as a couturier.

Léon-Paul Fargue, *Portrait de famille*, 1947

Preceding double page
ILL. 7, P. 108

ILL.1 Anonymous, *Der Bart aus Nägeln* [The Beard of Nails], 1931, gelatin silver print. Mask of Paul Poiret created by Victor Goursat. Paris, Musée des Arts décoratifs

The word 'couturier' closes this delightful list of Paul Poiret's array of talents, set down in no particular order of importance by his friend the poet Léon-Paul Fargue.[1] Reflecting this extraordinary man's insatiable curiosity and the diverse range of his passions, this portrait, which may seem splintered, fragmented and incoherent, captures a character who defied classification – just as he defied all the traditional definitions of the various artistic disciplines, in particular that of a couturier, a term that first emerged in the specialist press around 1870.

It was Charles Frederick Worth, widely known as the 'Father of Haute Couture', who first established the role of a couturier in the mid-19th century. He added a label to his original creations, signing them like an artist or an author, which elevated him above the status of a mere supplier. The couturier also set his sights on new goals: introducing novelty and setting out a rhythm for the seasons.

Next came Jacques Doucet, whom Poiret started working for as an 'overawed student' in 1898.[2] The young man admired his employer's taste as an art collector, combined with his work as a designer of the 1900s. A prosperous and well-managed family business, Doucet's fashion house gave him the financial means to acquire works of art and display them in appropriate settings. Soon surpassing his mentor, Paul Poiret shook up the definition of a couturier's role, bringing together the various activities connected to creating elegant women's clothing, while remaining in step with his era.

Poiret was interested in all the artistic disciplines (theatre, textile printing, book illustration, parties, cinema, painting) and, like a 'prophet of fashion', he innovatively branched out into new business areas (furniture, decoration, perfumes, cosmetics, gastronomy). This allowed him to broaden his knowledge and his field of activity. Like a modern-day all-powerful creator, Poiret 'invented this great symbolic figure, the couturier',[3] who brought his genius to bear on all the areas connected to women's dress and appearance, as well as to marketing and brand communications. Nowadays, this is the all-encompassing conception we have of the role of artistic director, couturier or designer, a catalyst for movements in fashion and contemporary lifestyle.

Paul Poiret saw himself as a 'true Parisian'. He was born in 1879 into a middle-class family of drapers in the Les Halles quarter. By the age of thirty, he was a great couturier, reigning over the city 'where fantasies of fashion flourish, precisely because Paris is the city where the life of the senses can thrive most freely'.[4] In 1912, he developed 'a Parisian silhouette', supple and easy to move in, which would be adopted by the queens of elegance who were drawn to the great couturier's name. Seeking to allow his clients' individuality to blossom, he advised them to do away with corsets, a real instrument of torture, in favour of a 'simple sheath, beneath which their sinuous elegance, the physicality of the modern woman, is set free'.[5]

What did Paul Poiret look like? His physical appearance changed over the years. He was thin before the First World War, growing more portly after it ended. Illustrators and writers sketched his expressive face, such as his friend Jean Oberlé: 'He was fairly short, fairly pudgy, with an oval face, like an African mask, from which his light, buggy eyes stuck out. His distinctive feature was a beard cut very short, as if it was still growing. He looked a bit like a conker with its spikes, and his big, staring eyes gave him the look of a deep-sea fish.'[6] In the postscript to Poiret's memoirs, Henry Muller described his gaze as having 'a strange intensity, it could grow hard or soft'.[7] His great friend the painter André Dunoyer de Segonzac paid tribute to 'Poiret the Magnificent' after his death in 1944, composing an intimate portrait of this multifaceted figure who 'remained proud and isolated': 'His name will always be evocative of a heroic personality that is typically French, completely original, gifted with a disconcerting creative force, a force that, unfortunately, sometimes turned self-destructive.'[8] Despite his struggles, Paul Poiret brought an injection of joy into his era, through his zest for life, his love of parties, his colourful experiments and his magnificent imagination, so much so that it came to be dubbed 'the epoch of Paul Poiret' by those around him.[9]

[1] Léon-Paul Fargues, Portraits de famille (1947), Fontfroide-le-Haut: Fata Morgana, 1987, p. 114.

[2] Paul Poiret, 'En habillant l'époque', L'Art vivant, 1 February 1939, p. 28.

[3] André Calas, 'Mort oublié, il y a dix ans, aujourd'hui célébré aux U.S.A.', Samedi soir, 29 July 1954, p. 2: 'l'Amérique lui consacre actuellement une exposition à Los Angeles au County Museum.'

[4] André Doderet, 'Ce que nous devons à Paul Poiret', Vogue, 1 January 1931, pp. 50 and 80.

[5] Paul Poiret, 'Une silhouette parisienne', Le Miroir des modes, June 1912, pp. 242 and 243.

[6] Jean Oberlé, La Vie d'artiste, Paris: Éditions Denoël, 1956, p. 127.

[7] Henry Muller, postscript, in Paul Poiret, En habillant l'époque, Paris: Grasset, 2022, pp. 267–269.

[8] André Dunoyer de Segonzac, 'Une figure française Paul Poiret', Comœdia, 13 May 1944, pp. 1 and 4.

[9] Muller, in Poiret, En habillant l'époque, p. 269.

CAT.198 Germaine Krull, publicity shot for Paul Poiret, 1926, gelatin silver print. Paris, Centre Pompidou–Musée national d'art moderne–Centre de création industrielle

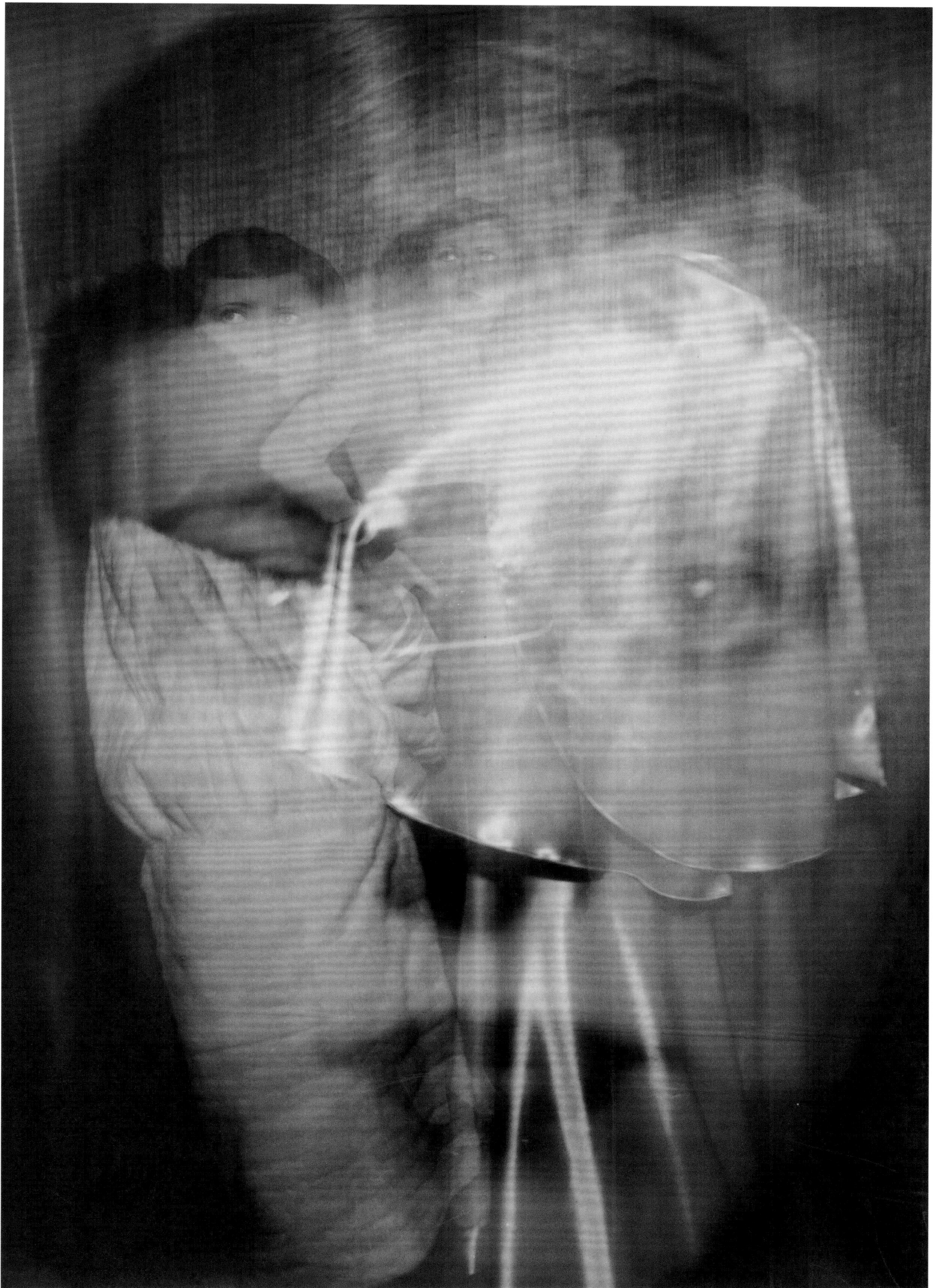

Christine Peltre

An Oriental soul

1
Apollinaire, 'La vie artistique. Albert Besnard', *L'Intransigeant*, 25 April 1912, *Œuvres en prose complètes*, Paris: Gallimard, 1991, p. 455.

2
Paul Poiret, *En habillant l'époque* (1930), Paris: Grasset, reissued 1986, p. 57. The turban as an accessory is linked to Orientalist fashions that were popular after the Egyptian campaign (1798–1801).

3
Ibid., p. 76.

4
Paul Poiret, *Revenez-y*, Paris: Gallimard, 1932, pp. 48–49.

5
M. de Mirecour, 'Les collections de la couture', *L'Art et la mode*, 28 August 1926, pp. 1182–1184.

6
Lucie Delarue-Mardrus, 'La mille et deuxième nuit chez le grand couturier', *Femina*, 1 August 1911, p. 415.

7
Poiret, *En habillant l'époque*, p. 40.

8
Unpublished, undated letter from Joseph-Charles Mardrus, quoted in Dominique Paulvé and Marion Chesnais, *Les Mille et Une Nuits et les enchantements du docteur Mardrus*, Paris: Musée du Montparnasse–Éditions Norma, 2004, p. 63.

9
Rémi Labrusse, 'Paris, capitale des arts de l'Islam? Quelques aperçus sur la formation des collections françaises d'art islamique au tournant du siècle', *Bulletin de la Société de l'histoire de l'art français*, année 1997, 1998, p. 286.

10
Poiret, *En habillant l'époque*, p. 142.

In 1912, when reviewing an exhibition of works by the painter Albert Besnard inspired by his travels around India, Apollinaire praised 'the vivacity, the picturesque, the charm that contemporary artists are obliged to seek in exotic countries because there is scarcely any remnant of the European picturesque left in the plainness and austerity of the costumes'.[1] This was already a common lament: the texture of the fabrics and the appeal of the clothes in the East inspired a craze for this world in the West, which was revived in the 19th century by the publication of collections of lithographs depicting costumes, scenes painted while travelling or the accessories shown in portraits, such as the cashmere shawls in the works of Ingres.

Paul Poiret was aware of this tradition and drew on it when, for the premiere of Jacques Richepin's *Le Minaret* in 1913 (ILL. 3), he crowned his wife's outfit with a turban – 'a style that had not been seen on a Parisian lady since Mme de Staël'[2] – most likely inspired by depictions of the writer, such as the portrait of her by François Gérard.

While this interest in the 'exotic' was still strong in the early 20th century, and while Paul Poiret was aware of older references, it was not Orientalist paintings that provided the inspiration for his designs. Although he had 'always liked painters' and 'felt he was on an equal footing with them',[3] his personal collection of paintings does not seem to feature this genre: he railed against the 'bland stew of painters seen as "bigwigs"', which included Benjamin-Constant, Georges Rochegrosse and Léon Bonnat, famous for their conventional depictions of the East, and likened the Musée du Luxembourg to 'a college for all the errors of taste, a temple to all the false gods of their time'.[4] He therefore had different sources for his 'marked penchant […] for Orientalism',[5] as highlighted by *L'Art et la mode* in 1926, which took on a new, modern expression.

The 'trace of the real'

Far from being the outflowing of a romantic dream inspired by an abstract geography, in Poiret, this 'penchant' was driven by the 'trace of the real',[6] to use the expression coined by Lucie Delarue-Mardrus when describing the 'real' characters from distant lands who were given pride of place at the 'Persian party' held by the designer in 1911. In many ways, Poiret's work was inspired by a quest for authenticity in his knowledge of Asia. He recalled his time spent studying 'modern Oriental languages, learning modern Greek, Tamil, Hindustani, Malagasy, Javanese, Arabic […]'.[7] This openness and curiosity were also clear from his interactions with figures in Paris who were ushering in a fresh approach to the East, the most prominent of whom was Joseph-Charles Mardrus (ILL. 5). Born and raised in Cairo, Mardrus studied at Saint Joseph University in Beirut, where he qualified as a doctor. He shot to fame as the author of a new translation of *The Thousand and One Nights* (1899–1904), which was imbued with greater freedom and sensuality than Antoine Galland's version published in the 18th century. In 1904, Mardrus was commissioned by the Ministry of the Colonies and the Ministry of Public Education and Fine Arts to work on a new translation of the Qur'an. He and his wife, the poet Lucie Delarue-Mardrus, travelled to Tunis, before going to Algeria to 'see […] certain holy men, Qur'an scholars and skilled commentators'.[8] *Le Koran*, 'a literal and complete translation of the essential suras by Dr J. C. Mardrus', was published in 1926, and Poiret had a copy in his library.

This intellectual and literary context fed the designer's interest in the artistic works of Eastern civilizations. Influenced by Jacques Doucet, for whom he had worked since 1898, soon becoming head tailor, he was interested in the Persian miniatures that the 1912 exhibition at the Union centrale des arts décoratifs introduced to a wider audience. Although we cannot say that 'Poiret was counted among the ranks of renowned Oriental art collectors at the time, whether because his taste, considered a little gaudy, put them off, or because the objects in his collection were not top quality',[9] his familiarity with this world is clear, as can be seen from his suggestion to a friend who was holding a party: 'I saw a fairly wide gallery and I advised her to turn it into an avenue of cypress trees taken from Persian miniatures.'[10]

The 'study trips' where he 'furnished [his] mind with precious memories and treasures' were, for Poiret, a vital aesthetic adventure: 'The principal work of a creator, during the hours when he is not creating, is precisely to decorate his mind as you decorate a house and to accumulate riches of art borrowed from museums or from all

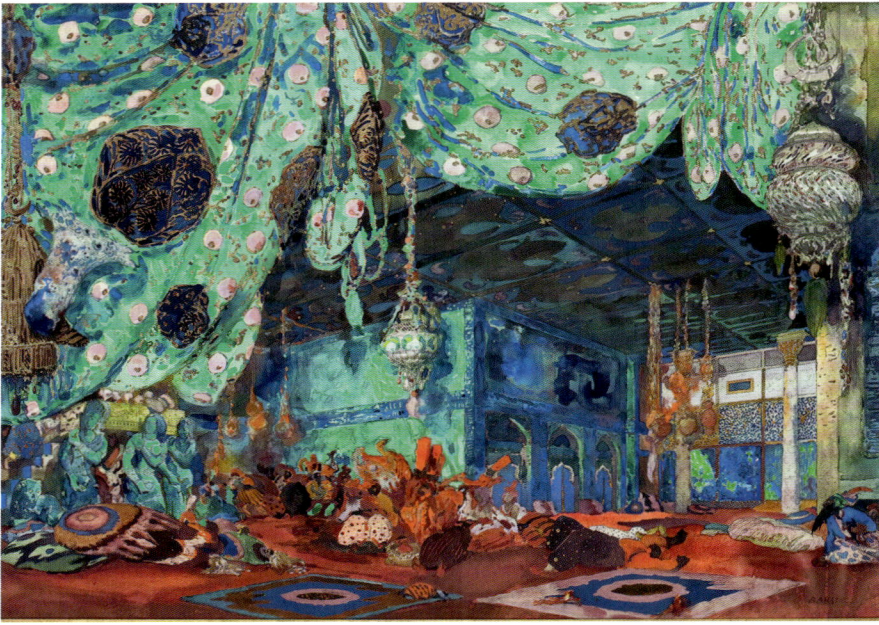

CAT.199 Léon Bakst, set design for the ballet *Shéhérazade*, 1910, graphite, watercolour, gouache and highlights in gold on vellum paper. Paris, Musée des Arts décoratifs

ILL.1 Raoul Dufy, *Moroccan Door*, 1925, gouache and watercolour on paper. Bordeaux, Musée des Beaux-Arts, inv. AM 2923 D(474)

ILL.2 André Suréda, *The Blue Pavilion*, 1923, oil on canvas. Autun, Musée Rolin, inv. H.V.233

11
Ibid., p. 125.

12
Expression by Paul Poiret that appeared on the invitation to a presentation of his designs in New York on 25 September 1913, quoted in 'Chronologie', Guillaume Garnier (ed.), *Paul Poiret et Nicole Groult. Maîtres de la mode Art déco*, exh. cat., Paris: Union Centrale des Arts décoratifs-Musée de la Mode et du Textile, 1986, p. 182.

13
Paul Poiret, *En habillant l'époque*, p. 105.

14
A letter from an anonymous correspondent published in *Revenez-y* confirmed this friendship: 'I had Jérôme and Jean Tharaud to dinner [...]; two interesting, simple young men who have a taste for the new, for character, for colour. I told them how much you enjoyed 'Les Seigneurs de Marrakech', because they remembered meeting you over there.' Poiret, *Revenez-y*, p. 202.

15
Poiret, *En habillant l'époque*, p. 171.

16
Ibid., p. 172.

17
Ibid., p. 132.

18
Ibid., p. 175.

19
See Florence Müller, 'Poiret, rencontre Orient–Occident', in *Touches d'exotisme XIVe-XXe siècles*, Paris: Musée de la Mode et du Textile, Union centrale des arts décoratifs, 1998, pp. 136–137.

20
Khémaïs Ben Lakhdar, *L'Appropriation culturelle. Histoire, domination et création: aux origines d'un pillage occidental*, Paris: Stock, 2024, p. 53.

21
Ibid.

22
Müller, 'Poiret, rencontre Orient–Occident', in *Touches d'exotisme*, p. 141.

23
Poiret, *En habillant l'époque*, pp. 17–18.

24
Ibid., p. 18.

25
Ibid., p. 75.

26
Ibid., p. 65.

the beauties of nature.'[11] While the destinations that he chose were not exclusively Eastern, he showed a marked preference for the East, 'where the sun rises' and where 'all the aesthetic revolutions are born'.[12] A trip around the Mediterranean in the autumn of 1912 took him to Italy, North Africa and Spain, and ended thus: 'What I had seen in the Arab countries awakened in me an urgent need to return there. I felt I was an Oriental soul and I could not resist the attraction of these countries of the sun'.[13] This desire was fulfilled in 1919 when he spent a few weeks in Morocco. Although the trip was firmly anchored in the colonial context through his meeting with the brothers Jérôme and Jean Tharaud,[14] chroniclers of the French presence in Morocco, as well as his visits to French colonial administrator Lyautey and even the pasha El Glaoui, who dazzled him with the same luxurious dishes that Colette would later describe, Poiret dedicated more personal pages to Marrakesh (ILL. 2), which did not yet boast the lavish surroundings of the iconic hotel La Mamounia. Next he visited Fez, during the festival of Ramadan, which he said was 'the most beautiful thing that [he] had ever seen in this world'.[15] He described the colours and sounds in great detail, overwhelmed by a sense of ecstasy he had not even dreamed of at his party of 1911: 'What was the phantasmagoria of the Thousand and Second Night, compared with this dazzling reality?'[16]

This affection for the reality that he experienced on other trips, such as the one he took with Raoul Dufy (ILL. 1) in 1926, also to Morocco, was eventually translated into an understandable curiosity about the day-to-day world that was the setting for his own creations, the world of jewelry and clothing. At the Victoria and Albert Museum in London, probably in 1909, he described among the 'treasures of India' the 'logical and elegant shapes' of the turbans, which he was allowed to take out from their cases and 'caress': 'There was the tight little turban of the sepoys which ends in a strip of fabric, carelessly tossed over the shoulder, and there was the enormous turban of the rajahs, raised like an elegant pincushion to attach all the plumes…'[17] The trip to Morocco in 1919 had offered other charms: 'Ah! How I would have loved to wear those gandouras [Arabic tunics] layered with white silk and mousseline-de-laine and butter muslin.'[18] Paying attention to these varied sources sometimes allows us to identify, beyond any doubt, the original inspiration for a design, such as with the dress *Marrakech* (CAT. 4, PP. 126-129), which has been compared to a Tunisian tunic, perhaps brought back from Poiret's travels.[19] Today, these similarities could lead us to denounce Poiret's creations as examples of cultural appropriation: his coat *Ispahan* (CAT. 47, PP. 74-77) from 1907 is 'an exact copy (down to almost the smallest detail) of a traditional Indian coat worn by Muslim men in the Punjab, the choga'.[20] Other designs could lead us to conclude: 'Nothing that Poiret presents in his Orientalist designs is drawn from his imagination.'[21]

A dreamlike exoticism

However, this debate remains live and does not prevent us from viewing Poiret's designs as 'pure fashion objects'[22] that offer their own interpretation of the borrowed elements, as part of an aesthetic movement that throws fresh light on the evocative power of the East, breathing new life into it through imagination. While the 'real', in its various senses, inspired Poiret's thinking, fashion remained for him an opportunity for a performance, with the world of theatre introducing him to a dreamlike dimension, as in 1893: 'And Bartet, in *Antigone*, who wore a crumpled chiffon robe, so pure, so chaste, with all of the lower part seeming to be in shadow due to a curious effect of the footlights.'[23] The designer learned about the world of theatre at the Comédie Française, where he was enchanted by the Oriental sets, as in Victorien Sardou's *Gismonda* (1894), with the title character played by Sarah Bernhardt.[24] His involvement with the theatre, which continued throughout his career, often took the form of events associated with the Arabic or Asian worlds, such as, in January 1911, the play *Nabuchodonosor* by Maurice de Faramond, where Édouard de Max, crowned with a tiara that weighed 6 kilos (13 pounds), wore a 'huge coat' dyed 'Tyrian purple'.[25]

The 1913 production of *Le Minaret* by Jacques Richepin, playwright and director of the Théâtre de la Renaissance, was 'a triumph [...] of the art of staging'. While the programme '[was] a shabby thing', 'the true endeavour [lay] in the costumes and sets'[26] created for this comedy in three acts, which Poiret designed with two assistants, Erté and José de Zamora (ILL. 4). The outfit *Minaret*, especially, amazed the public: 'Here first of all, majestic and superb, in her silver gauze *serouail*, is Mme Cora Laparcerie,[27] whose "snow" white tulle coat, at the slightest movement, wafts like the beating of wings.'[28] Swell, who reviewed the event for *L'Art et la mode*, was in awe of 'this tale like those in *The Thousand and One Nights*, rendered poetic by the music of Jacques Richepin's verses and enlivened by the charming airs composed on this theme by the innovative Tiarko Richepin [...] which allowed great imaginative leaps in the costumes and sets.'[29]

The Thousand and One Nights had captured the imagination of the artistic scene, since 'the new humanity, applauding the Ballets Russes, rushed to the Opera, adorned with exotic plumed headdresses',[30] as Marcel Proust wrote. Inspired by the prologue to the tales, the ballet *Shéhérazade* took Paris by storm at its premiere on 4 June 1910, which Poiret attended with his wife (CAT. 199). The set and costume designer, Léon Bakst, dispensed with realism in favour of a violent array of colour, and drew heavily on the charms of Orientalism. Although disputed by Paul Poiret – 'it must be known that I already existed'[31] – Bakst's influence on his work can nevertheless be seen in the growing connections, during that time, 'between Orientalist fashion and theatre'.[32]

The connections between these different art forms are best illustrated by the famous party given for three hundred guests on 24 June 1911 in the private mansion on the rue du Faubourg-Saint-Honoré, which established a kind of rivalry: 'The most beautiful performance by the Ballets Russes could not be more successful than this celebration of art and splendour.'[33] The 'Thousand and Second Night' – as it was called – was designed to 'spark a fire in the imagination',[34] reflecting as it did the mythical vision of Persia that had permeated all areas of artistic creation (CAT. 236). Poiret wrote a long description of this magical extravaganza where the richness of the decorations, the mystery of the garden, the luxurious flavours, the graceful performances and even the surprise appearances, such as that of the favourite (Denise Poiret) escaping from a gilded cage wearing the tunic *Abat-jour* and a plumed turban (CAT. 178, 234 AND ILL. 6), all came together, during this night that aspired to be 'miraculous'.[35]

In a later work, published in 1932 under the title *Revenez-y*, Poiret detailed the various elements that made up his creative process, which included the need to 'go and seek unknown spices and flavours in exoticism'.[36] The East certainly played an essential role in this, but the term 'exoticism' is broader than that and the designer embraced other kinds of curiosity among these 'spices' and 'flavours': everything that testified to the evocative power of other places. Poiret was also interested in European ethnography, in the context of the wider movement embracing the study of folklore that was born in the late 19th century,[37] embodied by artists such as Paul Sérusier and Vassily Kandinsky and which sought to create a new kind of art. Brittany in northwestern France was, for Poiret, a chosen land that inspired the generous skirts and simple bodices with wide sleeves that appeared in his 1918 collections. A passage from *Revenez-y* gives a good idea of the emotions they inspired: '[...] the procession began, marvellous, sumptuous, shimmering with a touch of sun in all the velvets and taffetas of these colourful pinafores. There were purples embroidered in gold [...].'[38]

Poiret's creative imagination drew on a number of different sources, in an era that was rich in experimentation. Sensual and abstract, his inspiration followed the sinuous line – taken from the East – that he set out himself, in a passage worthy of *The Thousand and One Nights*: 'I tried to follow the line of the arabesque which seems to have unfurled around me since birth, like those ribbons that magicians twirl around a stick and which, as they trace rings and spirals that become progressively more off-centre, seem to blossom into enormous blooms.'[39]

27
The wife of Jacques Richepin, an actress and director of the Théâtre de la Renaissance.

28
Swell, *L'Art et la mode*, 29 March 1913, p. 331.

29
Ibid.

30
Marcel Proust, *La Prisonnière*, Paris: Gallimard, 'Folio' collection, 1954, p. 283.

31
Poiret, *En habillant l'époque*, p. 132.

32
Mathias Auclair and Manon Lavergne, 'Le théâtre de la mode', in *Bakst: Des ballets russes à la haute couture*, exh. cat., Paris: palais Garnier, Paris, Albin Michel-BNF Éditions-Opéra national de Paris- Arop-Les Amis de l'Opéra, 2016, p. 126.

33
Lucie Delarue-Mardrus, 'La mille et deuxième nuit', *Femina*, 1 August 1911, p. 415.

34
Poiret, *En habillant l'époque*, p. 137.

35
Ibid., p. 141.

36
Poiret, *Revenez-y*, p. 98.

37
See Jean-Marie Gallais and Marie-Charlotte Calafat (eds), *Folklore: Artistes et folkloristes, une histoire croisée*, Metz: Centre Pompidou Metz–Mucem-La-Découverte, 2020.

38
Poiret, *Revenez-y*, p. 224.

39
Poiret, *En habillant l'époque*, p. 238.

ILL. 3 Félix, Maïmouna (Mademoiselle Corbé) in the play *Le Minaret*, performed at the Théâtre de la Renaissance, published in the magazine *Le Théâtre*, 1 May 1913. Paris, Bibliothèque nationale de France, Literature and Art department, inv. FOL-YF-138

ILL. 4 José de Zamora, programme for the play *Le Minaret*, Théâtre de la Renaissance, Association des régisseurs de théâtre, 1913. Paris, Librarie Diktats

Et ce sera la Mille et deuxième Nuit

Et cette nuit là il n'y aura pas de nuages dans
le ciel et rien de ce qui existe n'existera
Il y aura des clartés & des parfums & des
flûtes & des timbales & des tambours des
soupirs de femme & le chant de l'oiseau
Bulbul
Droite et d'un jet comme la lettre alephmince
& flexible comme le rameau de l'Arbre ban,
elle dansera belle comme la Lune, absolument
ta vue et ton ouïe seront réjouis à l'extrême
limite de la réjouissance Des mimes
savants & fertiles en artifices improviseront
des scènes belles & bien jouées et plus doux
que le gâteau échevelé au miel seront
les vers du poëte Pour ce qui
est du vieux potier myope, il sera dans
sa boutique comme y seront dans la leur
& le marchand d'esclaves, dont la moins
belle vaut mille dinars d'or et le savetier
pouilleux et le tailleur cacochyme et le devin
aveugle et le cuisinier du pays de Sindh
Et voila pour eux Et l'on verra des
choses bien extraordinaires & des prodiges
stupéfiants Il y aura un vase de cornaline
blanche Et il y aura encore bien
d'autres choses qu'il serait interminable
d'énumerer
Et de plus
On entrera par le Faubourg St. Honoré

Et ce sera la Mille et deuxième Nuit

CAT. 236 Raoul Dufy, combined invitation and programme for the 'Thousand and Second Night' party, 1911, woodcut with gouache. Paris, Bibliothèque nationale de France, Performing Arts department

ILL. 5 Paul-Charles Delaroche, *Doctor Mardrus*, 1911, black pencil on paper. Paris, Bibliothèque nationale de France, Performing Arts department, inv. ASP 4-O ICO-3 (360)

CAT.178 Georges Lepape, *Les Choses de Paul Poiret vues par Georges Lepape*, 1911, phototype and pochoir print. Paris, library of the Musée des Arts décoratifs

ILL.6 Lucie Delarue-Mardrus, 'The Thousand and Second Night', *Femina*, 1 August 1911. Paris, Bibliothèque nationale de France, Literature and Art department, inv. AM 2923 D(474)

CAT.234 Georges Lepape, Denise Poiret at the 'Thousand and Second Night', 1911, graphite, gouache, black ink and highlights in silver on vellum paper. Private collection

ILL.1 Anonymous, photograph of a Paul Poiret design for the legal registry, 2 February 1920, gelatin silver print. Paris, Musée des Arts décoratifs, Archives de la Seine collection, 1940

Sébastien Quéquet
Legal records of Paul Poiret's designs

1
See Géraldine Blanche and Sébastien Quéquet, *La Mode en modèles. Photographies des années 1920–1930*, exh. cat., Paris: Musée des arts décoratifs, 2024.

2
The Paris Archives have a related collection of 4,000 photographs. The Palais Galliera and the Institut national de la propriété intellectuelle also have one.

3
La Loi. Journal du soir judiciaire quotidien, 19 December 1907, p. 1.

4
See André Allart and Paul Carteron, *La Mode devant les tribunaux. Législation & jurisprudence*, Paris: Librairie de la société du Recueil Sirey, 1914, p. 41–42.

5
See Paul Poiret, *En habillant l'époque*, Paris: Grasset, 1930, p. 241–243.

6
Les Élégances parisiennes, no. 3, June 1916, p. 54.

7
Man Ray, *Self Portrait* (1964), Boston: Bulfinch Press, 1998, p. 100.

8
See Alphonse Bertillon, *La Photographie judiciaire*, Paris: Gauthier-Villars et Fils, 1890.

Fakes have always plagued haute couture, despite intellectual property laws. During Poiret's era, there were two forms of protection available: copyright, as set out by the decree of 19–24 July 1793, and protections for designs and patterns, introduced by the decree of 18 March 1806. Anyone who wanted recourse to the latter had to register the pieces to be protected with the industrial tribunal, either by providing a copy of the item itself, or by submitting photographs or sketches, sometimes accompanied by a technical description and swatches of the fabrics used, all of which had to be stored in boxes that were numbered, dated and sealed.[1] These would be opened only in case of litigation, to demonstrate counterfeiting. A number of couturiers registered their designs in the interwar period, including Jeanne Paquin, Elsa Schiaparelli, Madeleine Vionnet and Jeanne Lanvin.

The Musée des Arts décoratifs has in its collection more than 70,000 records of designs, donated in 1940 by the industrial tribunal of Paris after their copyright period had expired. Three thousand of these relate to the Paul Poiret fashion house between 1919 and 1928, including some that were used as evidence to combat fakes.[2] In 1907, the designer accused two former employees, Boomkens and Bartalena, of having copied his coat designs *Strogoff* and *Théo*. The pieces, seized on 9 July of that year, had been registered four days earlier.[3] Poiret therefore won the case at the tribunal.[4] Such victories were not generally assured, as the judges did not always recognize the innovative and artistic character of fashion, which proved to be a significant stumbling block in using intellectual property law to combat fakes.

During his trip to the United States in 1913, the designer discovered a different kind of fake, created by using fake labels.[5] In all the major American cities, businesses were selling labels in their thousands, which could be modified to suit the counterfeiters' purposes. Then all they had to do was attach them to poor-quality clothes.[6] Stunned, Poiret decided, on his return, to join forces with Jacques Worth and set up a syndicate to protect French couture and its related industries. However, is it really possible to combat fakes? Have they not survived throughout every era by constantly adapting?

While the legal effectiveness of these photographic records was limited, for Poiret they took on another dimension, beyond their use as evidence. The designer's interest in photography is well known. He was behind the choice to commission Edward Steichen to provide the now iconic photographs for Paul Cornu's article 'L'art de la robe', published in *Art et décoration* in April 1911, which has long been considered the birth of fashion photography. He also admired the work of Adolf de Meyer and Boris Lipnitzki, whom he worked with, as well as Marianne Breslauer. He launched

Man Ray's career, buying his first rayographs. In *Self-Portrait*, Man Ray offers an insight into Poiret's approach: 'With an inclusive gesture, he pointed out that here was his house, the rooms, the dresses, the girls – photographers generally worked on the spot, which he preferred.'[7]

The private mansion on Avenue d'Antin, between 1909 and 1925, and later the one on the Champs-Élysées roundabout, did indeed provide the setting for photographs of the fashion house's designs, which also showed the collections of art and furniture, pieces by the Martine workshop (Atelier Martine) and the gardens (ILL. 2). The variety of backdrops is fairly unusual, compared to the photographic records submitted by competitors. Perhaps that might be explained by the fact that Poiret was one of the few designers to publish these images in the press, as these photographic records were traditionally used only by the industrial tribunal and any relevant legal bodies.

In photographs of Poiret's designs, the models pose elegantly and interact with the space around them, laying a hand on a statue, a pillar, a mantelpiece (CAT. 191 AND ILL. 1, 3). Their gestures and expressions are natural, which distinguishes these shots from others submitted to the legal register, which were generally taken quickly, without much attention to style or expressivity on the model's part, following the guidelines set out by Alphonse Bertillon in *La Photographie judiciaire*.[8] Far from emulating the stereotype of legal photography, Poiret's records of his designs are more reminiscent of photographs of actresses, such as those taken by Léopold-Émile Reutlinger, Henri Manuel and Gilbert René. In fact, Gilbert René was the main photographer used for these legal records – although most of the photographs are not signed. Some of them break with the legal register's norms in their poetic depiction of natural elements such as wind and light, or in their composition, which is reminiscent of the book *Les Choses de Paul Poiret vues par Georges Lepape*. In this way, the photographs form part of Poiret's overall approach to his work, in which all art forms were in conversation with one another.

ILL. 2 Delphi, photograph of a Paul Poiret design for the legal registry, 17 August 1920, gelatin silver print. Paris, Musée des Arts décoratifs, Archives de la Seine collection, 1940

CAT. 191 Anonymous, photograph of the Paul Poiret dress *Tulipes stylisées* for the legal registry, motif by Raoul Dufy manufactured by Bianchini-Férier, 29 March 1920, gelatin silver print. Paris, Musée des Arts décoratifs, Archives de la Seine collection, 1940

ILL. 3 Gilbert René, photograph of the Paul Poiret dress *Séléné*
for the legal registry, 11 February 1922, gelatin silver print. Paris,
Musée des Arts décoratifs, Archives de la Seine collection, 1940

Mary E. Davis

Poiret
in America

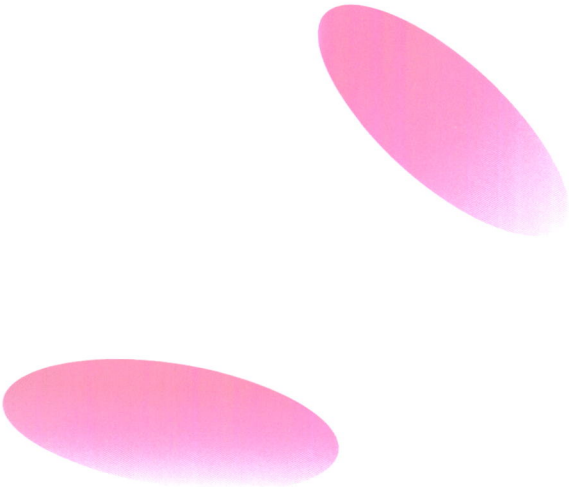

1
Paul Poiret, *En habillant l'époque*, Paris: Grasset, 1930, p. 236.

2
'Poiret, Creator of Fashions, Here', *The New York Times*, 21 September 1913, p. 93.

3
Paul Poiret, *En habillant l'époque*, Paris: Grasset, 1930, p. 236.

4
'To Bring 100 Gowns: Mme Poiret Will Wear in America Her Husband's Latest Gowns', *The New York Times*, 7 September 1913, p. 54.

5
'Ideals of Elegance in Dress', *Vogue*, 9 July 1909, pp. 35–36.

6
'Poiret on the Philosophy of Dress', American *Vogue*, 15 October 1913, p. 41.

7
Anne Rittenhouse, 'The Prophet of Simplicity', *Vogue*, 1 November 1913, pp. 42–43.

But what is charm for an American?[1]

'Poiret, creator of fashions, here!' *The New York Times* announced on Sunday 21 September 1913. The newspaper dedicated an entire page to the 'many-sided high priest of the beautiful' who had just arrived in the city for the first stage of a month-long trip around the United States. It described Poiret as a force of nature who 'is to be reckoned with every moment of the time':

> His brain teems with endless schemes, both good and new… if he had not turned out a dressmaker, he would have been an artist, or a musician, or an interior decorator, or a writer of ballads, or an actor. And the amazing truth is that he is all of those things now… A man of sports, a singer of ballads, a player of the violin, an Oriental scholar, a maker of rare perfumes, a decorator of houses and yachts, and now, the latest of all his achievements, he is to produce amazing ballets!

The article went on to say that this emissary of Parisian couture was not a champion of the 'new fashions' but a polymath who 'invents new movements in dress'.

'Oh, he is original, this many-sided artist,' the *Times* concluded. 'He travels like a comet, in an orbit all his own.'[2]

In the early 20th century, Poiret's reputation was only growing across the Atlantic. He sparked curiosity, regularly appearing in articles in American magazines and periodicals, whether as subject, author or advertiser. He had already made a name for himself as the purveyor of coveted products when he came to court the Americans in person, on his 1913 visit and the two that followed, in 1922 (ILL. 1) and 1927. Poiret made a splash, presenting himself as a provocateur from the outset: the day before his first visit, the Archbishop of New York condemned the 'diabolical' fashions of the moment, describing them as a 'social and moral danger'. Poiret, who had a nose for publicity, responded: 'His Excellency the Cardinal is correct!', adding that 'people of taste' would reject the 'scandalous necklines' in favour of his own, more modest creations.[3]

He began his trip in New York, where he and his wife, Denise, met executives from the fashion industry and visited the major department stores and tourist attractions. After giving lectures at Columbia University and the Pratt School of Design, they travelled along the East Coast, appearing in packed auditoriums and intimate salons from Toronto to Washington, D.C. When the highly anticipated film that Poiret had planned to project at his presentations was banned for obscenity, Denise, travelling with 'one hundred gowns for her to wear: gowns which are not even distant cousins to the fashions', took on the role of model.[4] Wherever the couple went, store visits and public lectures garnered widespread media coverage and drew enthusiastic audiences. On 15 October, when the Poirets set off to return to Europe on board the *Lusitania*, the great designer's fame in the United States was firmly established.

The American press had laid the groundwork for Poiret's celebrity long before he arrived. *Vogue* magazine, first and foremost, had been exploring his nonconformist approach since July 1909. An article entitled 'Ideals of Elegance in Dress' reported that Poiret believed clothing to be an art founded on 'one principle of elegance' that could be 'condensed in a word used by the Romans: *decorum*: that means the thing that suits!' *Vogue* also wrote that Poiret rejected trends, insisting that a woman must 'allow her clothes to express her individuality'.[5] A later article published in the same magazine, 'Poiret on the Philosophy of Dress', explained his guiding principles, particularly 'the search for the greatest simplicity, and the taste for an original detail and personality'.[6] The following month, in 'The Prophet of Simplicity', the magazine focused on Denise Poiret, presenting her as the muse and inspiration for her husband's 'dress theories' and principles, according to which 'it is what a woman leaves off, not what she puts on, that gives her cachet'. One of the fashions that Denise rejected was the corset; *Vogue* confirmed that she never wore them, preferring straight lines and a 'startling primitiveness' to a restricted silhouette.[7] Photographed wearing slouchy green boots and stockings in the same colour, her short hair wrapped in a turban, Denise was the embodiment of Poiret's ideal: a liberated Parisian woman, whose chic sense of style brave American women longed to imitate (CAT. 261).

Vogue's competitor, *Harper's Bazaar*, first started to feature Poiret a little later and chose a different approach: the magazine invited the designer to write about himself. His first article, published in September 1912, appealed to the American sense of originality: it is 'unfashionable to follow fashions,' he wrote. 'Choose whatever is most in harmony with your character.'[8] A month later, the magazine published 'Paul Poiret's Ten Commandments', and, starting in December 1913, he wrote a series of eight articles that culminated in 'From the Trenches', its title understood in the literal sense at the time, February 1915. 'Fashion! That appalling word!' was the first article's opening salvo. 'Dare to be individual, dare to be yourselves,' he entreated American women in the following one. 'There are as many styles of dress as there are women.'[9] Elsewhere, a photograph showed him putting 'the finishing touch' to a costume for the popular play *The Great Adventure*; after its opening night, he could add conquering Broadway to his long list of American triumphs.

After Paul Poiret was sent to the front in 1914, he had to shut up shop and enter a new phase of his relationship with the American fashion industry. When tensions between French couture houses and American interests intensified during the war, he found himself in the eye of the storm: the Americans were copying French styles, a practice that for many years had been accepted on both sides of the Atlantic. From 'authorized' copies to blatant fakes, the Americans adapted French designs for an American clientele; this practice indirectly confirmed the dominance of Parisian designers and couturiers. However, in 1913, after finding low-quality hats and dresses bearing an imitation of his label in a New York store, Poiret took issue with arrangement. Having learned that poor-quality copies were legal in the United States, he rallied his French colleagues with a view to creating an haute couture syndicate to protect original French designs. In 1915, he circulated the syndicate's declaration among his American counterparts — meeting with a muted response.

Reporting on this initiative, *The New York Times* wrote that Poiret, president of the syndicate, had published a 'diatribe' accusing 'Fifth Avenue couturiers [...] of stealing styles and clients and cutting prices' as well as 'vulgarizing [the] models' of French designers. The article detailed the syndicate's claims, particularly the accusation that Americans were procuring copies 'illicitly in dens where spy tailors smoke their German pipes', which the American industry unanimously (and correctly) rejected as a 'tissue of absurdities'.[10] The following day, the paper followed up with another article, entitled 'Won't Crown Poiret Czar of Fashion'. 'What is the real reason for Paul Poiret's attack upon American importers?' the paper asked. 'If, as several suggested, Paul Poiret is trying to make himself the fashion dictator of France and America through self-advertising, American importers will ignore him and deal with others of the 492-odd French designers who have not joined Poiret's syndicate'[11] [Le Syndicat de Défense de la Couture Française].

As the figurehead of the French initiative, Poiret was accused of trying to dismiss American competitors because he 'had lost prestige in the last two years because of radical tendencies'.[12] The approach suggested by *Vogue*, to form an American syndicate that could collaborate with the French organization, failed, as did the rival initiative set up by clothing store magnate J. M. Gidding, who sought to establish a 'Franco-American Council' to arbitrate the main disputes. 'If Mr Poiret wants to come into such an arrangement we will be glad to have him,' wrote Gidding. 'But if he thinks Paul Poiret is the only designer in Paris and can call us names and tell us what we should do, he will soon find himself in oblivion except for the free and paid advertising the press sees fit to give him.'[13] In late 1915, the partners in Poiret's syndicate started to desert him and the organization was ultimately dissolved. Poiret was held solely responsible for having refused to collaborate and having miscalculated 'the folly of antagonizing the American market'.[14]

Tensions around fakes were exacerbated by a new concern, seen by some as an American attempt to compete with Parisian haute couture. In reality, this was driven by necessity, as the war had put an end not only to haute couture shows, but also to the transatlantic trips undertaken by copyists, who sketched the latest trends and designs so they could be reproduced for the American market. This space had to be filled; but were the Americans, who for so many years had been relegated to reproducing French

8
Paul Poiret, 'Individuality in Dress: The Secret of the Well-Dressed Woman', *Harper's Bazaar*, September 1912, p. 451.

9
Paul Poiret, 'Paul Poiret Says', *Harper's Bazaar*, January 1914, p. 47.

10
'Paul Poiret Assails American Buyers', *The New York Times*, 19 December 1915, p. 17.

11
'Won't Crown Poiret Czar of Fashion', *The New York Times*, 20 December 1915, p. 11.

12
Ibid.

13
Ibid.

14
'Couturiers May Dissolve', *The New York Times*, 9 December 1915, p. 10.

CAT. 261 Geisler & Baumann, Denise Poiret wearing an ensemble by Paul Poiret at the Plaza Hotel, New York, 1913, gelatin silver print (1/3). Paris, Musée des Arts décoratifs

ILL. 1 George Rinhart, *Paul Poiret Sailing from New York*, 14 September 1922, gelatin silver print

CAT. 189 Anonymous, Paul Poiret in military uniform, c. 1914, gelatin silver print. Paris, Musée des Arts décoratifs

ILL. 2 Anonymous, Paul Poiret in denim overalls alongside Boris Lipnitzki, 1928

POIRET - GRAY SUIT (WANAMAKER)

POIRET MODEL GIMBEL'S

FLOOR

WITH FACES SET TOWARD THE
FASHION FÊTE—SMALL WON-
DER SOCIETY LOOKS CHEERFUL

Photographs copyrighted by
Underwood & Underwood

A smart suit of black velvet and
pointed furs of pointed fox were
worn on the Avenue by Mrs.
James Roosevelt, who harvested a
whole bookful of chances on gowns

Mrs. "Tommy" Shevlin, shown at
the upper left, the wife of the famous
football captain, Yale 1905, leaving
the Ritz-Carlton after attending a
matinée of the New York Fashion Fête

A vender of programs at the Fête
was Miss Muriel Winthrop, who
appears at the upper right in an in-
dubitably Russian suit and one of the
versions of the Tommy Atkins hat

A reputation for being one of the
smartest dressed women of New
York is possessed by Mrs. Hamil-
ton Cary, who is shown at the lower
left as she left the Ritz-Carlton

Miss Marie Tailer and Miss Margaret Andrews, who was one of the
hard-working book-makers on the
raffled gowns, arriving at the Fashion Fête with well-filled money bags

ILL.3 Underwood & Underwood, 'With Faces Set toward the Fashion Fête – Small Wonder Society Looks Cheerful', American *Vogue*, no. 12, vol. 45, 15 December 1914, p. 22.

ILL.4 Model wearing a grey Paul Poiret ensemble for the department store Wanamaker's, 1914, gelatin silver print. Washington, Library of Congress, inv. LC-USZ62-56679

ILL.5 Model wearing a Paul Poiret dress for the department store Gimbels, 1914, gelatin silver print. Washington, Library of Congress, inv. LC-USZ62-85524

15
Paul Poiret, 'From the Trenches',
Harper's Bazaar, February 1915,
p. 11.

16
'The Story of the Fashion Fête',
American *Vogue*, 1 November
1914, p. 38.

17
'Poiret: Audacious Color and
Naïve Line', American *Vogue*,
15 December 1917, pp. 42–43.

18
'The Blue Book of the Grandes
Maisons', American *Vogue*,
15 December 1915, p. 53.

19
Advert, *Vogue*, 1 October 1916,
p. 113.

20
Advert, 'Poiret, Inc.', *Vogue*, 15
February 1917, p. 5.

21
Janet Flanner, 'The Egotist',
The New Yorker, 21 October
1927, p. 25.

designs, capable of becoming fashion designers themselves? Poiret dismissed this idea, describing it as the 'dream of overthrowing the old French god which has reigned over the fashion world for three centuries'.[15]

These concerns grew after the 'Fashion Fête' held at the Ritz-Carlton in November 1914, a flashy show that lasted for several days, featuring pieces by New York designers. It was the event of the season: organized by *Vogue*'s editor-in-chief, Edna Woolman Chase, it was sponsored by high-society women, and the money raised went to support charitable causes. The press celebrated the arrival of 'good-looking clothes aplenty' and 'genuinely original' and 'smart' American styles[16]. With the end of the war not yet in sight, it suddenly seemed plausible that these American designers could find a place for themselves in the fashion landscape (ILL. 3).

In November of the following year, Poiret and his Parisian colleagues responded by holding their own fashion show in New York, the 'French Fashion Fête', also sponsored by *Vogue* and held at the Ritz-Carlton. This 'unprecedented exhibition of fashions' in America presented designs by all members of the syndicate – which was still intact at the time – featuring more than a hundred outfits, including twelve new looks created by Poiret. His designs, declared 'the only Poiret models in existence' by *Vogue*, were immortalized in ten photographs and four illustrations.[17] For those readers who might have forgotten that the couturier was doing his patriotic duty, a full-length shot showed Poiret in military uniform with a cigarette between his lips (CAT. 189).[18]

Although the 'French Fashion Fête' was not repeated, Poiret remained well known in America as the war dragged on. After his syndicate folded, he resolved to work in harmony with the interests of the American fashion industry instead of sowing discord. He sent pieces to the Panama-Pacific International Exposition in San Francisco in 1915, and in 1916 he partnered with the Max Grab Fashion Company, a Fifth Avenue business, to sell 'a collection of models exclusively for the women of America'. These 'authorized reproductions', as the advert called them, offered 'the opportunity to own a Paul Poiret creation without paying the usual excessive price'.[19] A year later, Poiret secured American funding to launch a New York business venture in his own right, opening a studio on Broadway and a shop on Fifth Avenue. 'PAUL POIRET, the world's greatest fashion genius, will be accessible to you!' an advert for Poiret, Inc. promised; 'specially designed for *La Belle Américaine*', these designs would be 'at prices to suit the average American pocketbook', marketed in a free catalogue, available on written demand or through a network of 'leading style shop[s]' around the country. Another advert told future clients: 'There is in your town a Poiret store.'[20]

However, the United States joined the war shortly after Poiret had launched this venture and he was not able to bring it to fruition; despite his efforts, he never succeeded in gaining a foothold in the mass American market. He briefly returned to the United States in 1922, to design the costumes for the successful Broadway show *Orange Blossoms*. With his financial troubles mounting, he was forced to restructure his fashion house in 1923, then to sign the business over to a manager the following year. Poiret had to vacate his much-loved studio on Avenue d'Antin in Paris and move to more modest premises, to sell his perfume business Les Parfums de Rosine and to give up his interior design business, the Martine workshop (Atelier Martine). The final blow came in November 1925, when he was left with no alternative but to auction off his precious collection of artworks.

In need of a break and to pursue new opportunities, Poiret returned to the United States five years later, in October 1927, for his final tour, after what must have seemed like an eternity. In *The New Yorker* that same month, an article by Janet Flanner, entitled 'The Egotist', reintroduced him to the American public as 'a spectacular public man of Paris'. Flanner wrote that, whatever the future held for him, Poiret 'remains one of the Continentals who has helped to change the modern retina'.[21] For more than a month, he travelled around the country, stopping in smaller towns – Akron, Ohio, and Chickasha, Oklahoma – as well as the major cities of Chicago, New York and Los Angeles. On these visits, he gave demonstrations in the art of draping, using textiles made in the United States; he remained loyal to the watchwords he had always cited in his lectures, 'simplicity' and 'originality', encouraging American women to always look for their own personal way of expressing themselves. His trip culminated in a gala dinner put on by New York fashion magnates, but overall it was not a success: Poiret returned to France with greater debts and without a single commercial contract. All he would bring back from his final American tour were his memories and his lecture notes, which at least provided him with material for two chapters of the first volume of his memoirs.

In the obituary published a few days after Paul Poiret's death on 30 April 1944, *The New York Times* recalled his first visit to the United States, around thirty years earlier. The 'famous dictator of fashion' had been 'acclaimed' and 'adored' across the United States; 'Americans always revolted against Poiret' because 'all sorts of controversies surrounded him'.[22] Acclaim and revolts: perhaps that might explain Poiret's enduring charm for a country that appreciates provocation and nonconformity – at least when it comes to fashion.

22
'Paul Poiret Dies', *The New York Times*, 3 May 1944, p. 19.

ILL.6 *Bretonne* dress by Paul Poiret, *Les Élégances parisiennes*, no. 7, 1 October 1916, plate 13. Paris, library of the Musée des Arts décoratifs

ILL.7 Georges Lepape, 'Vive la France!', cover of American *Vogue*, 1 November 1917. Paris, Librairie Diktats

CAT. 75 Paul Poiret, *Ice Cream Soda* evening coat, c. 1920, silk panne velvet and shot taffeta. Paris, Musée des Arts décoratifs

ILL.1 Man Ray, *Portrait of Elsa Schiaparelli*, c. 1934, gelatin silver
print. Paris, Centre Pompidou–Musée national d'art moderne,
donated by Mr Lucien Treillard, 1995, inv. AM 1995-281 (1399)

Marie-Sophie Carron de la Carrière

The 'Leonardo of Fashion', Poiret by Schiaparelli

1
Elsa Schiaparelli, *Shocking Life*, New York: Dutton & Co., 1954, p. 55.

2
When she was still very young, Schiaparelli wanted to escape a marriage arranged by her parents and break away from her family home, which, as she said, stifled her personality. However, she briefly returned to Italy in 1922 to obtain a new passport under the name 'Miss Schiaparelli'.

3
Schiaparelli, *Shocking Life*, p. 55.

4
Ibid.

5
American *Vogue*, 15 December 1927, p. 45.

It was then that I met Paul Poiret, whom I greatly admired and considered the greatest artist of all time.[1]

At the height of his fame, Paul Poiret became a mentor to the young unknown Elsa Schiaparelli, who had arrived in Paris penniless and eager for advice on how to forge her own destiny, little imagining that fashion could be her path.

Schiaparelli was Italian, born in Rome in 1890 into a family of privileged intellectuals. The daughter of an academic who specialized in Eastern civilizations, and granddaughter, on her mother's side, of a British consul to Malta, she was also the niece of Giovanni Schiaparelli, a famous astronomer who discovered the existence of channels on Mars. At the age of twenty-three, she left Italy, determined not to return,[2] and went to England, where she married Wilhelm de Wendt de Kerlor, before moving to the East Coast of the United States, where their daughter, nicknamed Gogo, was born. Soon separated from her unfaithful husband, Schiaparelli eked out a frugal existence with her daughter in New York. Her wealthy friend Blanche Hays, who was going through a divorce, persuaded her to come with her to Paris to try her luck there. She also started divorce proceedings and urgently needed to find work so she could provide for her child. She was free.

Taken along by her American friend, whom she lived with for a time, to the Boulevard de la Tour-Maubourg, she met the great designer. It was the first time that Schiaparelli had visited a fashion house. The meeting took place in the rooms at 107 Rue du Faubourg-Saint-Honoré, in the summer of 1922. In her autobiography,[3] Schiaparelli described it as a decisive encounter: 'While my friend was choosing lovely dresses , I gazed around moonstruck. Silently I tried things on and became so enthusiastic that I forgot where I was, and walked in front of the mirrors not too displeased with myself.' This initial meeting was the beginning of a warm and admiring friendship between Poiret and the young woman, who was wondering about her future: 'I felt the impact of our personalities.' Charmed by her nonconformist attitude, the designer remarked that Elsa had an impulsiveness and a sense of originality, which she used to create a colourful look for herself with limited means and a lot of imagination. For her part, she enjoyed the metamorphosis that came with trying on Poiret's designs: 'I put on a coat of large, loose cut that could have been made today. Really good clothes never go out of fashion. This coat was made of upholstery velvet — black , with big vivid stripes, lined with bright blue crêpe de Chine. It was magnificent.' Poiret generously offered to dress her, so that she could gain an intimate appreciation of how the clothes' colours and fabrics went together. Through their meetings, she built up a wardrobe of magnificent outfits that he had given her. Noting her growing understanding and how she blossomed with his gifts, he complimented her and encouraged her to explore the world of fashion: 'You could wear anything anywhere.' Finally, drawing on her Italian heritage, Schiaparelli compared the brilliant Poiret to the ultimate Renaissance artist. In her eyes, he was 'the Leonardo of fashion'.

During their sparkling exchanges, which were sprinkled with humour and learned references, they told each other news of their acquaintances, the American photographer Man Ray (ILL. 1), who had moved to the City of Light the year before, and the (now separated) wife of the painter Francis Picabia, Gabriële Buffet-Picabia, with whom Schiaparelli lived for a short time. They also shared a number of interests, such as Orientalism, travel and avant-garde art. Elsa Schiaparelli was a dedicated follower of the Dada group, in particular Tristan Tzara and Francis Picabia.

In late August 1922, Poiret, who had already travelled to North America in 1913, embarked on a second tour of the United States, with the aim of exporting his designs. He discussed the idea with Schiaparelli beforehand.

In December 1924, Poiret moved from Avenue Antin to a new address at number 1 on the roundabout of the Champs-Élysées. On Christmas Eve, Schiaparelli was invited to celebrate the move, in the form of a procession of multicoloured lanterns, from the former premises to the new 'ultra-modern' fashion house (ILL. 2).

In 1927, Elsa Schiaparelli was thirty-seven years old and still a self-taught designer. However, she had a great deal of intuition that allowed her to design clothes that suited the lives of elegant modern women who wanted to stand out. Her first success came when she designed hand-knitted sweaters with trompe-l'œil motifs. These were an immediate hit with clients seeking both novelty and comfort. According to American *Vogue*,[5] the young designer was inventing the modern woman's wardrobe. Schiaparelli's career had begun (ILL. 3 AND CAT. 108)! And Poiret had played a key role in launching her.

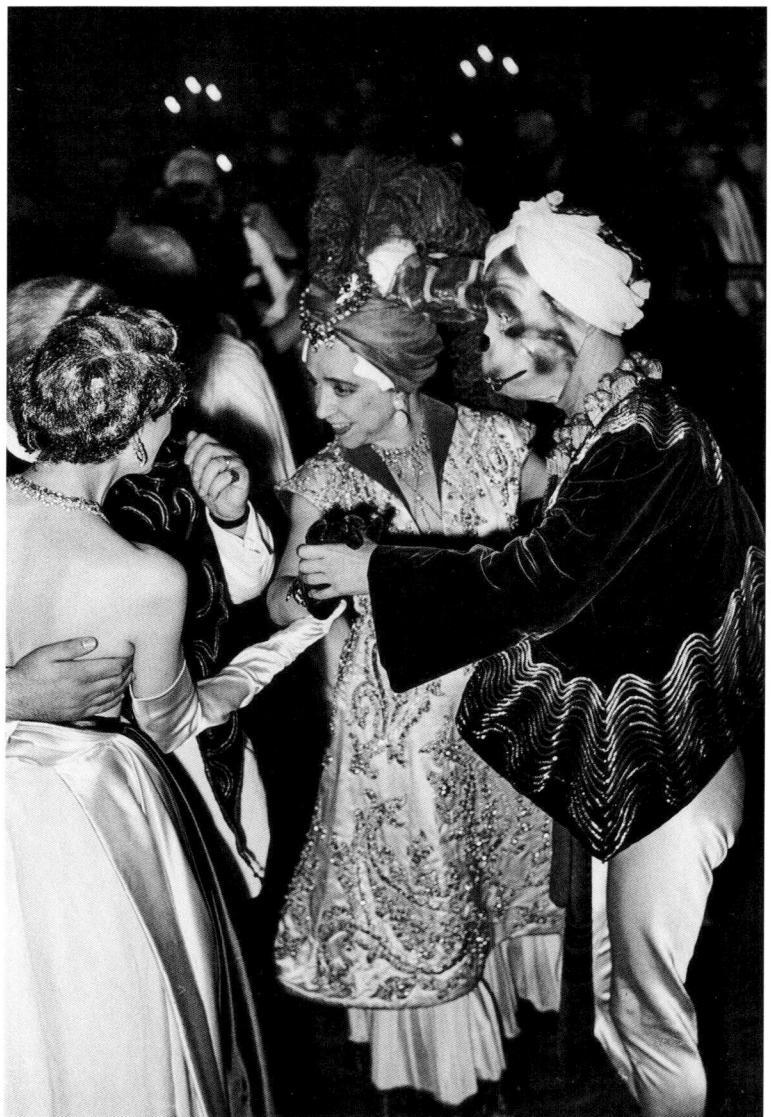

ILL. 2 Albert Harlingue, *The Great Night of Fashion*, 1924. Party to celebrate Paul Poiret's fashion house moving to new premises on the rond-point des Champs-Élysées

ILL. 3 Arik Nepo, Elsa Schiaparelli at the 'Ball of the Tableaux Vivants', held by Jacques Fath in June 1951 at the Château de Corbeville, Orsay, 1952, gelatin silver print. Paris, Palais Galliera–Musée de la Mode de la Ville de Paris, inv. GALK638

CAT.108 Elsa Schiaparelli, evening gown from the Winter 1950–51 'Ligne de face' haute couture collection, silk satin, silk velvet, embroidery by Lesage in metallic thread, cordonnet braid, beads and diamanté. Paris, Musée des Arts décoratifs

Colombe Pringle

A family of artists

Poiret and his sisters

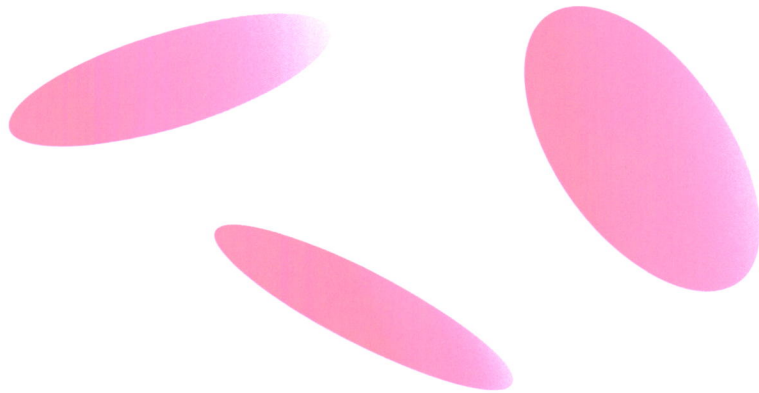

1
Flora Groult, 'Poiret couturier', lecture for the Friends of the Musée de l'Homme, December 1990.

2
Paul Poiret, *En habillant l'époque*, Paris: Grasset, 1930.

3
Flora Groult, *Tout le plaisir des jours est dans leur matinée*, Paris: Plon, 1985.

4
Ibid.

I did not know Poiret, but Flora, my mother, often told me about her 'mischievous, unusual uncle', who put on plays every summer with 'the troop of cousins' and whom she described as 'the only adult who knew how to remain childlike: weighing 100 kilos [220 pounds], with his sailor's beard prickly like a sea urchin and his big pale eyes which he tried not to blink, he still had that frantic desire to win at cards (in no time at all, he'd be pleading with Lady Luck to smile on him), he still indulged in feigned anger or real fits of giggles, as if he were the same age as us. All of that had a touch of incongruity, of the absurd, which is so much the territory of childhood. Poiret was like no one but himself.'[1]

While Paul was unique in many ways, I do not remember Nicole, my whimsical grandmother, the youngest sibling, ever talking about this gifted tyrant who praised his three sisters' artistic talents as long as they remained under his control, while not acknowledging them in his autobiography *En habillant l'époque*.[2] Perhaps the key to his personality lies in this anecdote of family legend? One day when, in front of Nicole's daughters Benoîte and Flora, their father lectured her about a chestnut preserve that had not turned out right, Nicole, in one of her opera singer's trills — as a child, she had dreamed of being a singer and she never stopped singing throughout her life — declared: 'In the Poiret family, we don't tolerate people playing the big man.' The seed of our 'feminism', a word not yet in common use, was planted.

In 1907, a time when Poiret reigned supreme over all of Paris, he wrote a letter to his 'Dear Maman' describing his visit to Nicole and André, who, after running around flea markets to buy furniture for their first apartment as a married couple, had just opened an antiques shop. 'They have a great talent when it comes to objects, I am going to send my wealthiest customers to them.' Which he did, and André Groult began his career as an interior designer, creating arrangements that would make his name. When the war started and her husband was sent to the front, Nicole came into her own, cutting and sewing, 'without a pattern, at the dining room table',[3] her first dresses, which had an 'elegant simplicity' that charmed her circle of friends among the intelligentsia (ILL. 4, 5 AND CAT. 271). But when Paul offered to hire her, an offer that, in a grand gesture of rebellion, she turned down, he forbade her from using their surname. After ending her collaboration with her brother, Nicole produced her first designs under the name of her husband André Groult, before opening her own couture house (CAT. 72).

Similarly, their sister Germaine — who, along with Paul's wife, Denise, set up the girls' clothing line for the daughters of Poiret's clients — broke away from her brother to open her own 'salon de couture', whose clientele included Madame Matisse and Kees van Dongen's lover. She also held concerts there by Les Six and exhibitions showing the work of her friends Fernand Léger, André Derain and Léopold Survage, exchanging paintings for dresses, before dedicating herself to painting.

As for Jeanne, the eldest — who hosted the traditional Christmas dinner in her huge grey and pink apartment, where she allowed Paul to live when he was financially ruined towards the end of his life, and who was married to the jeweller René Boivin — after her husband's death she hired Suzanne Belperron, who played a vital part in reinventing the Boivin style, which would be continued by Jeanne and René's daughter Germaine Boivin Sonrel, drawing on her passions for sculpture and shells.

While Poiret's sisters all had a similar proud look, with long legs, shining blue eyes like marbles, tomboyish haircuts, and, in the case of Nicole, kiss curls that emphasized the shape of her face, like one of Cocteau's paintings (ILL. 2), and all three were gifted with artistic talent, they were also enthusiastic in encouraging the talents of others. Nicole offered unflagging support to her ever-serious André (ILL. 1), whom she greatly admired, even naming their poodle 'Fric' (slang for money) during a difficult period — 'That will bring it in!' And throughout her life, she never stopped writing to her daughters, tender words or firm advice on her pink paper with the 'NG' letterhead designed by Paul Iribe. Letters that we, her granddaughters, and our children, still take great pleasure in reading, as they are still relevant today. 'Angel of my life, you should work on your writing, it's very bad to have weak writing', 'My treasures, make the most of the beautiful days, enjoy love', 'My dear bird, you must not say no to things, people invite you, you have to go and you will see, you will have fun', 'Don't let your gifts pass you by, my daughters, develop them! And keep your names!' Messages received by her daughters, who all kept the surname 'Groult'. Nicole, who refused to wear a watch or have a clock in her bedroom — 'I hate to see time passing'[4] — would not have the pleasure of seeing

ILL.1 Jacques Henri Lartigue, Nicole Groult and André Groult skating in Chamonix, January 1918, gelatin silver print. Groult family archives

ILL.3 Portrait of Nicole Groult and her daughters Benoîte and Flora, 1928, gelatin silver print. Groult family archives

ILL.2 Paul O'Doye, Nicole Groult in her Paris apartment, with a painting by Charles Martin behind her, c. 1928–30, gelatin silver print. Groult family archives

5
Benoîte and Flora Groult,
Journal à quatre mains, Paris:
Denoël, 1962.

that name enjoy its first literary success,[5] succumbing, ironically, to the passing of time, which she feared so greatly.

In turn, I also benefited directly from this family spirit and this precious advice, a gift from Nicole. One day, when we were walking at her usual brisk pace along the Rue de Bellechasse, to go to the 'faubourg' (Saint-Honoré), where she had her fashion house and André had his straw marquetry workshop, and she was wrapped in her sealskin or beaver coat – I never knew which it was, but I liked to rub my cheek against it – some house painters called out to her. Without a second thought, she turned round to thank them, offering them her most beautiful smile, while I scuffed my feet, blushing. Noticing my embarrassment, she admonished me gently: 'My little treasure, you have to learn how to accept compliments. One day, people stop wolf-whistling at you in the street, and then there is nothing left to smile about.' I was seven years old; today I understand her and am grateful to her for this life lesson and the love of beauty that she instilled in me.

ILL. 4 Louis Suë (illustrator), Devambez (printer), invitation for Nicole Groult's fashion house, c. 1920. Groult family archives

CAT. 72 Nicole Groult, dress, 1912, silk crepe, silk satin, embroidered netting and taffeta. Paris, Musée des Arts décoratifs

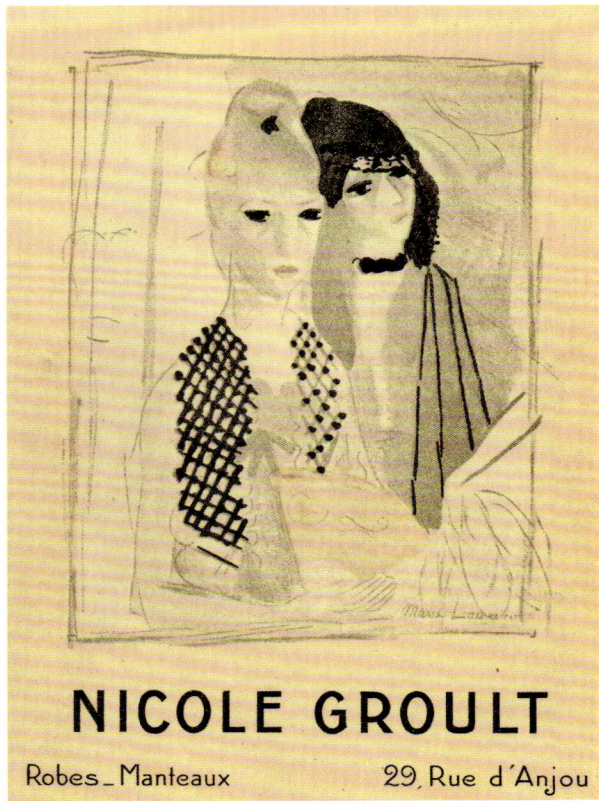

ILL. 5 Marie Laurencin, invitation to view Nicole Groult's summer collection, 1930. Groult family archives

CAT. 271 Marie Laurencin, *Women with Dove*, 1919, oil on canvas. Self-portrait of the artist with Nicole Groult. Paris, Centre Pompidou–Musée national d'art moderne–Centre de création industrielle

Sophie Fontanel

'She can have everything'

Denise Poiret and fashion

It was 1903. Paul Poiret was sick and tired of 'frivolous, shallow courtships'. He later said, 'I was dreaming of happiness.' And he found it, in Denise Boulet, the daughter of his parents' friends. She did not care about fashion. Or Paris. She loved Elbeuf. He was smitten; he wanted to marry her. At that point, his rare gem was only sixteen years old.

So he waited. He proposed two years later. He was lucky, she loved him too. He designed her wedding dress, inspired by this 'slim, brunette [girl], pale and untouched by make-up or powder'. It is difficult to tell whether he was describing the dress or his wife. She would go on to give him five children, a common size for a family at the time. And she blossomed. Very soon, she knew how to wear anything, and even how to make it her own! He was constantly designing dresses for her, impassioned by this extraordinary woman who defied all classification. What category did she belong to? She was not a coquette. Or a former coquette (if you follow me). Nor was she a provincial woman, or a snob, or even a muse. She was a true original.

At first, they were very happy together. He designed dresses for her, in the Orientalist style but ultramodern. Everything he designed was ultramodern, whether it was a traditional Breton costume or a nun's habit. Everything was free, open. He was the one who liberated women from corsets, a highly symbolic act in itself.

When they visited the US, Denise disembarked from the ship wearing men's boots. Everyone was talking about her. As soon as she wore something, women wanted it. They recognized themselves in Denise immediately, although she was unlike anyone else. Another time, they held a party, the 'Thousand and Second Night' – a reference, of course, to *The Thousand and One Nights*. She wore a gold skirt over a voluminous sarouel (harem pants). Her crepe bodice was transparent. That evening, Paul Poiret thought it would be amusing to lock up his 'favourite', Denise herself, in a gilded cage. His plan was to open the cage once the three hundred guests had arrived. He did so. And she escaped.

It was a prophetic scene, because soon Denise would escape for real. A gilded cage, no matter how beautiful, cannot hold a woman who has been cheated on so many times, a woman as liberated as Denise. She filed for divorce. Her husband – argumentative, impossible to live with, prone to fits of temper – did not fight it. He had lost, he said: 'She can have everything.' A year after the divorce, Paul Poiret's fashion house went bankrupt. The man who had dreamed of happiness became so poor that he was sometimes dependent on help from friends to meet his day-to-day needs. He was absolutely wretched. And as for her, what did she live on? It is a mystery. One day, she donated the clothes he had designed for her to the Musée des Arts décoratifs. She died in Paris in 1982, at the age of ninety-six. Liberated from all the corsets in the world, whatever form they took.

CAT. 272 Delphi, Denise Poiret wearing the Paul Poiret dress *Linzeler*, which she wore to a party at the Oasis, 1919–20, gelatin silver print. Paris, Musée des Arts décoratifs

ce tableau 1913 photographié en 1974

Ce tableau photographique ne date pas de 1913, mais il a fallu, en mars 1974, des centaines d'heures de travail et vingt-trois personnes pour l'esquisser puis l'achever.

Il eût été impossible de vous le présenter

si Madame Paul Poiret n'avait bien voulu, et pour la première fois, prêter des robes de sa collection personnelle ;

si Helmut Newton n'avait su et voulu réaliser pour vous la couverture de ce numéro et la photographie de cette double page ;

si Richard Blareau, chef de l'Orchestre de l'Opéra de Paris et Michel Cron, 1er violon du même orchestre n'avaient revêtu leur habit et sorti leur archet ;

si Maurice Franck n'avait si bien réussi à coiffer les mannequins de ces deux pages et des quatre qui les suivent ;

si les agences Christa, Elite, et Paris-Planning ne nous avaient aidés avec une élégance toute bénévole ;

si Annabelle, Chiffon, Dominique, Eija, Eva, Haude, Héloïse, Jeannette, Laurel Lee, Susan et Sophie ne nous avaient aussi fait cadeau de leur beauté et de leur temps ;

si Michel Souillac et Jacques Denoël ne nous avaient confié trois de leurs sublimes chaises d'époque ;

si l'Union française des arts du costume et Yvonne Deslandres ne nous avaient apporté leur concours ;

et Violette Gérard son talent de styliste.

ILL.1 Helmut Newton, tribute to the designs of Paul Poiret, featuring Denise Boulet-Poiret, Richard Blareau (conductor of the Paris Opéra orchestra) and Michel Cron (first violin) in *Magazine Réalités*, April 1974, no. 339. Stéphane Perl Collection

THE
POIRET
STYLE

Dare to be individual, dare to be yourselves.
There are as many styles of dress
as there are women.

Paul Poiret, 'Paul Poiret Says', *Harper's Bazaar*, 1914

CAT. 219 Lumière NY, Mademoiselle Spinelly wearing a design by Paul
Poiret, 1919–20, gelatin silver print. Paris, Musée des Arts décoratifs

1811 evening gown

1907

Pekin silk, metallic lace and chiffon

Paris, Musée des Arts décoratifs

CAT. 13 [REPR. PP. 66-67]

1

The design *Lola Montés* worn by Denise to her daughter Rosine's christening in autumn 1906.

2

A green dress with a crisscross bodice, which appears on pl. 2 of the book *Les Robes de Paul Poiret racontées par Paul Iribe*, shares a number of similarities, in both its shape and its fabric, with a dress from the Directory period that is in the collection of the Musée des Arts décoratifs, inv. 11840, acquired in 1905.

3

Not present on this example, perhaps lost.

4

We should mention the designer Margaine-Lacroix who, in 1898, presented dresses to be worn without a corset, such as the famous *Sylphide* design; however, this dress, which has a traditional structure, features a kind of flexible inbuilt corset made up of a boned silk knit lining that provides the necessary support to create the 'S' silhouette that was in fashion at the time.

5

'Modes artistiques', *Le Figaro-Modes*, 15 December 1905, p. 4.

This evening gown, called *1811*, is from the wardrobe of Paul Poiret's wife, Denise. It brings together the designer's experiments in style and form, which led to his creation of a new silhouette in 1906.[1] This sheath dress, which appears in the book *Les Robes de Paul Poiret racontées par Paul Iribe* in 1908, displays some characteristics of the vintage fashions from the Empire and Directory periods of France's history, from which Poiret drew inspiration for his collection: a square neckline and a high waist, gathered beneath the breasts. A slit in the left side of the skirt, making it easier for the wearer to walk, also allows a fleeting glimpse of mauve chiffon beneath. The designer accentuated the vertical lines of his composition by choosing a luxurious Pekin silk in very bright colours, using one of his favourite combinations, violet and fuchsia. Poiret also liked to combine different styles and added decorative elements borrowed from the 18th century, such as metallic lace, gold passementerie buttons and even striped fabric that was reminiscent of fashions during the Louis XVI era and the Revolution. The designer was particularly interested in historical sources and even went so far as to imitate the designs of earlier periods in his own creations.[2]

This silhouette is characterized by its surprisingly soft lines, created by its flat cut, loose around the waist, which means it can be worn without a corset, although there is one caveat: the Paul Poiret dresses from this period that are in the collection of the Musée des Arts décoratifs have an internal belt made of grosgrain, about 10 cm (4 in) wide, which is boned.[3] This feature is not comparable to a corset, but it does provide support. Poiret was certainly not the first French designer to present a dress to be worn without a corset, but it was very unusual, and only a few brave women, of whom Denise was one, did away with their corsets so early on.[4] Indeed, around this time, in autumn 1905, the fashion press, including *Femina*, *Le Figaro-Modes* and the very chic *Les Modes*, reported on the growing trend for high-waisted empire-line dresses created by the fashion houses Paquin, Lachartrouille and Bechoff-David, which had to be worn with a corset.[5]

M.-P. R

CAT. 160 Paul Iribe, *Les Robes de Paul Poiret racontées par Paul Iribe*, 1908, phototype and pochoir print. Paris, library of the Musée des Arts décoratifs

PAUL
IRIBE

**Joséphine
evening gown**

1907

Silk satin, silk netting,
metallic braid embroidered
with satin stitch

Paris, Musée des Arts
décoratifs

CAT. 2 [REPR. PP. 70-71]

1
See Yvonne Deslandres,
Paul Poiret, 1879-1944, Paris:
Éditions du Regard, 1986,
p. 110.

2
When this dress was donated,
the rose was missing; an
identical one was recreated
with the collaboration of
Denise Boulet-Poiret. See the
correspondence between
Yvonne Deslandres and Denise
Boulet-Poiret, December 1970,
Ufac collection.

3
See Nicole Biagioli, 'Prêtresses
de Flore: botanique et
émancipation des femmes
du 18ᵉ au 19ᵉ siècle', in Pierre-
Joseph Redouté (1759-1840),
Le Pouvoir des fleurs,
exh. cat., Paris: Musée de la
Vie romantique, Paris, Paris
Musées, 2017, p. 134.

4
Paul Iribe created the first
version of this rose design for
the perfumier Lubin in 1908.

5
Used for a dress in the
collection of The Metropolitan
Museum of Art, New York,
inv. 2005.198a, b.

6
Al. Terego, 'Les Opinions
de monsieur Pétrone', *La
Grande Revue*, 10 May 1909,
pp. 158–159.

There can be no doubt that *Joséphine*, created in 1907,[1] represents the culmination of Paul Poiret's aesthetic experiments, in its reinterpretation of period silhouettes taken from the Directory era and the First French Empire. This dress with a short train is made up of a plain white satin sheath overlaid with a tunic of fine square-mesh tulle, made by Maison Racine, edged with a decorative strip of spirals of gold braid, created by the workshop of the Monnot brothers. Another narrow braid accentuates the neckline and the high waist, which is adorned with a unique and delicate rose in the centre.

This flower was included on the original design. It was recreated for this dress in 1970 by Camille Amiot,[2] former head seamstress of the fashion house's 'embellishments' studio.

This embellishment recalls the great couturier's interest in women's engagement with botany at the turn of the 19th century;[3] Empress Joséphine, a knowledgeable botanist, was the inspiration for a new variety of rose, which was named after her. Poiret's tribute to the Empire era is part of the Neoclassical approach that is also explored by Paul Iribe in the book *Les Robes de Paul Poiret racontées par Paul Iribe*, printed in 1908, in which this dress appears, worn by a young woman with short, curly hair in the style of the Merveilleuses, a group of fashionable, decadent aristocratic women in Paris during the French Directory era (1795–1799).

Around the same time, this motif of the 'rose d'Iribe',[4] with its stem and two leaves, became the symbol of Paul Poiret's fashion house, appearing first on his logo and then on his letterhead. It also later appeared on a printed fabric by Raoul Dufy.[5]

The very deliberate placement of the rose on the bodice of the *Joséphine* dress draws on the 'science of detail' that Poiret, or rather 'Monsieur Pétrone', explored in an article published in *La Grande Revue* in 1909: 'This is the definitive expression of elegance and feminine simplicity; a plain dress [...] and the detail, the treasure, I would say almost the surprise: it's the slightest thing, a ribbon, a pleat, a tab used to fasten it [...] a gold tassel, a buckle, a little embroidered lapel, a lace collar, nothing, next to nothing, but it is just right and fits perfectly!'[6]

This rose symbolizes a broader interest in flowers on the part of Poiret, who named his first daughter Rosine and went on to create a perfume company named after her.
M.-P. R.

CAT. 160 Paul Iribe, *Les Robes de Paul Poiret racontées par Paul Iribe*, 1908, phototype and pochoir print. Paris, library of the Musée des Arts décoratifs

Ispahan coat

1907

Embroidered silk velvet and appliquéd cordonnet braid

Paris, Musée des Arts décoratifs

CAT. 47 [REPR. PP. 74-75]

1
Reproduced in Sylvie Legrand-Rossi, 'Paul Poiret, le couturier explorateur – la révolution de la coupe droite', in *Touches d'exotisme, XIVᵉ-XXᵉ siècles*, exh. cat., Paris: musée de la Mode et du Textile, Union centrale des arts décoratifs, 1998, p. 117.

2
See Françoise Cousin, 'Ispahan', in *Touches d'exotisme, XIVᵉ-XXᵉ siècles*, pp. 125–127.

3
See Sylvie Legrand-Rossi, 'Introduction', in *Touches d'exotisme, XIVᵉ-XXᵉ siècles*, p. 14.

4
Paul Poiret, *En habillant l'époque* (1930), Paris: Grasset, reissued 2022, p. 146.

5
Khémaïs Ben Lakhdar, *Paul Poiret l'orientaliste: un exotisme en question*, master's thesis, École du Louvre, supervised by Denis Bruna, May 2017, p. 33.

6
See Harold Koda and Andrew Bolton (eds), *Poiret*, exh. cat. for the Metropolitan Museum of Art New York, New Haven: Yale University Press, 2007, pp. 162–165.

7
See Paul Poiret, *En habillant l'époque*, pp. 151–152.

This coat, designed in 1907, was donated to Ufac by Denise Boulet-Poiret in 1963. Its label reads: 'Paul Poiret – 37, rue Pasquier.' She also wrote a letter that is held in the collection's archives: 'Huge success winter and summer. It was repeated in serge cloth and velvet in every colour.'[1] It appears again in 1908, in green embroidered with gold, in one of the illustrations in the book *Les Robes de Paul Poiret racontées par Paul Iribe*. Françoise Cousin analysed its cut, comparing it to coats from Central Asia.[2] She noted that there were similarities to Uzbek designs, while Paul Poiret also added Western elements. This incorporation of Eastern influences was made possible by Poiret's access to the collections of the Musée de l'Homme in Paris[3] and the Victoria and Albert Museum in London, which displayed the treasures of India, as he recalled in his memoirs.[4] Although he does not mention studying the coats, he recalls seeing the turban collection. More recently, Khémaïs Ben Lakhdar commented on *Ispahan* in his master's thesis.[5] He believes a possible inspiration might be the *chogas* of Rajasthan, which have a similar cut to the Uzbek *chapan*, but their embellishments are closer to those of *Ispahan*. The tone-on-tone embellishment draws on Indo-Persian motifs, such as the *boteh* (from the Hindi and Urdu *buta*, which means 'flower'). This motif is believed to date to the late 16th century, when the Mughal emperors annexed Kashmir. On its back, *Ispahan* has a large V-shaped design filled with plant motifs. Paul Poiret revisited this motif on the back of a dress worn by his wife in 1923, which he called *Persane*, and which is in the collection of Francesca Galloway Ltd.[6] All of the embellishments are created using satin stitch and in cord sewn on using blanket stitch. They give the piece a sumptuous feel that evokes the splendour of the Safavid court. The mystery and elegance of Persian art was a source of fascination to Poiret. That is why, in 1922, he chose it as the theme for his 'Thousand and Second Night' party.[7] In his memoir, he writes that he had put aside Persian outfits for any guests who arrived without a costume and that authentic Persian songs were performed. In 1923, the designer created a dress that was also called *Ispahan*, which was sketched by Georges Lepape for *Vogue*'s 1 April issue. The *Ispahan* coat is therefore one of the first signs of the designer's long-standing obsession with ancient Persia and 'exoticism'.

H. R.

CAT. 160 Paul Iribe, *Les Robes de Paul Poiret racontées par Paul Iribe*, 1908, phototype and pochoir print. Paris, library of the Musée des Arts décoratifs

MOSAÏQUE.

ROBE EXÉCUTÉE
CHEZ POIRET D'APRÈS MODÈLE
DE V. LHUER

Mosaïque evening gown

C. 1910

Chiffon embroidered with silk thread and beads, gold braid, mink fur and silk satin

Paris, Musée des Arts décoratifs

CAT. 26 [REPR. PP. 78-79]

1
'Poiret on the Philosophy of Dress', American Vogue, 15 October 1913, p. 41.

2
Paul Cornu, 'L'art de la robe', Art et décoration, 1 January 1911, p. 111.

3
However, the dress shown here has a number of differences from the drawing, especially in the bust and in the cut of the tunic.

4
See Bénédicte Gady, 'Dessins de mode de Victor Lhuer', in Bénédicte Gady (ed.), Le Dessin sans réserve. Collection du musée des Arts décoratifs, exh. cat., Paris: Musée des Arts décoratifs, 2020, p. 233.

5
Donated by the artist between 1943 and 1950.

This evening gown is typical of Paul Poiret's designs in the late 1910s. Made up of a lemon-yellow satin sheath overlaid with a floaty green chiffon tunic, it has a particularly high waist, in a crossover style, accentuated by a narrow braid. This characteristic look illustrates the great designer's words, as published in American Vogue: 'I like a plain gown, cut from a light and supple fabric, which falls from the shoulders to the feet in long, straight folds, like thick liquid […]. In a fourreau of supple satin, the plastic form of the modern woman is disclosed in its undulating svelteness […] which is an evidence of the oriental influence. It is, to my mind, the normal and rational vestment; one might say it is the original from which all dress sprang […] The first ornament that it seemed necessary to put on it was a girdle.'[1]

Here, the subtle combination of yellow and green reflects Poiret's taste for pure colours and his talent as a colourist who sought to revitalize, in his own words, the 'bland' 18th-century-inspired palette that had long been in fashion. The embroidery, in the same colours, gives shape to the composition and is organized into geometric strips, including one of Greek frets, reminiscent of architectural embellishments. Might this perhaps have been a reference to the new premises of the Maison Poiret, which had moved to a private mansion on the Avenue d'Antin in October 1909? Decorated over the course of a few months by the architect and interior designer Louis Süe, the rooms used to present the collections on the ground floor had a number of columns; cherry-red rugs and curtains and Empire furniture combined to form a setting with a Neoclassical feel and a touch of modernity, which complemented the style of the dresses, as described by Paul Cornu in 1911:[2] 'we view them, these dresses, in a modern setting, where the design of the furniture and the colours of the wall coverings reflect the same aesthetic tendencies.'

A variation of this piece,[3] called Mosaïque, was sketched by one of Paul Poiret's assistants, Victor Lhuer (1876–1952).[4] During this period, the great designer sought out and recruited a number of young artists, including Erté (1892–1990) and José de Zamora (1889–1971), who sketched designs under his direction. A significant number of Lhuer's drawings are in the collection of the Musée des Arts décoratifs:[5] they include day and evening coats, dresses and suits, some simply sketched, others painted with gouache in bright colours. The many annotations that Lhuer wrote on his sketches, which are sometimes signed, detail the choice of cuts, colours and fabrics, which makes them very valuable resources. He worked for the designer in the 1910s, as well as for Jean Patou and even the shoe designer André Perugia, another talented collaborator discovered by Paul Poiret.

M.-P. R.

CAT.172 Victor Lhuer, sketch of a dress for Paul Poiret, c. 1910, graphite and watercolour on vellum paper. Paris, Musée des Arts décoratifs

Lavallière
evening gown

c. 1910

Silk satin embroidered
with cylindrical glass beads

Paris, Musée des Arts
décoratifs

CAT. 3 [REPR. PP. 82-83]

1
Letter from Paul Poiret to
Denise Boulet, 5 September
1905, quoted in Palmer White,
Poiret le magnifique, Paris:
Payot, 1986, p. 66.

2
See Paul Poiret, *En habillant
l'époque*, Paris: Grasset,
1930, p. 69.

3
Ibid., p. 69.

4
See Guillaume Garnier (ed.),
*Paul Poiret et Nicole Groult,
Maîtres de la mode Art déco*,
exh. cat., Paris: Palais Galliera,
Musée de la Mode
et du Costume, 1986, p. 178.

5
Sylvie Legrand-Rossi,
'Paul Poiret, le couturier
explorateur', in *Touches
d'exotisme, XIVᵉ-XXᵉ siècles*,
exh. cat., Paris: musée de la
Mode et du Textile, Union
centrale des arts décoratifs,
1998, p. 121.

6
'The Prophet of Simplicity',
American *Vogue*, 1 November
1913, p. 43.

7
Idem.

8
Inv. GAL2008.1.1 (1 and 2).

This design, called *Lavallière* in homage to the famous actress Ève Lavallière, who often wore Poiret's designs both in town and on stage, is an evening gown from the wardrobe of Denise Boulet-Poiret. Wife and mother but also collaborator, muse and model, Denise was inextricably linked to her husband's work and success. He saw in her the ideal partner: 'I dream of marrying you, because I see in you something more than a devoted companion, of course. You are the lovely creature who constantly provides my imagination with assistance, who gives me encouragement and a vital purpose in my work.'[1] She dressed boldly and posed elegantly for photographers' cameras, wearing some of her husband's most avant-garde creations, and he drew inspiration from her slender, feline silhouette, both to design and to show off his clothes. Was this not the woman who dared to wear *Lola Montés*, a dress with no corset, to her daughter Rosine's christening in 1906? Or the first woman to appear in public wearing a turban in the Eastern style?[2] According to Poiret, 'she was discovering herself. She was meant to become one of the queens of Paris. Her appearances in elegant settings were remarked upon and many times she sparked a true sensation.'[3]

Denise Poiret is reported to have worn *Lavallière* to the opening night of the ballet *Shéhérazade*, staged by Diaghilev at the Palais Garnier on 4 June 1910.[4] For that extraordinary evening, she chose this particularly innovative outfit, inspired by the East,[5] with its straight and flowing line that also pre-empted the fashions of the following decade. Cut from a large rectangle of ivory silk satin and embroidered with silver tubes, the dress is unusual in that it can be slipped on easily and is worn with a belt draped around the hips, which was originally embellished with a line of small diamante buttons. A photograph by the studio Davis and Sanford shows that Denise also wore this design in New York, on the trip she took with her husband in 1913. 'Denise Poiret has never worn corsets [...]. Every garment falls free of her body[6],' American *Vogue* declared, describing her avant-garde wardrobe designed by Paul Poiret, whom it dubbed 'the Prophet of simplicity'.[7]

Denise Poiret had a number of variations of *Lavallière*, including one version designed to be worn as daywear, which is now in the collection of the Palais Galliera.[8]

M.-P. R.

ILL. 1 Davis & Sanford, Denise Poiret wearing the Paul Poiret dress *Lavallière*, 1913, Paris, Bibliothèque nationale de France, Prints and Photography department, inv. OA-702-FOL

Evening coat

c. 1910

Trimmed gros de Tours
with brocade design in gold
thread and silver strips,
shot taffeta, passementerie
and silver-coloured metal

Paris, Musée des Arts
décoratifs

CAT. 16 [REPR. PP. 86-87]

1
See Sylvie Legrand-Rossi,
'Paul Poiret, le couturier
explorateur', in *Touches
d'exotisme, XIVᵉ-XXᵉ siècles*,
exh. cat., Paris: musée de la
Mode et du Textile,
Union centrale des arts
décoratifs, 1998.

2
See Gustave Babin, 'Une
leçon d'élégance dans un
parc', *L'Illustration*, 9 July 1910,
pp. 21–22.

3
Ibid.

4
The Palais Galliera in Paris has
a similar example, *Révérend*,
dated 1905, inv. 1963.30.3.

5
See the description by Hélène
Renaudin, p. 77.

6
See Guillaume Garnier (ed.),
*Paul Poiret et Nicole Groult.
Maîtres de la mode Art déco*,
exh. cat., Paris: Musée de la
Mode et du Costume-Palais
Galliera, 1986, p. 16.

7
Paul Cornu, 'L'art de la robe',
Art et décoration, 1 January
1911, p. 111.

8
New York, The Metropolitan
Museum of Art, inv. 2005.199.

This evening coat donated to Ufac by Marcel Piccioni was worn by his mother Valentine, née Eiffel, an early customer of Paul Poiret's fashion house. For this piece, imbued with a sensual, dreamlike Orientalism, the designer chose a very valuable fabric, a bright orange gros de Tours with a brocade of gold and silver thread, which is reminiscent of the 'bizarre silks' of the 18th century, fabrics with patterns featuring sinuous curves and plant motifs combined with various surprising embellishments, with a possibly Eastern influence.[1] Here, Poiret combined this historicist fabric with thick fur around the wrists and wide collar; the fastening, consisting of bright green frogging and six silver buttons, reveals the full splendour of the design, offering a glimpse of the green shot-silk lining.

Contrasting colours are one of the designer's stylistic signatures, as a journalist from *L'Illustration* noted when invited to attend the show for the summer 1910 collection launched by the fashion house on the Avenue d'Antin.[2] This illustrated article is also the only known place where an image of this coat appears, presented alongside other pieces worn by a group of models walking through the gardens 'with gliding steps, like those women of the Orient who balance full vases on their heads'.[3] Made from a slightly different fabric, this coat was the couturier's original design, which he accessorized with a bicorne-like hat and, in one of the photographs, a Japanese parasol.

For Poiret, coats were particularly rich ground for self-expression, in terms of both shape and embellishment. From the earliest days of his career, it was coats that he experimented with and created new shapes for: first generous and draped like a kimono, such as the famous *Confucius* design,[4] created when he was working for Worth, although he also released a version under his own label; the *Ispahan* coat of 1907,[5] with a cut inspired by the traditional Rajasthani *choga*; or even the *Battick* design, with a triangular silhouette created by gathering it in tightly around the hips or knees,[6] photographed by Edward Steichen in 1911;[7] finally, we should mention the *Perse* coat,[8] worn by his wife, Denise, and the actress Ève Lavallière in 1911, its fabric printed with a spectacular design by Raoul Dufy.

M.-P. R.

ILL. 2 Henri Manuel, group of models in front of a trellised portico, illustration for the article 'Une leçon d'élégance dans un parc' ('A lesson in elegance in a park') by Gustave Babin, published in *L'Illustration*, no. 3515, 9 July 1910, p. 22. Paris, library of the Musée des Arts décoratifs

Evening gown

1910

Silk satin, chiffon embroidered with cylindrical glass beads and silk velvet

Paris, Musée des Arts décoratifs

CAT. 36 [REPR. PP. 90-91]

1
Femina, 15 October 1910, p. 537.

2
See Guillaume Garnier (ed.), *Paul Poiret et Nicole Groult. Maîtres de la mode Art déco*, exh. cat., Paris: Palais Galliera–Musée de la Mode et du Costume-Paris Musée, 1986, p. 222.

3
L. de L. 'La broderie à Galliera', *Le Figaro*, 29 June 1912, p. 3.

4
Paul Cornu, 'L'art de la robe', *Art et décoration*, 1 January 1911, pp. 114–118.

5
Georges Henri Pissarro (1871–1961), a painter, engraver and illustrator of two tales from the *Thousand and One Nights* (1910–1923).

6
Paul Poiret, *En habillant l'époque*, Paris: Grasset, 1930, p. 166.

In October 1910, a variation of this evening gown design was featured in the fashion magazine *Femina*,[1] which described it as: 'Imperial green Liberty sheath, overlaid with a chiffon tunic in the same colour, with a strip of black velvet with embroidery inserts of tubular glass beads.' This very precise description highlights the characteristics of Poiret's designs in the early 1910s, which drew on the Neoclassical line that he had launched a few years earlier and which had made his name.

Here, the particularly dense, structural embroidery, of a thickness that contrasts with the transparency of the chiffon, evokes stylized Persian-inspired floral motifs. Its arrangement in geometric borders, as well as the contrast between black and white, also draws on the decorative style of the Vienna Workshops (Wiener Werkstätte), which the couturier visited the same year that he designed this piece. These embellishments were most likely created by the studio of the brothers Maurice and Henri Monnot, whom Poiret had met through Jacques Doucet.[2] Based at number 5 Rue Godot-de-Mauroy in Paris, they were described as 'Orientalists of embroidery';[3] the great skill shown in their creations was also praised by the journal *Art et décoration* in an article illustrated by famous photographs of Poiret designs taken by Edward Steichen:[4] 'Fabrics, embroidery, passementerie, lace, everything here testifies to the same desire for renewal, and the Monnot brothers have a wealth of talent at their disposal [...]. The richness of the gold and silver embroidery gives certain [dresses] the sumptuous and refined feel of a painting by Manzana-Pissarro.'[5]

These varied inspirations form the essence of Poiret's style, which charmed both clients and muses who were particularly receptive to his groundbreaking vision. Among them were the Ballets Russes dancer Tamara Karsavina (1885–1978), who played the title role of the *L'Oiseau de feu* (*The Firebird*), first performed on 25 June 1910 at the Paris Opera. Indeed, around the same time, she posed for a photograph wearing a similar design, paired with a turban.

In his memoirs, Poiret wrote of his admiration for Sergei Diaghilev, founder of the Ballets Russes, and for Léon Bakst, who designed the sets and costumes, and whose flamboyant aesthetic shared similarities with Poiret's work; he also insisted that his style was his own: 'I was struck by the Ballets Russes, I would not be surprised if they'd had a certain influence on me. However, it must be known that I already existed and that my reputation was made before that of Monsieur Bakst [...]. There was little to draw from his designs for the stage [...] too extravagant to inspire a couturier who works in the real world.'[6]

M.-P. R.

ILL. 3 Anonymous, Tamara Karsavina wearing a design by Paul Poiret, 1910. London, Victoria & Albert Museum, inv. 2010EA6775

**Flammes
shawl and
culotte-dress**

1911

Shawl made from hand-
embroidered silk crepe (cut
into Manila shawl style);
culotte-dress made from
silk velvet, chiffon and
passementerie

Paris, Musée des Arts
décoratifs

CAT. 50 [REPR. PP. 94-95]

1
On close inspection, it is clear
that the cut is unfinished and
the finishes were very rushed.

2
See Sylvie Legrand-Rossi,
'Paul Poiret, le couturier
explorateur', in Touches
d'exotisme, XIVe-XXe siècles,
exh. cat., Paris: musée de la
Mode et du Textile, Union
centrale des arts décoratifs,
1998. p. 117.

2
'Les quatre manières de
culotter une femme',
L'Illustration, 18 February 1911,
p. 103.

3
See Paul Poiret, En habillant
l'époque, Paris: Grasset, 1930,
p. 276.

4
Quoted in JF, 'Les costumes de
Nabuchodonosor', Excelsior,
3 February 1911, p. 8.

This evening-wear outfit, carefully preserved by Denise Poiret, is an exceptional example of Paul Poiret's creative output in the early 1910s. Called *Flammes*, this 'culotte-dress' is made up of a draped backless bodice embellished with a tassel, and a pair of voluminous trousers made of bright red silk velvet, paired with a large shawl with a fur border, made from multicoloured embroidered silk, a style known as a 'Manila' shawl. This outfit, which was put together quickly for a party,[1] brings together a number of Orientalist influences that shaped the designer's style, an interest partly inspired by the cultural and aesthetic infatuation with the Ballets Russes towards the end of the first decade of the 20th century.

Poiret caused a stir by featuring in his collections accessories and clothes adapted, in the broadest sense, from traditional Eastern clothing. In 1909, he presented an Indian turban, then in the winter of 1911, a year after the first performance of the ballet *Shéhérazade*, he launched the culotte-skirt, also called 'harem pants' or the 'sultan skirt', among other names. This style of trousers is derived from the sarouel, with a low-hanging crotch but tight around the ankles. In February 1911, the magazine *L'Illustration* published sketches of a number of variations on the style, drawn by Poiret himself.[2] For the designer, this was first and foremost a luxurious garment only to be worn indoors, unlike the versions designed to be worn out in public released by the fashion house Bechoff-David in 1910, which caused a scandal.[3]

This bold style was also associated with parties and theatre. In the winter of 1911, Poiret designed the costumes for the play *Nabuchodonosor*, which ran at the Théâtre des Arts and for which he created various versions of the culotte-skirt: 'As for the costumes for *Nabuchodonosor*, they seemed particularly interesting to design because I found in them very specific similarities with contemporary women's fashion. I endeavoured to express only the very fantastical vision that we have of Chaldea, and to adapt the costumes to suit the modern aesthetic.'[4]

The enthusiasm sparked by this fantasy version of the East infused all of Parisian high society, and there was a spate of private parties with this theme. Poiret hosted the most iconic one, the famous Persian party the 'Thousand and Second Night', held on 24 June 1911: his wife, Denise, wore an outfit designed by her husband, made up of a 'lampshade' tunic worn over a voluminous culotte-skirt. This costume, of which there were a number of variations in Poiret's collections from September 1911, was a critical success but, it must be noted, only adopted by high society.

M.-P. R.

ILL. 4 Henri Manuel, *Denise Poiret looking out of the window*, 1911,
gelatin silver print [1973], printed from the positive. Paris, Bibliothèque nationale de France, Prints and Photography department

Mélodie dress

1912

Silk damask, silk velvet, galalith and piping

Paris, Musée des Arts décoratifs

CAT. 37 [REPR. PP. 98-99]

1
Paul Poiret, 'The Logic of Dress by Paul Poiret', *Harper's Bazaar*, December 1913, p. 45.

2
American *Vogue*, 15 February 1914, p. 21.

3
See De Lange, 'The Tango Fashion', *Women's Wear Daily*, 9 January 1914, p. 1.

4
See Paul Poiret, 'Le chapitre des chapeaux', *Le Journal*, 29 December 1913, p. 7.

This afternoon dress from Denise Poiret's wardrobe, called *Mélodie*, has a highly innovative cut and pattern. Dating to 1912, it is made up of a surprising triangular silk velvet pinafore-tunic with a pocket, combined with a damask sheath dress in bishop's purple, its narrow, split skirt embellished with a line of six large, purely decorative covered buttons. Another button, made of galalith (a type of plastic) with a simple concentric motif in yellow and red, appears to fasten the tunic (which is sewn at the collar) and is the focal point of the composition. Although they are not functional, these buttons are placed so as to complement the clean geometric lines, which are also emphasized by the red piping on the tunic, contributing to the overall visual harmony of the piece. Indeed, in his designs, Poiret places great importance on buttons: 'A button is an object of utility. If it does not serve any purpose, then do not put it on. [...] A button should button or be placed so that it might button; but placed haphazard on a dress it spoils the logic and consequently the ensemble.'[1]

The amazing composition of this dress, which does not draw in at the waist, creates a groundbreaking silhouette that is both straight and flowing, 'the straightest waistline in Paris', according to an article in American *Vogue*.[2] That is most likely why Poiret proposed a variation on this design for the costume to be worn by one of the actresses in the play *Le Tango* by Jean and Marianne Richepin, which was performed in Paris at the Théâtre de l'Athénée from 30 December 1913.[3] After the critical success of the costumes that he designed that same year for Jacques Richepin's play *Le Minaret*, Poiret also designed the set for *Le Tango*, which was made by the Maison Martine, as well as all of the costumes for the play, which was set in 1925; his designs embraced simple lines and minimal embellishments.[4]

The actresses Ève Lavallière and Andrée Spinelly, the stars of the play, regularly wore designs by Poiret around town as well as on stage, especially Spinelly, his friend and muse. They enjoyed a mutual admiration: the actress, who asked him to decorate her Paris apartment, regularly appeared in his designs up until the mid-1920s; she even chose the *Mélodie* dress when posing for photographs by the Rol agency in 1913, alongside Ève Lavallière.

The *Mélodie* design, sketched by Romain de Tirtoff, aka Erté, who assisted Paul Poiret between 1912 and 1914, seems to have been a hit; it certainly charmed the high-society figure Daisy de Broglie, who wore it when posing for the painter Jacques-Émile Blanche.

M.-P. R.

ILL. 5 Anonymous, Denise Poiret wearing the *Mélodie* dress by Paul Poiret, 1913, gelatin silver print. Paris, Bibliothèque nationale de France, Prints and Photography department, inv. OA-702-FOL

Bretonne dress

1919

Embroidered silk velvet, silk crepe and silk netting

Paris, Musée des Arts décoratifs

CAT. 53 [REPR. PP. 102-103]

1
Yvonne Deslandres, 'L'influence du costume traditionnel sur les créations de Paul Poiret', in *Vêtements et sociétés*, symposium at the Musée de l'Homme, 2–3 March 1979, pp. 49–52.

2
'La mode au jour le jour, visite chez les couturiers – M. Paul Poiret de la rue Auber expose une robe en drap noir rappelant assez par sa forme et ses détails le costume des femmes bretonnes', *New York Herald Paris*, 22 March 1904, p. 5.

3
The collection of Alain Charlemagne, son of Paul Charlemagne and Agnès Jallat, a former 'Martine', held in the Musée des Arts décoratifs, inv. 2019.116, includes accounts of these trips to Brittany, particularly to Île-Tudy.

From the wardrobe of Denise Poiret, this afternoon dress, called *Bretonne*, dates to 1919 exactly. The clothes that Paul Poiret was designing at the time, an average of two hundred pieces per collection, embraced a blended style that combined Orientalist and 'exotic' references, in the broadest sense of the word, but also reinterpreted Western historical and folk styles. These varied inspirations became his signature and the designer, who was constantly seeking to innovate, came up with pieces that were often put together in an unexpected way.

Indeed, while the line of this dress was in vogue at the time, its cut is unusual, because it looks like it is made up of three separate pieces. Cut in black silk velvet, it boasts an unusual false blouse front with a high turtleneck collar and a crepe georgette blouse with a wide band of grosgrain for internal support at the waist. The apron-like look, which is certainly deliberate, is also accentuated by a long ribbon of bright red jersey, tied at the back and hanging down. However, this is a variation on the original design: a photograph of *Bretonne* for the legal register, in the collection of the Musée des Arts décoratifs, shows the designer's original intention – he had added velvet half-sleeves with slashes to let the crepe underneath show through.

The use of black velvet and, especially, of the floral embroidery created by the Monnot brothers, which follows the cut of the garment, are reminiscent of a traditional Breton bodice, but, according to Yvonne Deslandres, the style of this dress draws more on Slavic embroidery.[1] As was typical in his work, Poiret did not present a literal interpretation of regional costumes, but an innovative combination of their rich and original range of embellishments. He had also built up a large collection of fabric swatches, braids, embroidery and even traditional costumes in their entirety, from which he borrowed shapes or details.

This reinterpretation of picturesque, charming Breton costume had been present in his work from his earliest days as a designer, as the *New York Herald – Paris* noted in 1904,[2] and it would be a recurring theme throughout his career. Poiret had a particular affection for Brittany. He visited the region with his family and friends; he also took members of his team on holidays there, including a group of young women from the Martine School (École Martine) in the 1910s.[3]

M.-P. R.

ILL. 6 Anonymous, photograph of the Paul Poiret design *Bretonne* for the legal registry, 1919, gelatin silver print. Paris, Musée des Arts décoratifs, Archives de la Seine collection, 1940

Jacket
that belonged to Paul Poiret
c. 1920

Woodblock-printed linen, based on a design by the Martine workshop, figured silk crepe and braided leather

Paris, Musée des Arts décoratifs

CAT. 93 [REPR. PP. 106-107]

1
The Musée des Arts décoratifs has a very small number of accessories from Paul Poiret's wardrobe, including a few stiff collars, donated by his ex-wife, Denise.

2
Jean Oberlé, 'Quelques dandys', *Adam*, 15 December 1931, p. 40.

3
A similar plain yellow jacket is in the collection of the Palais Galliera, inv. 1985.148.3.

4
Photographs of Paul Poiret by Thérèse Bonney, dated 1927, in the collection of the Bibliothèque historique de la ville de Paris.

5
Paul Poiret, *En habillant l'époque*, Paris: Grasset, 1930, p. 96.

Donated by his ex-wife, Denise, this jacket is one of the few remaining items of clothing worn by Paul Poiret himself,[1] a man who, throughout his life, stood out from the crowd for his elegance and sophistication. He co-founded the men's fashion magazine *Monsieur* in 1919; his personal style was the subject of a charming description written by his friend the painter and illustrator Jean Oberlé: 'In general, he wears on his striking head, which is spiked with the thousand prickles of a short beard, grey felt hats, from which he takes care to remove the hatband. […] He is wrapped in Norfolk-style belted jackets, in every fabric and every colour, in tussore, in velvet, in white with royal blue. […] These are paired with ties in bright colours, purple or bright red, when they are not made of batik fabric. Dark trousers lead down to elasticated shoes […] with no laces, with no seams, without anything. But their toe is square, with stitching that forms two interlaced Ps, their owner's initials.'[2]

This practical, comfortable belted work jacket, which accentuated his stout figure, is an interpretation of the English Norfolk jacket, made of tweed and traditionally worn for hunting and other outdoor activities. Poiret, who owned a number of variations on this design,[3] seems to have dressed in it in a variety of different settings, especially during the 1920s. Worn under a fur-trimmed coat or an outdoor coat, it is strongly associated with the designer's public persona as an artist. Indeed, a number of drawings and photographs, including those taken by the American Thérèse Bonney,[4] show him wearing it while at work, as well as while indulging in his hobby of painting, as can be seen from the small paint spots visible on the surface of the fabric.

This example, which boasts a collar in imitation reptile skin, features a range of embellishments drawing on various references and sources of inspiration that were important to the designer. The motif of the fabric, in particular, printed following a design by the Martine workshop (Atelier Martine), is made up of dense foliage through which does (or gazelles) are leaping. This graceful animal evokes the iconography of Persian rugs or miniatures, of which Poiret was a connoisseur, but also recalls the ancient bronze statuettes of does, 'two wonders brought back from Herculaneum',[5] displayed on either side of the front steps of his couture house on the Avenue d'Antin. The density of this pattern is also evocative of jungle scenes by the painter Henri Rousseau (1844–1910), whose work Poiret greatly admired.

M.-P. R.

ILL. 7 Thérèse Bonney, Paul Poiret and the model Renée at his fashion house at 1 rond-point des Champs-Élysées, 1927, gelatin silver bromide print. Paris, Bibliothèque historique de la ville de Paris, number NN-006-02707

Summer dress
that belonged to
Martine Poiret
c. 1920

Block-printed silk satin after
a drawing by the Martine
workshop and cordonnet braid

Paris, Musée des Arts
décoratifs

CAT. 88 [REPR. PP. 110-111]

1
Invitation designed by Bernard
Naudin, around 1907.

2
See Guillaume Garnier (ed.),
*Paul Poiret et Nicole Groult.
Maîtres de la mode Art
déco*, exh. cat., Paris: Palais
Galliera–Musée de la Mode
et du Costume-Paris Musée,
1986, p. 209.

3
The Musée des Arts décoratifs
has two other outfits worn
by Paul Poiret's children in its
collection: inv. 2005.37.1.1-2
and 2005.37.10.1.

4
Auction 'La création en
Liberté, univers de Paul et
Denise Poiret 1905–1928', held
at the auction house Piasa in
2005.

5
Vogue, 1 November 1921, p. 39.

This summer dress was worn by Martine Poiret (1911–1953), the couple's second daughter, who, like her sisters Rosine (1906–1915) and Perrine (1916–1997) and her brother Colin (1912–1998), was dressed in clothes designed by their father. Indeed, Paul Poiret was designing children's clothes from the middle of the first decade of the 1900s, as can be seen from an invitation to attend the presentation of the collection at the fashion house,[1] at that point located at 37 Rue Pasquier, now held by the library of the Musée des Arts décoratifs. These first pieces would actually have been the result of the short-lived collaboration between Paul Poiret and his younger sister Germaine Bongard (1885–1971),[2] who set up her own couture salon in 1911.

However, there are very few remaining examples of children's clothes designed by Poiret,[3] who seems to have pursued this only up until the 1920s, with the notable exception of the children's clothes from the Poiret family archives, which were auctioned off in 2005.[4] While some of these embrace the norms of traditional children's clothing, such as the sailor suit, others, much like his designs for adults, also reflect the diverse inspirations that shaped the designer's creative output; those particularly worth mentioning include a burnous-dress, a miniature kaftan, a blouse with a Chinese collar and even a dress cut from a cashmere shawl.

The silk satin bodice of this dress is printed with a floral motif created by the Martine workshop (Atelier Martine). Named after his daughter, the fashion house's interior design studio, which was founded in April 1911, remains a fairly unusual experiment in this area. Young girls, with names such as Gabrielle, Agnès or Martiale, without any artistic background, were recruited and trained according to an innovative pedagogical approach that placed great emphasis on the spontaneity of drawing from nature. Numerous sketches of these designs, characterized by, among other things, stylized, dense and highly coloured floral motifs, have survived. They were used on a range of different items created by the studio: transposed onto furniture fabric, wallpaper or packaging paper, or block-printed on crepe, silk satin or linen to be used for clothing.

This charming motif of branches with blue leaves combined with small flower bells and buttercups, which dates to around 1920, was created in a number of colourways. It was used on 'Oriental' silk cushions,[5] was printed on the bottle for the Rosine perfume *Jardin d'Enfant* and even appeared on the curtains in the salon of the barge *Amours*, which was used for the International Exhibition of Modern Decorative and Industrial Arts in 1925.

M.-P. R.

CAT. 313 Auguste Léon, interior of the barge *Amours*, which Paul Poiret used to exhibit his works at the International Exhibition of Modern Decorative and Industrial Arts in 1925. Interior design by Ronsin and Laverdet. Fabrics and decorative elements by the Martine workshop, 1925, autochrome, Boulogne-Billancourt, Archives de la Planète collection, Musée Albert-Kahn/Département des Hauts-de-Seine

CAT. 86 Martine workshop, *Les Anémones* fabric (detail), 1912, roller printed on linen after a drawing by the Martine Workshop. Paris, Musée des Arts décoratifs

Martinique dress

1922

Crepe marocain and printed crepe de chine

Paris, Musée des Arts décoratifs

CAT. 57 [REPR. PP. 114-115]

1
Poiret, *En habillant l'époque*, Paris: Grasset, 1930, p. 58.

2
'Chez Poiret', *Officiel de la couture et de la mode*, no. 17, 1922, p. 13.

3
See Marie-Jo Bonnet, *Les Deux Amies. Essai sur le couple de femmes dans l'Art*, Paris: Éditions Blanche, 2000, p. 215

This dress, *Martinique*, dating to 1922, is a remarkable design: in appearance it is reminiscent of a kimono, a garment that Paul Poiret reinterpreted, inspired by the widespread interest in clothes and fabrics from the Far East that had been growing since the late 19th century. Popular with elegant women of the era for its comfort and the wide range of movement that it permitted, the kimono was first designed to be worn indoors, and its characteristics were gradually combined with elements of Western clothing. Poiret, a trailblazer when it came to experimenting with new cuts, had drawn inspiration from it since his earliest designs. In 1903, when he was working at the prestigious Worth fashion house, the young designer came up with a highly innovative coat: 'a large square kimono made of black serge, trimmed with a bias strip of black satin; the sleeves were wide, all the way down, with embroidery embellishments on the end like the sleeves of Chinese coats.'[1] This description also shows Poiret's stylistic eclecticism, freely combining Chinese and Japanese inspirations in the same piece.

The introduction of new cuts based on the geometric simplicity of the Japanese kimono played its part in reinventing the female silhouette, as women were gradually liberated from restrictive corsets. Designers such as Madeleine Vionnet and Jeanne Lanvin took inspiration from it in the late 1910s and early 1920s, as did Paul Poiret, whose collections regularly featured clothes that drew on this aesthetic. This piece, designed as an afternoon dress, is an especially interesting example of this influence, with its crossover fastening, its characteristic sleeves and no collar. It is a wrap dress made of black crepe marocain with two inset panels of block-printed crepe with naive floral motifs in seven colours, in the style of designs by the Martine School (École Martine); the bodice is loose-fitting and the skirt has two ruffles on the sides. Its long, generous sleeves, made of yellow crepe de chine, are reminiscent of kimono sleeves, and they accentuate the flowing lines and relaxed look, 'well draped, wraparound: a silhouette traced with true artistry'.[2]

This dress was donated to Ufac in 1953 by the American artist Louise Janin (1893–1997). The daughter of a collector of Chinese art, her paintings, inspired by the Far East, were the subject of a highly successful exhibition at the Bernheim-Jeune Gallery in Paris in 1924. She moved in literary and artistic circles in the capital and opened her own salon on the Rue des Beaux-Arts, to which she invited Paul Poiret, among other well-known personalities.[3] It is not surprising, therefore, that this avant-garde artist shared certain intellectual and aesthetic interests with the designer, which could explain why she chose this dress, which had been in her wardrobe for many years.

M.-P. R.

ILL. 8 Henri Manuel, photograph of a Paul Poiret design for the legal registry, 1922, gelatin silver print. Paris, Musée des Arts décoratifs, Archives de la Seine collection, 1940

Ballon
travel coat

C. 1923

Peau de tortue fabric,
silk velvet and silk pongee
lining by Dagobert Peche
(textile designer)

Paris, Musée des Arts
décoratifs

CAT. 43 [REPR. PP. 118·119]

1
Paul Poiret, 'Der Sturmlauf
gegen Poiret', *Neues Wiener
Journal*, 4 March 1924, p. 3.

2
As well as the article cited
above, see also the following
sources: 'Die Wiener
Schneider drohen den Poiret-
Ball zu stören', *Der Tag*, 29
February 1924, p. 5; 'Poiret, die
Schneider und die Schreiber',
Die Stunde, 6 March 1924,
p. 3.

3
'Der Sturmlauf gegen Poiret',
p. 3.

4
Idem.

5
Berta Zuckerkandl, 'Paul Poiret
und die Klimt-Gruppe', *Neues
Wiener Journal*, 25 November
1923, p. 5. This article is not
without errors: Zuckerkandl
claims that Poiret's first visit to
Vienna was in 1912, whereas
the designer had visited
Vienna in 1910 and again in
1911.

6
This fabric was made in a
number of colourways. Poiret
also used other fabric designs
from the Wiener Werkstätte:
Diomède (1919) by Dagobert
Peche and *Kanarienvogel*
(1910) by Mizzi Vogel.

7
See Peter Noever, *Yearning
for Beauty: The Wiener
Werkstätte and the Stoclet
House*, exh. cat., Vienne: MAK,
Ostfildern: Hatje Cantz, 2006,
p. 149.

8
'Der Sturmlauf gegen Poiret',
p. 3.

'*Before the war, I proved in Vienna that I had never sought to compete with Viennese business. On the contrary, I think I contributed a great deal to ensuring that everything that Vienna has created in the world of fashion, elegance and decorative arts was recognized abroad.*'[1]

These were the words of Paul Poiret when, in March 1924, he was asked about the protests being held in the Austrian capital against his upcoming promotional trip. The local press detailed the grievances of Viennese tailors, hit by unemployment, who complained of favouritism in the treatment of the French designer.[2] Poiret defended himself against accusations that he was creating 'unfair competition', insisting that he promoted Viennese designs in his fashion house and his interior design studio.[3] He argued that he did not try to hide the provenance of the embroidery, laces and fabrics that he used and went on to say that he was against 'protectionism'. In his view, this policy contributed to the impoverishment of creativity, by cutting it off from international support.[4]

The *Ballon* travel coat – a visual and referential patchwork – should be understood in the light of this last declaration. Poiret combined a rare, valuable fabric, simulated tortoise skin, with the *Regenbogen* fabric created by the designer Dagobert Peche in 1919 in the fabric department of the Wiener Werkstätte. Discovering these workshops founded by Josef Hoffmann, Koloman Moser and Fritz Wärndorfer in 1910 was a pivotal moment in Poiret's career – at least, that was the contention of the Austrian art critic and salon hostess Berta Zuckerkandl in an article published in 1923.[5] The designer shared a certain aesthetic taste with the Vienna Workshops, as well as an interest in the idea of the *Gesamtkunstwerk* ('total artwork'), which he drew on in his various businesses (Martine and Rosine). It was also after his visit to the Wiener Werkstätte that he set up the Martine school (École Martine) and workshop (Atelier Martine). The use of the *Regenbogen* fabric,[6] most likely purchased in Vienna in late 1923,[7] is therefore very intentional. It exemplifies the designer's claim that Viennese decorative arts had an impact on fashion[8] and serves as a reminder of the importance of the international art scene in his work.
A. N.

ILL. 9 Anonymous, Paul Poiret surrounded by his models and Lars Christiansen at the station, 1925, gelatin silver print from the *Photographic Album of Paul Poiret's visit to Copenhagen*. Paris, Palais Galliera–Musée de la Mode de la Ville de Paris

CAT. 42 Louis Vuitton, hat box in Monogram fabric, formerly belonging to Paul Poiret, 1911, coated canvas, wood, brass and iron. Louis Vuitton Collection

154

La Source coat

1924

Roumécla fleuri fabric
by Rodier (cotton, machine
embroidery in gold thread
and cotton thread), buckle
by Paul Kiss (metalworker)

Paris, Musée des Arts
décoratifs

CAT. 59 [REPR. PP. 122-123]

1
Inv. 3414.

2
Inv. MT 26443, mentioned
in Armen Tokatlian, *Soies
de paradis*, Paris: Gourcuff
Gradenigo–Musée des Tissus
de Lyon, 2008, p. 62.

3
Étienne Blondeau, 'Précieuse
alliance: le bleu et l'or dans
les arts islamiques au Moyen
Âge', in Étienne Blondeau
(ed.), *Les Routes bleues.
Périples d'une couleur de
la Chine à la Méditerranée*,
Limoges: Musée national
Adrien-Dubouché-Les Ardents
Éditeurs, 2014, p. 122.

This coat was created by Paul Poiret for the spring/summer 1924 collection. The Musée des Arts décoratifs also has, in its collection of Ufac photographs, two original prints of the legal register photographs of this coat, dated 6 February 1924. It also featured in *Vogue*'s 1 July 1924 edition with the following caption: 'Poiret endows the simplest dress with the stamp of originality: a Poiret design is never ordinary and, in his hands, a simple cotton dress takes on the feel of the most luxurious designs. This one, made of "Roumécla fleuri", a mix of silk and cotton, is embellished with Persian motifs by Rodier. The entire look: the skirt with multiple godets, the fitted bodice with darts, drawn in at the waist, gives a charming, nostalgic impression that is somewhat evocative of the silhouette of the 1840s. A strip of plain fabric runs along the hem and the fastening.' At the waist, this mid-length coat also features a silver-plated metal buckle created by the artisan metalworker Paul Kiss. The coat's shape is reminiscent of certain Asian garments, such as the Persian *khalat*, one example of which, from the 17th century, is in the collection of the Royal Armoury Museum in Stockholm.[1] As for the techniques used, *La Source* is decorated with machine embroidery in blue and gold. The *Vogue* article highlighted the similarities with Persian motifs. Although the embroidery technique was not the same, from a stylistic perspective this design certainly does evoke the image of the 'Persian fabrics' that were so popular in the 17th and 18th centuries. These fabrics, which were attributed to Persia but could also come from India, were embellished with floral arabesques inspired by the decoration on Persian rugs, or imitated printed or painted fabrics imported from India. Westerners were major consumers, as can be seen from the ban on importing these fabrics that was in place in France between 1686 and 1759. This meant they were widely imitated throughout Europe. During the reign of the Safavids, these motifs were designed to evoke the eternal garden of paradise.[2] The choice of colour is equally revealing: Poiret's use of blue and gold was in all likelihood not random... He was probably aware of the spiritual importance of this colour combination in Islamic art. Étienne Blondeau explains this well in his article on the subject, writing that the combination of blue and gold is common in the sumptuous arts of medieval Islam and was more than a simple question of fashion.[3] Safavid architecture testifies to this taste, with the blue and gold domes of the magnificent mosques in Isfahan and other cities of Persia. The name of this design is also a reference to water, which is a symbol of life in the Qur'an: it is the way in which God caused 'gardens and harvest-grain to grow, and tall palm-trees' (Surah 50: 9–10). It is likely that, thanks to his research and travels to the area, Poiret was well aware of such symbolism.

ILL. 10 Anonymous, photograph of the Paul Poiret design *La Source* for the legal registry, 1924, gelatin silver print. Paris, Musée des Arts décoratifs, Archives de la Seine collection, 1940

Marrakech evening gown

1924

Silk satin, silver strip embroidery in Tsel stitch, chinchilla fur and silk velvet

Paris, Musée des Arts décoratifs

CAT. 4 [REPR. PP. 126-127]

1
See 'Da Poiret viste Kobenhavnerinderne sine Vidundere', *Kobenhavn*, 14 November 1925; 'Poirets opvisning paa modeudstillingen', *Berlingske Morgen*, 14 November 1925; 'Fra Poiret-Opvisningen pass Modeudstilingen', 14 November 1925; 'Da Poirets mannepuiner igaae viste de sidste Skrig for Koben', *BT*, 14 November 1925.

2
See Isabelle Denamur and Marie-France Vivier, 'Introduction', in Rémi Labrusse, Fatima Lévèque and Émilie Salaberry-Duhoux (eds), *Tarz. Broder au Maroc, hier et aujourd'hui*, exh. cat., Angoulême: Musée d'Angoulême, Paris: Skira, 2022, pp. 14–15.

3
Inv. 74.1973.2.1 and inv. 74.1975.1.12.

4
Rémi Labrusse, 'Fils noués, fils rompus dans les regards d'Occident', in Isabelle Denamur and Marie-France Vivier, 'Introduction', in Labrusse et al, *Tarz...*, p. 26.

5
Poiret, *En habillant l'époque*, Paris: Grasset, 1930, reissued 2022, pp. 187–195.

6
Florence Müller, 'Poiret, rencontre Orient-Occident', in Legrand-Rossi, *Touches d'exotisme, XIVᵉ-XXᵉ siècles*, exh. cat., Paris, musée de la Mode et du Textile, Paris, Union centrale des arts décoratifs, 1998, pp. 135 and 137.

7
Information taken from the Pacific Biodiversity Institute, document written by S. Murray (available online).

The *Marrakech* evening gown, created in 1924, was presented at a runway show of Paul Poiret's designs in Copenhagen in November 1925.[1] This white silk satin evening gown is embellished with strips of metallic silver using the Eastern technique of Tsel stitch (a flat, double-sided stitch using flat gold or silver thread). The name given to this piece, which refers to Morocco, suggests that Poiret was inspired by the traditions of that country. Morocco has an embroidery tradition that draws on many different influences.[2] One of the most pervasive is a legacy of the encounter between the art of Al-Andalus and that of the Berbers. Tsel stitch is commonly found on women's veils. One very fine example, which dates to the 19th century and was created in Fez, is in the collection of the Musée du Quai Branly, Paris.[3] This means it is possible that Poiret might have seen this kind of work and drawn inspiration from it. He may well have attended the Exhibition of Moroccan Art held in 1917 at the Musée des Arts décoratifs in Paris, where embroidery featured prominently.[4] But the designer also travelled to Morocco, as he recalls in the 'Morocco' chapter of his memoirs.[5] He spent some time in Fez, where he was enchanted by the city and its atmosphere. The designer certainly brought back a number of fabrics, which may have sparked his imagination, and which he may even have reused. In her article on Paul Poiret[6], Florence Müller wrote that the *Marrakech* dress features a number of embroidered silk satin panels, which she describes as 'cobbled together', and which may suggest the use of fabrics from the Maghreb. Poiret put the finishing touch to the outfit by adding a wide strip of chinchilla fur to the hem at the front. This was not a reference to the East, but a form of embellishment that was very fashionable in the 1920s. Highly prized for the softness of its fur, this small animal from the Andes was subject to intensive hunting in the 19th century. A protection treaty was signed in 1910 between Chile, Bolivia, Argentina and Peru, which drove prices up; they increased fourteenfold.[7] In this context, the addition of this precious fur made the dress a true luxury product bringing together East and West.

H. R.

ILL. 11 Studio Lipnitzki, photograph of Paul Poiret, undated

ILL. 12 Anonymous, embroidery swatch, late 19th–early 20th century, silk, cotton and gold lamé. Paris, Musée du Quai Branly–Jacques Chirac, inv. 74.1975.1.12

Christian Lacroix

Poiret the Magnificent

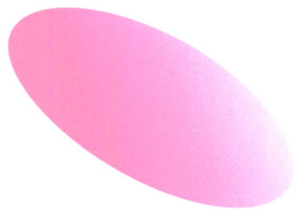

There are some names that seem made to be inscribed in memory, rolling off the tongue, beautiful to look at and ponder, because they are endowed with such perfect simplicity, radiating charm, full of verve. We smile whenever we speak them aloud, and 'Poiret' is one of these names.

There must have been a question mark in my mind, along with the smile on my face, the first time I read this name, stopped short by an illustration in Henny Harald Hansen's *Costumes and Styles*. I must just pause to give this author the praise she deserves! In 1956, this Swedish woman wrote the book *Costumes and Styles: The Evolution of Fashion from Early Egypt to the Present. With 700 Individual Figures in Full Color*, which was later translated from English into French and which, as a very young boy, I saw in a Christmas catalogue and immediately asked my grandmother to buy for me. The book, which boasted a violet cloth cover embossed with a gold silhouette of Louis XVI, and a jacket illustrated with a double row of images depicting the evolution of fashion from ancient times up to the 1950s, became my daily bible, the source of my inspiration and the place I turned to for my fevered research, up until the publication, ten years later, of François Boucher's major tome *L'Histoire du costume en Occident* (*The History of Costume in the West*). This did not, however, take the place of my 'Hansen', now in a pitiful state, but still there! Hard to believe now, when books about costume, fashion and designers are everywhere, but at that time, unless you owned or could go to the library to consult Maurice Leloir's huge collections, they were almost the only books available to satisfy an almost pathological passion for the history of silhouettes and clothing. And at the end of one of these rows of illustrations, between a kimono-style evening coat by Paquin and a skiing outfit by an unknown designer from 1913, was this tunic ('half-crinoline'), embroidered or printed with stylized flowers, edged with fur, worn over a long, narrow pleated skirt, designed by Poiret, later discovered to have been based on an Iribe sketch (CAT. 211).

I am not sure why, but at the time this name was more evocative for me of a jet of water than a fruit (*poire* means 'pear' in French); it conjured up images of watering plants, or of the pear-shaped perfume bottles that I saw on my grandmother's dressing table.

While this fairly simple, naive drawing did not seem more sublime to me than some of the others, which I preferred and which fascinated me more, nevertheless I could feel how it broke away from the previous pages, a link in the chain of silhouettes from the 1910s that was suddenly very different from the others.

I had very few opportunities to learn more about the period that inspired such curiosity in me (1910–1945), I was only around nine or ten years old, and it would be many years before the advent of Google. Around that time, Lartigue's photographs were being rediscovered, and they captivated me, with the huge Babylonian hats, like cakes bristling with feathers and bows, their shadows and veils obscuring the faces of the mushroom-women, hemmed in by frills and fur, garlanded with ribbons and guipure lace. They 'amused me', like young 'Madwomen of Chaillot', but I did not yet realize the extent to which they were the opposite of Poiret's women, as at the time I did not have enough information about them, finding them neither in family albums nor in the journals I discovered in attics and at flea markets, where I spent all my modest pocket money.

In terms of interior design, Hector Guimard's work was being rediscovered at the time, with his 'noodle-like' style and his Paris Métro station entrances. Unlike in the countries of northern and central Europe, this style did not leave much of a mark on French tastes or flourish in our cities, where people were keen to destroy the few remaining traces of it – the last surviving remnants, overgrown with winding plant motifs and writhing creatures, were reduced to objects of curiosity. Guimard does not really occupy the same place that Charles Rennie Mackintosh does for the British, or Horta and Henry Van de Velde for the Belgians. H. H. Hansen mentions Van de Velde's voluminous dresses, inspired by the Italian Renaissance, fastened simply at the shoulders and the high collar, with motifs that are evocative of Rorschach tests.

I gorged myself on the work of Alphonse Mucha and Georges de Feure, then sank body and soul into Aubrey Beardsley and, a little later, the London of Michelangelo Antonioni's *Blow-Up*, Portobello Road, Kensington, Carnaby Street, King's Road, and so on, so much more innovative and daring than Paris, somewhere between Wildean camp and psychedelia.

However, my senses pricked up at the slightest hint of Poiret's famous 'half-crinoline' or 'fish' silhouette, often spotted in old American silent films, before I was swept away by *My Fair Lady*, with its graphic black and white costumes in the Ascot scenes and its schmaltzy pastel shades at the ball, designed by Cecil Beaton.

In the mid-1960s, everything was either very modern and geometrical, or rippling psychedelic curves. One side was all Scandinavian and Zen, high-tech and ahead of its time, with Yves Saint Laurent's Mondrian dresses and Courrèges' cosmonauts, while the other was exploring the beginnings of 'retro' fashions, and I drew nothing but androgynous creatures, drowning in floaty concoctions in the style of Sarah Bernhardt, or eclectic jumbles, very 'kitsch' – a word that was in vogue in the late 1960s. In the early 1970s there was a new wind blowing, a change in the air. It was all about Art Deco, a catch-all term that covered everything, without distinction, from the 1910s to the 1930s. After the winding, smoky feel of Mucha and Théophile Steinlen came the 'clean line' of André-Édouard Marty and Georges Barbier or Georges Lepape and Paul Iribe, who all drew Poiret's designs. This wave even reached a great 'servant of the state', sadly forgotten despite a long, heroic and inspired life: Julien Cain, director of the Musée Jacquemart-André, who, along with Yvonne Deslandres, decided in 1974 to dedicate an exhibition to 'Poiret the magnificent'…

We went along like worshippers attending mass. It was as much an exhibition of Raoul Dufy's work as of Poiret's, with hundreds of drawings and paintings from his collection and a few dozen designs, true relics to kneel before (even more so because the descriptions were placed low down!), taken straight from the wardrobe of Denise Poiret. And she was there, Denise Poiret! Accompanying (or accompanied by) a respectful and attentive group, Julien Cain, Yvonne Deslandres, around the exhibition mannequins. I remember, although it is probably a false memory, a small woman dressed in black, a little childlike, who reminded me of Cecil Beaton's 1965 portrait of Cléo de Mérode. Doubtless because they both had slender profiles, with a purity that was almost unchanged by age.

The pieces were certainly a little worn, as Geneviève Breerette wrote in *Le Monde* on 24 January 1974, misshapen by the department store mannequins, which often consisted of a child's body – to match the sizes of times gone by – combined with an adult head, giving them a slightly 'hydrocephalic' look, crowned with wigs made from crepe paper (the art of invisible 'mannequin dressing', using transparent bodies that were made to measure, did not appear until the reopening of the Musée de la Mode in 1987, thanks to Azzedine Alaïa and Jacques Grange).

Exhibiting clothes has always seemed like a dishonest practice to me, eternally utopian. I remember that, beyond the joy of discovering these miraculous 'vestiges', I was struck by a certain fragility, a precarity, a great – perhaps too great – simplicity and naivety, a sense that it was almost 'cobbled together'. The same childlike naivety that we find in the creations of the Martine workshop (Atelier Martine). The excessive speed of execution that we see in certain stage costumes, their ephemeral quality, their sometimes bizarre appearance, which I was reminded of when, years later, François Lesage told me about Jacques Fath's designs, all very 'chic' but with none of Balenciaga's perfectionism.

But with my simple faith, the unconditional belief of a worshipper of the past, despite the decayed embroidery and the slightly worn embellishments, I could recognize the flamboyance and innovation that these outfits had exemplified when they were brand new.

One of the wonders of fashion, both regrettable and inevitable, is the way that, the moment we feel that shock of something we have never seen before, that flash of novelty, it is taken away, slipping through our fingers as soon as it appears. Sadly, it is impossible for us to feel or quantify the sudden chill that must have run through our peers in the past when they witnessed something being created almost out of nothing, like the appearance, in the salons of 1908, of this woman now standing before me, Denise Poiret, wearing these dresses that she had lent to the exhibition, her head wrapped in a lamé turban bristling with sprays of feathers, the hoop of her translucent 'minaret lampshade' rippling around her hips with its trembling fringe. The shy modesty of this simple young woman dressed in outfits that were so cutting edge must have held a certain charm, splashed as she was with all the 'resurrected' pigments of the Orient – 'tango' orange, emerald green, turquoise, Indian pink, purple, scarlet, like the precious gems in Aladdin's garden – and wearing it all with such disconcerting naturalness, with none of the contortions that we see elegant women of the period undergoing in contemporary photographs or engravings.

There was a hint of Orientalism in the air, from the Ballets Russes to the 'Thousand and Second Night' party, harem pants, veils, turbans, Indian miniatures and illuminations. But not only that.

ILL.1 Christian Lacroix, portrait of Paul Poiret, March 2025, digital media.

Because before these Scheherazade-like figures appeared in the Faubourg Saint-Germain, as early as Poiret's time working on the Rue Pasquier, or at least from the opening of the fashion house on the Avenue d'Antin, with the publication of Iribe and Lepape's sketchbooks, we saw figures drawn not from mysterious far-off lands, but from times or centuries past. The era of the Palais-Royal, the Merveilleuses (decadent fashionable aristocratic women) of the Directoire period (1795–1799) and the elegant women of the First Empire (1804–1814/15), moving on from the ladies of the 17th-century court, the refinements of the Regency era (1715–1723) and the creations of Rose Bertin, fashion designer to Marie-Antoinette, which Jacques Doucet reinterpreted beautifully in his illustrations for the *Gazette du Bon Ton*, with their high waist, small busts and diaphanous shirt-dresses. These notebooks drew on the style of engravings from exactly a hundred years earlier, but were more stripped back, with minimalist black and white backgrounds and neo-Directory settings like the salons of the Faubourg Saint-Honoré. Bright colours as well, for Iribe and Lepape, as if the young students of the Martine School (École Martine) had been let loose to colour in these plates depicting immaculate fashions from the Napoleonic era. They recall the colours of certain portraits or drawings by Ingres that Denise Poiret reminds me of in photographs, the direct gaze, somewhere between 'smiling with the eyes' (an expression of my grandfather's!) and melancholy, impassive and inviting, wearing no make-up, unlike the heavily powdered women of the era, with their pink cheeks, red lips and brownish-yellow pigment around their eyes. I like to read the account, in *En habillant l'époque*, of her arrival from the countryside, when she was appraised by the models at the fashion house, while it was she, more than any other, who was the inspiration for and embodiment of her husband's creative vision, wearing his designs so naturally and making them seem timeless and far removed from all historical folklore.

The harem of the 'Poiret oasis' was revived, then stretched throughout the 1970s and 1980s, from the Musée Jacquemart-André to the Palais Galliera. And here, I would like to pay an affectionate tribute to one of the curators who does not enjoy the recognition today that his passionate, knowledgeable and devoted work deserves. I am thinking of Guillaume Garnier, curator of the exhibition 'Paul Poiret et Nicole Groult. Maîtres de la mode Art déco' ('Paul Poiret and Nicole Groult: Masters of Art Deco Fashion').

In the mid-1980s, I was still working at Patou, but I was starting to picture myself 'in my own place', perhaps, one day... I amused myself by imagining what Jean Patou, who had died half a century earlier and who, along with Chanel, had ushered in a modernity that had become the norm seventy years later, might have designed if he had still been with us. Patou, Chanel, everything that Poiret hated, everything that he railed against in his New York lectures, everything that led to his downfall, after the interruption of the war stymied his creativity. What a surprising, fascinating paradox is to be found in the approach of this man who, after offering the corseted 'marchionesses' of 1908 the freedom of simple tunics – similar to 18th-century dresses in the English style – returned in 1920 with formal brocades, nostalgic folklore-inspired designs, skirts that were too long, too round, 'frilly'. Jeanne Lanvin, for her part, continued to explore her interest in the Far East and her *robes de style*, but with a more natural touch, making them more up to date and lighter, while Patou and Chanel emulated her pared-back lines with tunic-blouses. At that time, a generation of female couturiers were coming of age, such as Alix Grès and Madeleine Vionnet, who would, along with Chanel, reach the top of the industry. Often – although there were exceptions – male couturiers created a fantasy version of women, as they were not women themselves, paying tribute to them by creating dresses that they would only ever wear in their dreams, while female couturiers designed for themselves, with full awareness of their bodies and their desires...

The pared-back 'Patou' line did not come naturally to me; despite all my 'mercenary' loyalty, I did not want to be restricted, in a decade overflowing with extravagance and eccentricity. I was therefore not the only one who was delighted by the exhibition at the Galliera, the opulence of the ethnic embroidery, the colours of the travelling caravan, the theatricality, the historicism, the extravagance of the Poiret years, which spoke to and finally entered into such an intimate dialogue with the eccentricity of the 1980s.

These kinds of exhibitions certainly had an influence on my creativity and, even at Patou's studio on the Rue Saint-Florentin, I must have felt encouraged to express my intimate kaleidoscope, my personal vision, giving free rein to my passion for all folklore and all eras, throwing them all together in patchworks, collisions and collages, a prelude to opening Maison Lacroix two years later.

Then, in 2005, came another triumph for Paul Poiret's work in the form of the exhibition, hosted by Azzedine Alaïa, of pieces put up for auction by his family. An 'epiphany' in the sense that I still recall the feeling of being dazzled, as if by white laundry hanging in the sun, a trousseau of spotless linen, by the light that streamed through the glass roof of the building on the Rue de la Verrerie, which was filled with these small masterpieces of organdie, chiffon and organza that seemed to have only just left the delicate, expert hands that had created them, hemmed with fine embroidery and passementerie. Poiret had once again left an impression, on design studios as well as magazine editors, and the editor of American *Vogue* asked some designers to create tributes to Poiret, whose work was soon to be celebrated by the Metropolitan Museum of Art in New York in the exhibition 'Poiret: King of Fashion'.

I remember feeling invigorated by this 'exhilarating', playful commission. What did we have in common, Poiret and I? Black and white stripes? Exoticism? The oxymoron of a futurist nostalgia and a nostalgic futurism? Our impermeability to Surrealism and Cubism? Painting as a driving force? In any case, what was needed was a 'lampshade' silhouette, colour and a flower to evoke the quintessence of 'Paul Poiret's dresses seen by Iribe'. It was made of Indian pink cigaline (a translucent silk fabric), with a bow of the most intense green, and dotted, in the absence of the Iribe roses that were still being made by the Maison Lemarié, with large graphic buds, a little like artichoke hearts or huge white peonies. This is still one of my favourite pieces, of all the thousands that I have designed.

A grand finale for Poiret, a testament and an inventory. First the official, inescapable caricature of him as the vanquisher of the corset, although bras have been around since the Middle Ages and the Musée des Arts décoratifs has in its collection a dress worn by a Merveilleuse, with its matching embroidered bag, that has a lace-up bandeau inside. How paradoxical that, on the one hand, he liberated women's busts after decades of the 'S-shaped' silhouette, when curves were restricted to create a tiny waist and a large backside, and on the other hand, created narrow 'hobble' skirts that made it difficult to walk. Although soon afterwards women were set free by the invention of the culotte-skirt.

France was never receptive to the social reforms that flourished in Britain, where some groundbreaking figures promoted the wearing of bloomers as early as 1851, or Belgium, with Van de Velde's 'sack dresses' and 'smock dresses', or even Austria, with the Wiener Werkstätte. This last was a Viennese workshop bringing together artisans and artists from the Secession movement, such as the ceramicists Reni Schaschl, Lotte Calm and Hilda Jesser, the illustrators Mela Köhler and Maria Likarz-Strauss, the architect Josef Hoffmann, of course, but in particular Eduard Josef Wimmer-Wisgrill, whom Poiret visited many times from 1911 onwards, bringing back fabrics created by him and other Viennese graphic designers.

The two couturiers clearly influenced one another, their designs often so similar that Wimmer-Wisgrill was nicknamed 'the Viennese Poiret'. There is a surprising similarity in the silhouettes they created, and also in their furniture, which is more geometric and refined in the Austrian's work, more 'rustic' in Poiret's. In the designs created with the Martine workshop, he drew on the same graphic repertoires as those found at the Werkstätte, especially naive floral motifs, although again these were more sophisticated in Vienna and more childlike in Paris. It was as if Poiret had brought back in his luggage the spirit of an entire 'secessionist' generation, which was not widely embraced in France, except by Iribe and Lepape – who some gossips suggested were the true creators of the designs reproduced in their respective collections, as Paul Poiret wrote his 1930 book *En habillant l'époque*. A dangerous suggestion…

Here I must make a confession: I expected that these memoirs, which I read with curiosity tinged with disappointment, would include chapters on his inspirations, his creative process, the genesis of his most groundbreaking ideas, his way of working with his 'studio', when drawing or draping, and so on. Perhaps I am mistaken, but there is no information of this kind in any of the chapters dedicated to so many varied activities, from yachting to travel, from lectures to meetings, which are imbued with a kind of flamboyant egotism as, throughout this self-portrait, he creates a likeable image of himself, which is as much playful self-caricature as it is a bitter, bad-tempered performance, however joyful and 'resilient' he may be.

In his article about the 1974 exhibition at the Musée Jacquemart-André, published in the *Revue des deux mondes*, Georges Charensol wrote: 'I knew Paul Poiret after his failure at the Exhibition of Decorative Arts in 1925 […]. Whether because his creative genius was already on the wane at the age of forty-five, or because this man who had always worked for an elite clientele did not know how to adapt to the tastes of the wider public, these designs in which he had invested a fortune only met with limited success. He felt a deep bitterness about this. […] instead of reacting appropriately, he tended to brood over his glorious past. However, his reputation remained high, but he considered it demeaning to work for a department store or to be forced to entrust businessmen to manage his fashion house, which was on the verge of bankruptcy.'[1]

These memories bring him vividly to life, as if we too were sharing the exchange that Charensol had with Poiret when he was in decline, poignant, if a little arrogant, even more so because I also walked along paths similar to those that he considered demeaning – although I forced myself to 'react appropriately'! Perhaps Poiret's importance does not lie in the gaudy image of the maharajah couturier, the liberator of women, but in the very modern extravagance of this groundbreaking creative mind, who was so ahead of his time, who, before anyone else, including those who would later dethrone him, had such innovative ideas: in no particular order, copyright, the flexible corset, the idea for a fashion academy with a museum, the very up-to-date idea of naming the short-lived fashion house that he opened near the Place de l'Étoile after its telephone number, and finally, the quest for a kind of *Gesamtkunstwerk*, a total work of art, created throughout his life and career, which brought together all art forms, from painting to music, literature, theatre, gastronomy, dance, even cinema and the recitation of La Fontaine's fable 'The North Wind and the Sun', which I find deeply moving.

Businessman, collector, actor, traveller, artist, promoter, producer, inventor, lecturer, Poiret embraced all the areas now explored by contemporary designers – Yves Saint Laurent, Karl Lagerfeld, Jean Paul Gaultier, and so on.

Now that I have looked at him a little more closely, the image that emerges for me, beyond all the familiar images, is one of a giant, a genius, a kind of ogre who devoured everything around him with an all-consuming hunger, a blind passion that went beyond ambition, a fierce courage, a zealot's elation, right up until the end of a life in which reality surpassed fiction. After seeing so many, too many, promotional biopics on streaming platforms, we might dream of a biopic of Paul Poiret. But who could play him? Great actors such as Harry Baur are now few and far between.

'1974: a Poiret year? Who knows. The next collections will perhaps show us,' concluded Geneviève Breerette in her article on 24 January 1974 in *Le Monde*. Will 2025 be a Poiret year too? On the Rue de Rivoli, definitely! And beyond!

1
Georges Charensol,
'Poiret à Jacquemart-André',
in *Revue des deux mondes*,
November 1974.

LASSITUDE
Robe de dîner, de Paul Poiret

Gazette du Bon Ton   N° 1. – Pl. VIII

CAT. 211 Georges Lepape, '*Lassitude*, a dinner gown by Paul Poiret', *Gazette du Bon Ton*, no. 1, 1912, plate 8, Paris, Librairie centrale des Beaux-Arts, 1912, photogravure and pochoir print. Paris, library of the Musée des Arts décoratifs

ILL. 2 Steven Meisel, Christian Lacroix gown worn by Natalia Vodianova for American *Vogue*, May 2007, p. 244

THE POIRET LIFE-STYLE

*I have searched through countless museums,
decoded bas-reliefs, collected vintage fabrics,
pieces of embroidery, trinkets of all kinds,
I have sought to live in artistic environments.*

Paul Poiret, qucted in *Le Miroir des modes*, June 1912

ILL.1 Philippe Jullian, Madame Haugoult-Dujour wearing a *Minaret*
dress by Paul Poiret, in Philippe Jullian, *Les Styles*, Paris: Plon, 1961.
Paris, library of the Musée des Arts décoratifs

Wanting to stand out at the International Exhibition of Modern Decorative and Industrial Arts in 1925, Paul Poiret paid to present his creations on three barges moored on the Seine, between the Pont des Invalides and the Pont Alexandre-III, which were open to the public. 'The creative vision on display here is reminiscent of that seen in some of the couturier-decorator's dresses.'[1] Called *Amours* (*Loves*), *Délices* (*Delights*) and *Orgues* (*Organs*), the three barges, in the colours of the French national flag – one was covered with blue carnations, the second with red anemones, the third decorated in white and gold – housed the creations of his three companies, Maison Martine for interior design, Maison Rosine for perfumes and Maison Paul Poiret for the couture collections, arranged against a backdrop of fourteen wall hangings created specially by Raoul Dufy, while 'shapes, figures and shifting colours' were projected on a screen.[2] The barge *Délices* was dedicated not only to the sense of smell, but also to taste, in the 'restaurant Délices', decorated by the painter Eugène Ronsin. An official luncheon was held there to celebrate the opening of the barges,[3] to which Poiret invited, among other eminent figures, the exhibition's director, Fernand David, and the director of the Musée des Beaux-Arts, Paul Léon. They both praised the designer as the 'instigator' or inspiration behind the International Exhibition of Modern Decorative and Industrial Arts, which, in their view, was the next step in the story that had begun with the creation of the Maison Martine in 1911. With its innovative approach, responding to the demands of modern life, this venture, as Poiret recalls, 'gave rise to a flourishing movement of ideas in interior design' and sparked a number of imitators (ILL. 1). The designer therefore took great satisfaction in being recognized for his pioneering work: '[I was] right.'[4]

In 1925, the financial situation at Paul Poiret's fashion house had deteriorated significantly. There was friction between the designer and his business partners, who accused him of profligate spending and cut him off financially. His barges were an opportunity to celebrate his contribution to couture; in some ways, they were a 'prestigious swansong',[5] coming as they did before the sale of the Martine company. Although he was ever-present on the roof terraces of his boats, Poiret lamented how 'chaotic and difficult' they were to run. To make up for their out-of-the-way location on the Left Bank, far away from the Grand Palais, he put on entertainment, such as light shows, 'a magical, wonderful spectacle, the pinnacle of light shows',[6] to draw in visitors.[7] He was also 'very disappointed' when it came to the works created by his friend Dufy: 'Who remembers them? No one noticed them.'[8] In his memoir, he commented on his strategic miscalculation: 'I was wrong to rely on a luxury clientele who eschew popular pleasures; they did not come.'[9] Poiret never recovered from the costs he incurred in realizing this bold venture.

This all-encompassing approach, embracing a highly refined way of life in a charming setting, in harmony with the clothes he designed, traces its origins back to 1910, when the designer travelled to Berlin, Vienna and Brussels. Seeking to invent a French model for the decorative arts, Poiret travelled there to learn about new approaches in neighbouring countries. In Vienna, he was inspired by the creations of the Wiener Werkstätte (Vienna Workshops), and he saw the all-encompassing approach to art developed by their founder, the architect Josef Hoffmann, as an example to follow. On his return, convinced of the need for a stylistic reinvention of the decorative arts in France, which would be rooted in education, in April 1911 he branched out from his fashion label to found the Martine School (École Martine), named after his third daughter, who had just been born. Situated at the same premises as his fashion house and run by Marguerite Sérusier, the wife of the Nabi painter Paul Sérusier, this school offered an experimental approach to teaching the decorative arts, the aim being to create unusual motifs to be used on 'works displaying youthful charm and boldness'.[10]

A few months later, Poiret opened the Martine boutique, 'Choses à la mode', which sold cushions, rugs, wallpaper, lamps, hand-decorated glassware, ceramics and marionette dolls. It also featured furniture and decorative objects designed by the artist Guy-Pierre

1
Paris, arts décoratifs, 1925,
exhib. guide, p. 357.

2
Idem.

3
As can be seen from the menu for the opening of the barge *Délices*, 24 April 1925.

4
Poiret, *En habillant l'époque*, Paris: Grasset, 1930, p. 154.

5
Palmer White, *Poiret le magnifique. Le destin d'un grand couturier*, Paris: Payot, 1986, p. 242.

6
Paris, arts décoratifs, p. 358.

7
See Paul Poiret, *Art et phynance*, Paris: Lutetia, 1934, p. 131.

8
Poiret, *En habillant l'époque*, p. 153.

9
Ibid., pp. 153–154.

10
René-Jean, exhibition brochure, 'Tapis, paravents et travaux de l'école Martine', Barbazanges Gallery, 1917.

11
Paul Poiret, *En habillant l'époque*, p. 162.

12
See 'Le Home exotique et moderne d'une artiste', *L'Illustration*, 12 April 1921, pp. 335–336.

13
See Léon Moussinac, 'L'Atelier Martine', *Art et décoration*, August 1924, p. 33.

14
Pierre Lévy, 'Stratégies économiques de la création', in *Le Monde selon les créateurs*, exh. cat., Paris: Palais Galliera–Musée de la Mode et du Costume, 6 June – 15 September 1991, Paris: Paris-Musées, 1991, pp. 41–47.

Fauconnet (1882–1920), 'the most gifted and the most devoted' of Poiret's collaborators.[11] Under his direction, the pupils at the Martine School worked on every aspect of interior design projects for living rooms, bedrooms and children's rooms for an avant-garde clientele, which included Jacques Doucet and Mademoiselle Spinelly, who wanted to create an elegant, distinctive home that reflected her personality.[12] The specialist press commented that the ephemeral, moveable nature of the Martine workshop's interior design projects was shaped by its founder's background as a fashion designer. Everything he did, everything he worked on, existed for a season.[13]

Poiret's incredible modernity lies in his ability to create, as early as 1912, an entire world, sharing his imagination with his client. Today, this has become common practice for many fashion brands, which have adopted an 'all-encompassing marketing' strategy.[14] The kind of approach espoused, for example, by the American designer Ralph Lauren with his 'Home Collection', which allows customers to completely embrace every aspect of his way of life.

Cécile Pichon-Bonin

The Martine School

Artistic creation
and educational innovation

1
See Margaux Granier-Weber's article 'Paul Poiret (1879-1944): le couturier et les arts', 9 March 2022 (available online).

2
See Hee-Jeong Moon, 'L'école "Martine" de Paul Poiret', in Stéphane Laurent (ed.), *Une émergence du design: France, 20e siècle*, pp. 84–85 (published online October 2019).

3
See especially Yvonne Deslandres, *Poiret*, Paris: Éditions du Regard, 1986; Anne Stauffacher, *L'Évolution stylistique de la fleur dans l'industrie du textile. Un exemple: l'Atelier Martine*, master's thesis, supervised by Bruno Foucart and Jean-Louis Gaillemin, Université Paris-Sorbonne, 1998. For more information about La Maison Martine, the sale of students' designs and their reception, see Moon's article in Laurent (ed.), *Une émergence du design. France, 20e siècle*, pp. 69–85.

4
Paul Poiret, *En habillant l'époque*, Paris: Grasset, 1930, p. 147.

5
See Guy Brucy and Vincent Troger, 'Un siècle de formation professionnelle en France: la parenthèse scolaire?', *Revue française de pédagogie*, vol. 131 (*Les Formations professionnelles entre l'École et l'Entreprise*), 2000, pp. 9–21 (available online).

6
See Jean-Claude Marquis, *Le Travail des enfants au XIXe siècle, en Seine-Inférieure*, Rouen: CRDP, p. 9. This age was later raised to fourteen by a law passed on 9 August 1936, and later to sixteen by ruling no. 59-45 of 6 January 1959, which did not come into force until 1967.

7
See Guy Brucy, 'L'apprentissage ou… les apprentissages?', *Revue française de pédagogie*, no. 183, April/May/June 2013, p. 12 (published online 16 December 2016, accessed 10 December 2020).

8
Sylvie Gayan, 'Créations de petites filles chez Paul Poiret', *Sorcières: les femmes vivent*, no. 17, 1979, p. 42 (available online).

Against a backdrop of greater enthusiasm for the decorative arts around Europe, and drawing inspiration from the dynamism of artistic life in Germany and his discovery of the Wiener Werkstätte (the WW, or Vienna Workshops), Paul Poiret launched a new initiative in April 1911, when he founded the École Martine, or Martine School, named after his youngest daughter (ILL. 1). This decorative arts school accepted girls aged twelve and over (CAT. 285). In the autumn of that year, he also created La Maison Martine, Choses à la mode ('Fashionable things'), a boutique in Paris that sold pieces designed by the 'Martines', as he liked to refer to his pupils, as well as by various artists, including Raoul Dufy (1877–1953) and the interior designer Guy-Pierre Fauconnet (1882–1920). Fauconnet was also artistic director of the studio up until the outbreak of the First World War, and worked with the girls to design interiors for bedrooms and children's rooms.

From around fifteen pupils in 1912, the numbers had gone down to seven by 1917. The school then struggled to get back on its feet after the crisis that followed the war, and to survive the commercial failure of the three barges —'Amours' ('Loves') was used to present designs by La Maison Martine, 'Délices' ('Delights') for pieces by La Maison Rosine, and 'Orgues' ('Organs') for the Paul Poiret collection— moored on the Seine that the designer used as sites to present his work at the International Exhibition of Modern Decorative and Industrial Arts in Paris in 1925.[1] That same year, the Martine company was taken over by an administrator, but his hostile relationship with Paul Poiret, who remained artistic director,[2] spelled the end for the organization, which finally closed its doors in 1929.

While there have already been a few books dedicated to the school and the designs created by its students,[3] here we will seek to understand the innovative nature of this pedagogical and artistic experiment, by situating it within the history of women's professional training in decorative arts and the educational and artistic context of the 1910s and 1920s.

The Martine School: an experiment in professional decorative arts training for girls

The designer's decision to recruit 'from among the working classes on the outskirts of the city girls of around twelve, who have finished their studies'[4] must be seen in the context of reforms ushered in by the Third Republic, which concerned primary education, professional training and the creation of new employment legislation designed to protect children physically. The 1880 law is seen as the beginning of French technical education. However, it was the culmination of a government interest in professional training that went back to the early 19th century, a consequence of the decline of guilds and the profound changes brought about by the Industrial Revolution (especially technical advances and changes to the division of labour).[5] The Jules Ferry laws of 1881 and 1882 made primary schooling free and compulsory. From 1892, children were no longer allowed to work before they had obtained their primary school certificate, which raised the age when children entered the workforce to around twelve or thirteen.[6] Therefore, in 1911, when Paul Poiret opened his school, twelve was generally the age when a girl from a modest background started work, to bring in another income for her household as soon as possible; at best, she started an apprenticeship. Daughters of employees or shopkeepers, whose families were less dependent on a daily wage, could enrol in a professional school, for example training to be teachers. Only a small number of girls from the middle classes attended secondary school or higher education. In general, only a minority of children over twelve were in education; it should be noted that even in 1939, 75 per cent of individuals in each age group did not go on to pursue any education beyond primary school.[7]

The creation of the Martine School therefore had a philanthropic aim: it was a way of giving young girls from modest backgrounds a means to continue their training. For most of them, this would come to an end when they married. Paul Poiret enrolled the daughter of one of his employees, alongside one of her friends whose mother was a 'stitcher of shoes'.[8] However, as the designer recalled, the parents of these young pupils soon came to believe they were wasting their time. That is when he started to give out prizes to the best designs, establishing a reward system in order to keep the girls at the school. He found his own solution to a problem that had concerned the economic elites since the French Revolution: how to train workers and ensure they could improve their position in society. Inviting the girls into a few rooms in his house for six hours a day, Poiret also gave them a sympathetic and welcoming place to work,[9] in comparison with conditions for young girls employed in the workshops of milliners, lacemakers and embroiderers, or even those recruited by the textile industry. These were the sectors that traditionally hired women, while boys worked in mines, glass factories, metal workshops or the construction industry. Working conditions remained particularly gruelling in all these industries. New laws on the age of workers, weekly working hours and rest periods were difficult to enforce and often met with fierce resistance from employers, who saw them as restrictions that would lead to lower profits for their business. In November 1892, the maximum weekly working hours were limited to ten for a child of thirteen, and sixty for those aged sixteen to eighteen. Further measures in this area were introduced in 1905.

The designer's experiment should also be understood in the context of the growing female presence in the decorative arts industry. Aside from one young boy who briefly studied at the Martine School, all of the pupils were girls. Since the beginning of the 19th century, a few private initiatives had offered young girls access to training in the decorative arts, with the dual aim of improving their condition in life and meeting the needs of the industry. These aims were confirmed in 1863 and 1864 by two professional schools that combined general education and workshop training: the Montizon School, which was restructured to fit this pattern, and Élisa Lemonnier's school, a new establishment that became known as the 'Duperré School' from 1882 onwards, when it moved to the street of that name.[10] In the 1880s, the Jules Ferry laws allowed municipalities to create professional schools that were open to pupils from the age of twelve, some of which were exclusively for girls. However, this tendency for greater government involvement in professional training was designed to increase school education rather than workshop training.[11]

As it went against the grain of this drive to increase school education, Paul Poiret's private initiative seems unique in France. The designer was inspired by the example of industrialists, especially in Switzerland and Germany, who commonly offered employees classes to complete their training. The WW, the association of artists and artisans founded in Vienna in 1903 and often cited as a model, owed its existence to the financial support of a rich patron, Fritz Wärndorfer. At the same time, the Martine School was an amalgamation of a number of French practices. The students were trained in techniques such as fabric printing, and some of the pieces that they created went on to be sold (CAT. 84, 87). In return, they were given a small payment. This combination of training and working in the studio was similar to an apprenticeship.[12] Student Alice Ruty recalled being on the premises for six hours a day,[13] which matches the working hours in the first year of a practical school for young girls.[14] As well as his philanthropic aims, Poiret said he was looking for 'gifted teenagers',[15] just like a master chooses his apprentice based on innate individual qualities.[16] The rewards given to the best designs drew on the school system of giving out prizes, although they took the form of financial compensation rather than books. The school was Paul Poiret's personal solution to the shortage of qualified workers and designers, and a response to the debate about the roles of schools and workshops, and of the private and public sectors, in professional training.

The freedom enjoyed by these kinds of institutions was the result of the informal nature of training in the luxury sector[17] and weak regulation of professional training in general.[18] It can be seen particularly strongly in the pedagogical choices that Poiret made to serve his artistic ambition of creating a new style of decorative arts.

An innovative teaching approach used to create a new style

The desire to create new styles sprang up in a number of European countries, in response to the crisis in the industrial arts that began in the 1890s. The Wiener Werkstätte manifesto, drawn up by Josef Hoffmann in 1905, argued that the Workshops should be an alternative to both low-quality mass production and artistic creations that simply imitated old styles. Against a backdrop of intense international competition, the movement was also a way to create a Viennese style that was free from the Parisian influence.[19] Inspired by this Austrian experiment, Poiret in turn dreamed of 'creating in France a new fashion in decoration and furniture',[20] with a style that would be set apart from the highly geometric style of the WW, the basis for Art Deco.

9
Ibid., former student Alice Natter describes a happy, relaxed atmosphere.

10
For more information about the history of decorative arts training for young girls in France, see Stéphane Laurent, 'Teaching the Applied Arts to Women at the École Duperré in Paris, 1864–1940', Studies in the Decorative Arts, vol. 4, no. 1, Autumn/Winter 1996–1997, pp. 60–84; Rossella Froissart, 'L'Ecole à la recherche d'une identité entre art et industrie (1877–1914)', in Rossella Froissart, Renaud d'Enfert, Ulrich Leben and Sylvie Martin (eds), Histoire de l'École nationale supérieure des arts décoratifs (1766–1941), Paris: Éditions de l'Ecole nationale des arts décoratifs, 2005, pp. 108–147.

11
See Guy Brucy and Vincent Troger, 'Un siècle de formation professionnelle en France: la parenthèse scolaire?', Revue française de pédagogie.

12
Agnès Jallat's certificate of service describes her as 'employed at the Martine School as a designer', from 1 April 1911 (when the school first opened) to 3 August 1914 (Paris, Musée des arts décoratifs, inv. 2019.116.48).

13
See Sylvie Gayan, 'Créations de petites filles chez Paul Poiret', p. 42.

14
Article 7 of the decree of 28 July 1888, see 'Apprentissage (Écoles manuelles d')', Ferdinand Buisson (ed), Nouveau dictionnaire de pédagogie et d'instruction primaire, 1911 (available online).

15
Moon, 'L'école "Martine" de Paul Poiret'.

16
See Guy Brucy, 'L'apprentissage ou… les apprentissages?'.

17
Idem.

18
It was not until 1928 that apprenticeship contracts became true work contracts, with apprentices receiving professional training and a certificate, the CAP (certificat d'aptitude professionnelle). See Guy Brucy, Florent Le Bot, Cédric Perrin and François Wassouni, 'Pour une histoire culturelle du siècle du Technique', Artefact, no. 3, 2015, p. 18 (published online 5 May 2021, accessed 12 May 2021).

19
See Werner J. Schweiger, Art nouveau à Vienne: Le Wiener Werkstätte, Paris: Herscher, 1990, p. 26.

20
Poiret, En habillant l'époque, p. 145.

CAT. 285 Anonymous, students from the Martine School, 1911–29, gelatin silver print. Paris, Bibliothèque nationale de France, Performing Arts department

ILL. 1 Boris Lipnitzki, *Martine Poiret*, 1924

CAT. 283 Martiale Constantini, design for the Martine workshop, undated, graphite, ink and gouache on vellum paper. Paris, Musée des Arts décoratifs

CAT. 290 Gabrielle Drapier, Martine Workshop, wallpaper and linen fabric design, *Les Radis [Radishes]*, 1913, gouache on thick paper. Paris, Musée des Arts décoratifs

21
In 1890, Mme de Montizon's
National School of Design
for Young Girls became the
'Girls' Section at the National
School of Decorative Arts',
and the School of Fine Arts
started accepting women from
1897. See Froissart, 'L'Ecole à la
recherche d'une identité entre
art et industrie' (1877-1914).

22
See Meredith Rob's article,
'Franz Cizek: Liberating the
Child Artist' (available online).

23
Gaston Arnaud, 'L'école
Martine. Une curieuse
méthode d'enseignement.
Ses résultats surprenants',
Comœdia, 31 March 1914.

24
For more information about
these events, see Franck
Beuvier, 'Le dessin d'enfant
exposé, 1890–1915.
Art de l'enfance et essence
de l'art', Gradhiva, no. 9, 2009,
(published online 2 September
2012, accessed 26 September
2024). For a detailed study
of children's drawings,
see Emmanuel Pernoud,
L'Invention du dessin d'enfant
en France à l'aube des avant-
gardes, Paris: Hazan, 2003.

25
See Jessica Boissel, 'Quand les
enfants se mirent à dessiner.
1880–1914: un fragment
de l'histoire des idées', Les
Cahiers du Musée national
d'art moderne, no. 31, 1985,
pp. 15–43; on the subject of
Nikolai Bartram, see Elitza
Dulguerova, 'Potentialité
du jouet dans la pensée de
Nikolaï Bartram', Strenæ,
no. 17, 2021 (published online
22 March 2021, accessed
27 September 2024); Cécile
Pichon-Bonin, 'La fabrication
du jouet par l'enfant chez
Nicolas Bartram: entre
création et travail manuel',
Josefffine, no. 12, 2021,
pp. 115–140.

The need to stand out from the competition led to the idea that an artisan could also be an artist and that the industry needed creative designers. Women, whose status as subordinates had never been questioned in the 19th century, soon found an opportunity to become designers, conceiving new pieces. In 1894, the Congress of Decorative Arts, organized by the Central Union, raised the question of women's access to artistic studies, sparking heated debates that brought together pragmatic arguments (the need for more workers in the art industries) and ideological taboos.[21] In 1910, the Second Congress on the Teaching of Design stressed the importance of encouraging the development of originality and creativity in girls, at all the municipal design schools. And it was precisely such creative and original designs that Paul Poiret expected from his students – creations that were both personal and inspired.

Poiret rejected the Viennese model's style and strict teaching approach, which, in his opinion, made its students into poor imitators. For the designer, the creation of a new style soon seemed to be inseparable from the pedagogical approach, as he went against the Vienna Workshops' strict methods. Perhaps he was also inspired in this by the free art school for children aged five to fourteen that the artist Franz Cižek opened in the Austrian capital in 1897, where he encouraged free expression, allowing each pupil to explore their own personality.[22] In the early days of the Martine School, Marguerite Sérusier, who also taught at municipal professional schools, led the drawing classes. When she left in 1912, Poiret decided not to replace her, instead adopting an innovative approach: the students would simply be allowed to follow wherever their inspiration took them, although they would be guided towards nature and pattern design. In 1914, the press praised this radical, innovative choice.[23] This pedagogical approach should be seen in the context of an international fascination with the originality and powerful freedom of expression shown in children's drawings. In Paris, this trend first came to the fore in publications by psychologists, the free drawing competition for children held at the Petit Palais in 1901–1902, and the promotion of the intuitive method – especially at an exhibition held in 1906 at the École pratique d'enseignement mutuel des arts. The year 1909 proved to be pivotal as it was when Gaston Quénioux's reforms to the teaching of drawing in primary school were adopted, Henri Matisse organized the Salon des enfants, and the children's exhibition was held at the Salon d'automne.[24] This formed the backdrop against which Paul Poiret and other groundbreaking artists developed.

The subjects in which the designer trained his students were part of a wider movement that sought a return to nature. The Martines mainly drew flowers, plants and animals, motifs that had been fashionable since the Art Nouveau movement and that were popular trends in the design industry and at all the schools (CAT. 288, 289). Quénioux's reform, which focused on primary schools but maintained the essence of training in decorative drawing to prepare children for working life, also took nature as its principal subject. In the 1910s, the Duperré School offered classes in zoology and botany, which allowed pupils to deepen their knowledge and trained them in creating printed designs – while the WW designed geometric versions of flora and fauna.

Instead of theoretical classes, Poiret gave priority to direct observation and drawing from nature; sometimes he and his wife brought the Martines bouquets to draw. The pupils' creations also drew on the modern pedagogical practice of excursions. The Martines regularly visited the Jardin des Plantes, the market at Les Halles and the aquarium at the Trocadero, and went on trips to the countryside. Museums and studios were other potential destinations, just as they were for students at the Duperré School.

Poiret's approach drew on the work of other pedagogues from the world of avant-garde art, such as the Russian collector and pedagogue Nikolai Bartram and the Swiss-born German painter Paul Klee, both of whom believed that children were naturally creative and that any form of teaching restricted the expression of their personality, corrupting their creative nature and their innate powers of imagination and observation.[25] Following the example of the Expressionists, Fauvists and Neo-Primitivists, the designer emphasized wildness, nature, inspiration, sensitivity, joy and creative freedom. He sought all the 'spontaneity and all the freshness of [the] nature' of each child, an authentic expression. Far from the fussy ornamentation of Art Nouveau and the geometric approach of Art Deco, the Martines' style embodied simplified forms and bright shades, in solid blocks of colour (CAT. 283, 284, 290). While painters collected, exhibited and drew inspiration

CAT. 289 Agnès Jallat, design for the Martine Workshop, 1913,
gouache with silver highlights on vellum paper. Paris, Musée des
Arts décoratifs

CAT. 288 Agnès Jallat, design for the Martine Workshop, 1913, gouache on vellum paper. Paris, Musée des Arts décoratifs

CAT. 284 Agnès Jallat, design for the Martine workshop, 1911–29, graphite, gouache, gold highlights on vellum paper. Paris, Musée des Arts décoratifs

from children's drawings to breathe new life into artistic expression, the designer had 'the courage necessary to manufacture, sometimes at great cost, these bold flights of fancy, whose value was not recognized by the public'.[26] At the same time, Nikolai Bartram was training teenagers in various Russian artisanal techniques, in order to preserve the traditional knowledge that was disappearing in the wake of industrialization. Poiret's insistence that the pieces should be made by the students who had designed them was a resolutely modern approach. While the technical training that these girls received was part of their apprenticeship, it was also, for the designer, a way of ensuring the pieces did not pass through the hands of workers who might misunderstand the initial idea and interpret it incorrectly.

26
Poiret, *En habillant l'époque*, p. 48; see Gaston Arnaud, 'L'école Martine...'.

CAT. 87 Kees Van Dongen, Martine workshop, rug, c. 1919, knotted wool. Paris, Musée des Arts décoratifs

CAT. 84 Paul Poiret, beach ensemble, c. 1912, linen block-printed with the design *Les Artichauts [Artichokes]* by the Martine workshop. Paris, Musée des Arts décoratifs

ill.1 Thérèse Bonney, bedroom in Paul Poiret's home, 1927, gelatin silver print. Paris, Bibliothèque historique de la ville de Paris, number NN-006-02717

Marion Neveu
The wallpapers of the Martine School

1
Part of the Musée des Arts décoratifs' huge collection of wallpapers, which includes around 400,000 works, this collection is made up of sixty-seven pieces, including forty different designs, and features a number of items: three rolls of wallpaper, six large-format swatches, nineteen small-format swatches, thirty-three small bags, five gouache designs and one painting on canvas.

2
Inv. 2005.37.11.

3
Inv. 2005.37.13.2.

4
Interview with Paul Poiret, published in *Mobilier et décoration*, 1 January 1934.

5
See essay by Sébastien Quéquet, p. 37.

6
Inv. 52391.1099, RI 2022.3.774 and RI 2022.3.775.

7
Inv. 52391.81, RI 2022.3.763 and RI 2022.3.764.

Created at the height of the Art Deco movement, between 1912 and 1925, the remarkable range of wallpapers designed by pupils at the Martine School (École Martine) and held in the collection of the Musée des Arts décoratifs in Paris[1] is testament to the creative freedom that reigned during that time at number 107 Rue du Faubourg Saint-Honoré, particularly under the direction of Guy-Pierre Fauconnet, who was at the school until 1914. Spontaneity of line, naive motifs, simplified treatment of shapes and bright, joyful colours are the defining characteristics of these designs based on flowers, plants, vegetables and even shells (ILL. 4). Only one of the young girls who had a hand in creating them is named: Gabrielle Rousselin, who designed the radish motif in 1913.[2] The designs are most often labelled 'Propriété Poiret', 'Paul Poiret', 'Société Martine' or simply 'Martine', with no mention of the individual student. A few wallpaper designs that bear the 'Martine' stamp in the margin were not printed Poiret's studio, but by renowned manufacturers. Two of these, who had been operating in the Paris area since the 19th century, are known to us: the Paul Dumas printing factory, which manufactured the radish and artichoke designs,[3] and the limited company of Desfossé & Karth, which manufactured thirty or so designs. It is in the collection of this second factory, which includes more than 13,000 different wallpapers acquired by the museum in 1982, that we find the majority of works by the Martine School, which include an interesting series of '*pochons*' (ILL. 2). These played a key part in the mechanical production process for wallpaper: they were the intermediate stage between the original design painted in gouache and the printed version (ILL. 3), allowing printers to find the right colours by trying out a range of options. The handwritten notes found on them, relating to the number of cylinders and colours needed to print the motifs, make them particularly valuable. The designs were then engraved onto as many copper cylinders as there were colours in the pattern. It is interesting to note that one of the engravers employed by Desfossé, called Dournel, also worked for Raoul Dufy. On average, the machines used in these two factories were made up of between ten and twelve cylinders, while the largest, such as the one used by Isidore Leroy in Ponthierry, had up to twenty-six. They printed on paper, but also on fabric, and the designs could sometimes be matching.

The Martine designs met with considerable success, thanks particularly to an ambitious approach to distribution. Sold in rolls of 10.05 metres at the Martine boutique, alongside other decorative items, they were also featured in the manufacturers' collections, which allowed them to reach a wider clientele. The Martine designs were also the subject of exhibitions and publications, which brought them wider recognition. Wallpaper designs were presented at the Salon d'automne in 1912, then at

the International Exhibition of Modern Decorative and Industrial Arts in 1925 – on the three barges that Poiret used to exhibit his works – and finally, in 1928, alongside pieces by all major players in the sector, at the exhibition 'Printed fabric and wallpaper' at the Palais Galliera. They also featured prominently, in the form of colour plates, in some of the 1923 and 1924 volumes of *Les Arts de la maison*, published by Albert Morancé, and in *Intérieurs français* by Jean Badovici, published in 1925. These publications depict an all-encompassing style of decoration, in which colourful, highly patterned decorative elements, created by the designer based on objects from the Martine universe, were placed in modern interiors to create a harmonious overall feel – wallpaper on the walls, curtains at the windows, rugs on the floor, cushions, and so on.

For Paul Poiret, 'art did not [come] from the desire to make things practical and comfortable, but from the desire to enhance the setting of our life'.[4] Many reception rooms in his private mansion on the Avenue d'Antin were decorated with Martine wallpapers, and he liked models wearing his designs to pose in front of them, especially for photographs of his clothes used for the legal register.[5] He even used the designs in private rooms: the shell wallpaper[6] was in his children's bedroom, photographed by Thérèse Bonney in 1927 (ILL. 1), while the chervil design[7] was in the living room, as can be seen in Boris Lipnitzki's photographs.

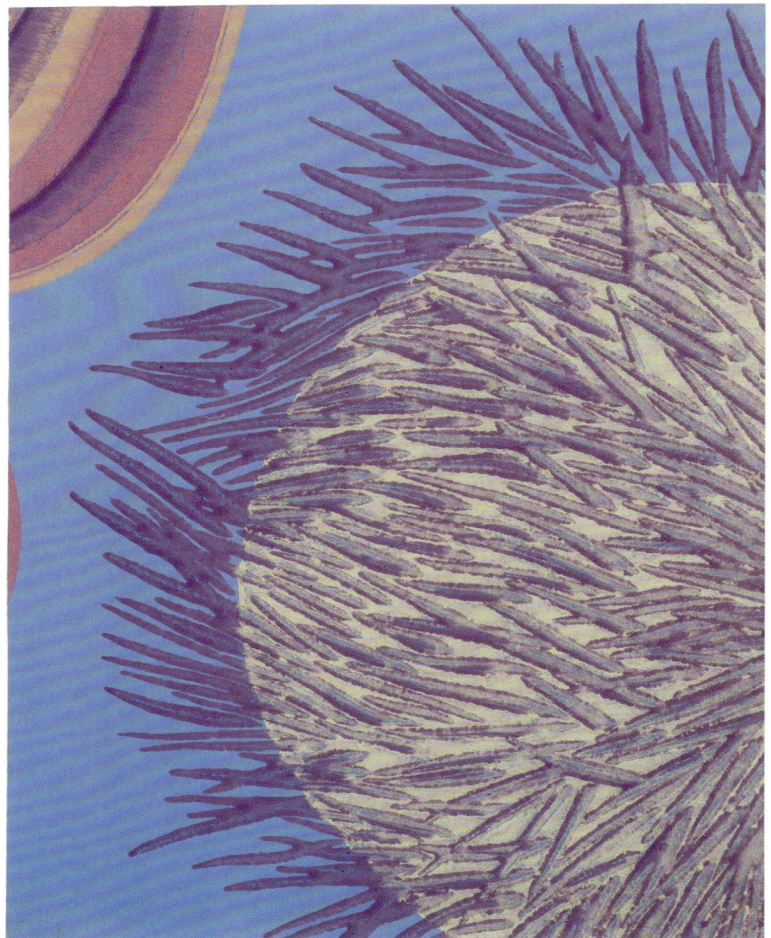

ILL. 2 Martine workshop, Société anonyme des Anciens Établissements Desfossé & Karth, *Coquillages [Shells]* pochon, 1919, gouache on paper. Paris, Musée des Arts décoratifs, purchased in 1982, inv. RI 2022.3.774

ILL. 3 Martine workshop, Société anonyme des Anciens Etablissements Desfossé & Karth, swatch of *Coquillages [Shells]* wallpaper, 1919, brushed texture on cylinder-printed ground on continuous paper. Paris, Musée des Arts décoratifs, purchased in 1982, inv. RI 2022.3.775

ILL. 4 Martine Workshop, Société anonyme des Anciens Établissements Desfossé & Karth, *Coquillage [Shells]* wallpaper, 1919, brushed ground and cylinder-printed colors on continuous paper. Paris, Musée des Arts décoratifs, purchased in 1982, inv. 52391.10899

Marie-Pierre Ribère

The couturier's last master strokes

Paul Poiret in the 1930s

1
Maison Paul Poiret finally closed its doors in 1932 (*Women's Wear Daily*, 12 March 1930, p. 1).

2
'No Definite Plans But to Go On Creating, Asserts Paul Poiret', *Women's Wear Daily*, 14 February 1930, p. 5.

3
Harper's Bazaar, September 1929, p. 162; *Women's Wear Daily*, p. 9.

4
See Guillaume Garnier (ed.), *Paul Poiret et Nicole Groult. Maîtres de la mode Art déco*, exh. cat., Paris: Palais Galliera–Musée de la Mode et du Costume/Paris Musée, 1986, p. 206; Poiret told *Women's Wear Daily*, in its issue of 22 May 1931, p. 9, that the fashion house was run by a number of silk and wool manufacturers from Troyes, Lyon and Roubaix, although he did not name them.

5
'Nouveau décor pour une reprise', *Le Figaro*, 12 July 1931, p. 4. According to this article, the room was furnished by J.-P. Sabato.

6
Idem.

7
Manuel Jacob, 'Paul Poiret et la Renaissance couturière', *Bravo*, September 1931, p. 28.

8
See 'Poiret Sees Return [...] with New Astral Signs', *Women's Wear Daily*, 24 June 1931, p. 3.

9
Idem.

10
Paul Poiret quoted by Jean Oberlé, 'Nouvelle incarnation de Paul Poiret', *Le Crapouillot*, 1 July 1931, p. 48.

11
Idem.

12
See Manuel Jacob, 'Paul Poiret et la Renaissance couturière'.

In January 1930, Paul Poiret was a famous designer, but one without a fashion house. A series of financial troubles that had intensified since 1925 had left him with significant debts and practically no funds at his disposal at the dawn of this new decade.

The late 1920s had been particularly difficult: despite his reputation as a great designer, founder of the prestigious eponymous fashion house on the roundabout of the Champs-Élysées, his collections started to meet with a more lukewarm response among a clientele that was growing less receptive to his creative vision. Moreover, his volatile relationship with the directors of the fashion house meant that his working conditions significantly deteriorated. In late 1924, Poiret's financial difficulties forced him to entrust the management of his fashion house to a businessman, M. Aubert, who belonged to a group of bankers led by the senator Lazare Weiler. However, the designer stayed on as artistic director of the new company, Maison Paul Poiret, designing its collections until 1928. He was removed from his role in 1929, at a time of global economic crisis. His departure culminated in a lawsuit in January 1930 and Poiret was replaced by Marc Claude in March of that year.[1]

Without a job or a home, and temporarily unable to operate a business under his own name, Paul Poiret left Paris and sought refuge, with his model Renée, at his ultra-modern but unfinished house in Mézy-sur-Seine, which he had commissioned from the architect Robert Mallet-Stevens in 1923. This 'modern ruin', which he later sold to the actress Elvire Popesco, was a haven during this time of exile and poverty. He painted a great deal and, with the help of his daughter Martine, wrote the first volume of his memoirs, *En habillant l'époque*, which he dedicated to his mother and published in December 1930; it was an international success. Paul Poiret was fifty-one years old and, for the wider public, his name was still synonymous with good taste and luxury.

The unfortunate designer would not admit defeat, declaring to the press: 'What are my plans? I don't have any but I intend to create!'[2] His business ambitions rested on developing collaborations with American investors, particularly a plan to open boutiques on the East Coast of the United States, which would follow the formula he had invented of bringing together 'couture, accessories, jewellery, perfume and furniture'. From 1929 onwards, Poiret worked with, among others, Whiting & Davis Co., for which he designed handbags.[3]

However, it was a French textile company, the silk manufacturer Chatillon-Mouly-Roussel,[4] that seized the opportunity to put Poiret's talent to good use, offering him the role of artistic director of a fashion house. Situated in the ground floor and basement of number 12 Rue de Presbourg in Paris, 'Passy 10-17', named after its telephone number, opened its doors in summer 1931 (ILL. 3). The 'clean, light' room[5] charmed journalists with its stripped-back style, its furniture made of steel tubes and its glass partitions; through its wide windows hung with multicoloured curtains, there was a glimpse of the flower-beds that could function as a catwalk, boasting majestic views of the Arc de Triomphe. Furthermore, 'on their way to the fitting rooms, customers can see the workers leaning over the masterpieces that they will be wearing tomorrow'.[6] It was a 'small house of great couture',[7] in Poiret's own words, which employed nineteen people, including a young girl, Zorah, who wore a turban, worked on reception and served tea. The designer had only one head seamstress, Mme Van Praag,[8] with whom he planned to design collections for an elite clientele.

The highly anticipated first runway show was planned for 9 July 1931, the date when the fashion house opened: seventy designs for daytime, evening and leisure, made from the most beautiful fabrics, were presented to buyers and the international press – who recognized the designer's signature sources of inspiration. Indeed, this was Poiret's intention, 'to do something new' while still drawing on the historicist and Eastern influences (ILL. 2) that had made his name.[9] He also announced: 'The first designs that I will present will be inspired by the Colonial Exhibition. This exhibition, which I think is wonderful, will provide new sources of inspiration for all branches of art [...]. I will infuse them with a touch of the Orient...'[10] He also wanted to bring back the culotte, renamed 'the double skirt', 'endless' or 'ottomane',[11] and included examples in both daywear and eveningwear. He even created an innovative day outfit that could be transformed into an evening dress. The excitement generated by his return boosted sales for a time and the designer reported a turnover of 250,000 francs for the first two weeks after the collection went on sale.[12]

ill.1 Boris Lipnitzki, Paul Poiret on the terrace of his apartment above the Salle Pleyel, in Paris, c 1934

ill.2 Lipnitzki studio, 'Day ensemble (Passy 10–17)', *Bravo: Tous les spectacles*, 1 September 1931. Paris, Bibliothèque nationale de France, Law, Economics and Politics department, JO-15890

ill.3 Emile Marcovitch, 'Paul Poiret in his fashion house (Passy 10–17)', *Bravo: Tous les spectacles*, 1 September 1931. Paris, Bibliothèque nationale de France, Law, Economics and Politics department, JO-15890

13
Gisèle de Biezville, 'Un numéro de téléphone qui a l'ambition de devenir le bistrot de la couture', *Paris-Midi*, 11 July 1931, p. 2.

14
Bettina Bedwell, 'Paris Autumn Styles Shift to the Street Scene', *Chicago Tribune*, 9 August 1931, p. 2.

15
'Poiret Leaves Passy', *Women's Wear Daily*, 28 December 1931, p. 1.

16
'La mode – Passy 10-17', *Bec et ongles*, 13 February 1932, p. 20.

17
See Palmer White, *Poiret le magnifique. Le destin d'un grand couturier*, Payot, 1986, p. 264.

18
The Musée des Arts décoratifs has in its collection an unfinished dress given to Ufac by a loyal client, the Countess of Hinnisdäl.
The note accompanying her donation suggests that it was commissioned from the designer when he was running his boutique in Passy. Ufac collection, inv. UF 56-46-2.

19
See 'Paul Poiret Carries On at Modest Scale for "Cash Only"', *Women's Wear Daily*, 20 April 1932, p. 20.

20
Paul Poiret, 'L'art de faire les fêtes par Paul Poiret', *Fantasio*, 15 June 1935.

21
'Poiret May Open London Establishment', *Women's Wear Daily*, 12 December 1932, p. 4.

22
See 'Mascotte', *Aux écoutes*, 4 March 1933, p. 10.

23
For example, the major department store Aux Trois Quartiers. See Marie-Pierre Ribère, 'L'esprit de la couture: mode et confection dans les grands magasins', in Amélie Gastaut (ed.), *Naissance des grands magasins*, Paris: Musée des arts décoratifs, 2024, p. 80.

24
See Fabienne Falluel, 'Poiret et le Printemps', in *Paris-Couture-Années trente*, exh. cat., Paris: Musée de la Mode et du Costume, 1987, pp. 216–218.

25
See 'Standardization of Women's Ready to Wear – Feature of Printemps Style Show in Paris', *Women's Wear Daily*, 10 March 1933, p. 5.

26
See Fabienne Falluel, 'Poiret et le Printemps'.

However, the style was seen as outdated and impractical for the demands of a modern wardrobe, and this took its toll on profits. 'Overall, the outfits presented are curious, even strange, admirable stage costumes but impossible to wear in town.'[13] '[C]an you imagine walking down the street in a blizzard, wearing Byzantine or Persian culottes?'[14] Confident of his own talent and creative vision, in early November Poiret presented a second, mid-season collection, in the same style but more practical. A month later, his departure was announced;[15] perhaps he was pushed out by directors who had grown 'weary of this famous designer's merits and flaws'?[16] He was replaced by a pair of designers, Apolline and Henry Delcourt, who had formerly worked for Maggy Rouff and Schiaparelli.

In the winter of 1932, Poiret moved to Passy. Charmed by the small boutique on Place Possoz, he set up shop there, with one employee. A sign reading 'cash only' greeted customers in this modest fashion house, named 'Elle', for which he created the following letterhead: 'Paul Poiret-Place Possoz-Passy-Paris'.[17] The boutique offered designs[18] made to order with the help of family members, but sold only two or three dresses a day.[19] The venture was not especially profitable and did not last long. As Poiret's situation did not improve, he sought to diversify his business interests.

The designer liked to write and give lectures. Gallimard published the second volume of his memoirs, *Revenez-y*, dedicated to his son Colin. He also wrote a number of press articles on a variety of themes, such as 'Paris without nights grows bored (1880–1910)', a series of nostalgic texts published in July 1932 in *Paris-Soir*, and an issue dedicated to parties for *Fantasio*.[20] Then he once again tried his hand at acting, in *Panurge*, a film by Michel Bernheim in which he had a small role as a cobbler.

Towards the end of 1932, Paul Poiret seemed to be setting his sights on the United Kingdom. As he had been approached to give a lecture for textile manufacturers in Bradford, rumours spread that he was planning to set up shop in London.[21] However, these proved to be unfounded. Other opportunities opened up after the liquidation of the Paul Poiret fashion house. However, he received offers from two major department stores, Printemps in Paris and Liberty in London, at almost the same time.[22] Poiret had already drawn on the commercial scope and influence of department stores in autumn 1923, when he held a runway show presenting his couture collection alongside designs by Les Grands Magasins Dufayel. Although he had always refused to work for 'the masses', he now agreed and, once again, caused a sensation. It was Pierre Laguionie, director of Printemps, who commissioned him to design four collections a year. The idea of combining the name of a great designer with that of a department store was not unprecedented,[23] but this choice proved to be particularly astute in this time of economic crisis.

The store wanted to make an impression so, at significant cost, it created a spectacular theatrical space[24] with hundreds of seats, equipped with a vast central catwalk lit by projectors, the Pont d'Argent (Silver Bridge), where it held first two, then four daily runway shows (ILL. 4, 5, 6). There was a publicity campaign around the event and the press flocked to it, along with Parisian women for whom Poiret's name was still iconic. The set decoration had a springlike feel, draped with pink fabrics and geraniums, and the amethyst-coloured velvet stage curtain[25] was raised on the first collection on 28 February 1933. Poiret appeared as master of ceremonies alongside the models, who included the actress Pépa Bonafé wearing a dress with a crinoline. The runway show followed, set to music, presenting his designs for day, leisure and evening, made to measure and shown alongside the department store's clothes (ILL. 7).

In its April issue, Printemps' in-house magazine, *Printania*, published the 'master designer's' somewhat effusive first impressions behind the scenes at the show: 'I am delighted, enthralled! Here in this house I have found one of the most beautiful joys of my career. I feel that we have invented the blueprint for the future, democratized couture and transformed luxury into a question of taste, no longer a question of price.' He went on to describe 'the death of couture' and the standardization of the 'mass-produced woman', comments that revealed a certain bitterness despite the show's success… Poiret designed three collections for Printemps, but they did not renew his contract, as they grew tired of his incessant demands for advance payments.[26]

At the same time, he embarked on a collaboration with Liberty, whose products he knew well, particularly their fabrics, which he had often used in his own collections.

He received an advance of 10,000 francs (rapidly squandered)[27] to design four collections intended to modernize the women's fashion department. The iconic Regent Street department store helmed by Paul Saint George Perrot had closed its Parisian branch on the Boulevard des Capucines in 1932, but wanted to maintain a link with Paris by capitalizing on Poiret's image as an avant-garde, luxury designer. A first runway show, presenting his designs alongside the store's clothes, was held in early March 1933. 'Poiret is nothing if not original!'[28] Voluminous sleeves, generous skirts with uneven hems and Renaissance-inspired dresses were the characteristics noted by the press, who also remarked gleefully on the fact that sitting by the designer's side in the audience was Margot, Countess of Oxford and Asquith, wife of the former prime minister Herbert Henry Asquith and a London client from the beginning (ILL. 8).

The following year, Paul Poiret was the most famous unemployed person in Paris.[29] From his huge apartment overlooking the rooftop of the Salle Pleyel (ILL. 1), this man who lived surrounded by the last remaining traces of his collection of artworks, antiquities and fabrics still had 'the illusion of ruling over his dear Paris'. He described his situation quite openly in an interview ('I am completely penniless!'),[30] also touching on his fascination with stars, his passion for painting and his love of good food. His nights out in Paris still drew attention, as did the parties that he held in his home, where he sometimes delighted his guests with his talent for giving readings from La Fontaine's fables.[31] Towards the end of 1934, he published *Art et phynance*, the story of his fashion house's demise, dedicated to 'my enemies'.

Poiret remained surrounded by loyal friends, some of whom, such as Colette, the journalist Léon Bailby, the princess Jeanne Bibesco, the actor Paul Bernard and Dr Joseph-Charles Mardrus, even offered him financial support.[32] The designer was seeking to relaunch his career by raising capital to set up a new business called 'Les Croisières de la Mode'; the idea was to present collections first on ocean liners, then in runway shows that would travel around France and abroad. Created in his apartment[33] on a modest budget, the designs, which were sold at more accessible prices than his former creations[34] and sometimes made from furniture fabrics (ILL. 9), were unveiled in the winter and spring of 1935, at events both outside the capital and in Paris, in his home, in tea houses, at dinners and dances, and in the dining room of the restaurant La Coupole, during service... In a short film shown at the Club de la publicité,[35] Poiret described his pursuit of modernity and commented solemnly on a few evening gowns and garden party dresses with remarkable prints of seascapes and flowers – which were reminiscent of designs by the Martine workshop (Atelier Martine).[36] This presentation culminated in three daywear outfits with clever coats that could be transformed into capes; in a neat twist of fate, it was a design for a cape that had been his first major success in his early days at Douce⁻. This is probably one of the last images we have of Paul Poiret as a designer, because, aside from a few stage costumes, he did not get the opportunity to design clothes again: 'I can no longer make a living from couture: the time for beautiful fabrics and vibrant colours has passed. Women wear a uniform. They no longer have time to love and to dress themselves. However, there has never been a time, a society that has placed as much emphasis on dreams.'[37]

Despite his struggles, Paul Poiret never lost his drive: 'The further you fall, the further you bounce back; what I mean to say is, hope lives in my soul.'[38] Indeed, these challenging years forced him to explore different approaches, such as classic couture and limited-edition runs, as well as mass-market fashions, and to experiment with new kinds of visibility – his constant presence in the media built up his fame and his image as a great couturier. The diversity of these approaches reveals his very broad conception of his profession as a designer, which drew on his ideal of modernity. It was this view, combined with a desire for intellectual recognition for his profession, that led him, shortly before his death, when his fame had dwindled, to come up with the ground-breaking, visionary idea of founding an academy of luxury and fashion.[39]

27
See Cecil Beaton, *The Glass of Fashion*, New York: Doubleday and Company Inc., 1954, pp. 144–145.

28
Yvonne, 'What Smart Women Are Wearing', *Aberdeen Press and Journal*, 10 March 1933, p. 2.

29
See Serge, 'Paul Poiret roi des chômeurs', *Comœdia*, 6 December 1934, p. 1; Maryse Dubois, 'Avec Paul Poiret, poète et mémorialiste', *La Liberté*, 27 January 1935.

30
See Maryse Dubois, 'Avec Paul Poiret, poète et mémorialiste', *La Liberté*, 27 January 1935, p. 4.

31
Le Figaro, 1 July 1935, p. 5.

32
Various newspapers and magazines mentioned that these figures had supported Poiret's company financially; also in 'La rentrée de Paul Poiret', *Aux écoutes*, 12 January 1935, p. 22.

33
See 'Paul Poiret to Stage Another Come Back', *Women's Wear Daily*, 12 February 1935, p. 9.

34
'Entre 300 et 1,000 francs – Serge, Paul Poiret a encore quelque chose à dire', (*Comœdia*, 1 March 1935, p. 1).

35
'Au Club de la publicité, Paul Poiret présente ses robes croisières', 3 March 1935, Gaumont Pathé Archives, AF 127 1.

36
According to the photographic archives of the department store Printemps, very similar designs seem to have already been presented by Poiret in 1933.

37
Paul Poiret, 'Le château des rêves', *Le Journal*, 8 August 1936.

38
'Les échos du jour', *Le Jour*, 15 August 1935.

39
See Olivier Quéant, 'Hommage à Paul Poiret', *Images de France*, 1 January 1944; Garnier (ed.), *Paul Poiret et Nicole Groult*, p. 24.

ILL.4 Anonymous, runway show of Paul Poiret designs for Printemps at the Pont d'Argent, 1933, gelatin silver print. Paris, Fonds patrimonial du Printemps

ILL.6 Anonymous, Paul Poiret surrounded by sales assistants and clerks from Printemps on the Pont d'Argent, 1933, gelatin silver print. Paris, Fonds patrimonial du Printemps

ILL.5 Anonymous, runway show of Paul Poiret designs for Printemps at the Pont d'Argent, 1933, gelatin silver print. Paris, Fonds patrimonial du Printemps

ILL. 7 Advertising leaflet for Paul Poiret's second collection of the season at Printemps, April 1933. Paris, Musée des Arts décoratifs, Ufac Collection, 1995

ILL. 8 Anna Zinkeisen, *Liberty* evening gown design by Paul Poiret (left) in *Harper's Bazaar* US, July 1933, p. 42

ILL. 9 Paul Poiret, dress from the collection 'Les Croisières de la mode', 1935, printed chintz. Paris, Palais Galliera–Musée de la Mode de la Ville de Paris, inv. 1983.12.1

CAT. 351 *Les Parfums de Rosine*, advertising catalogue, Cannes,
Imprimerie Robaudy, 1923. Agnès Mulon Collection

Marie-Sophie Carron de la Carrière

When fashion meets fragrance

1
'Les parfums de Rosine', marketing catalogue, 1923, unpaginated.

2
Paul Poiret, *En habillant l'époque*, Paris: Grasset, 1930, reissued 2022, p. 260.

3
See Palmer White, *Poiret le magnifique. Le destin d'un grand couturier*, Paris: Payot, 1986, p. 116.

4
Paul Poiret, *Revenez-y*, Paris: Gallimard, 1932, p. 99.

5
Paul Poiret quoted in Palmer White, *Poiret le magnifique. Le destin d'un grand couturier*, p. 115.

6
Poiret, *En habillant l'époque*, 2022, p. 302.

7
Ibid., p. 13.

8
Ibid., p. 304.

9
'Les parfums de Rosine', page 'La véritable eau de Cologne', unpaginated.

10
Les parfums à travers la mode. Rétrospective de 1765 à nos jours, exh. cat., Paris: Les éditions du Chêne, 1945, unpaginated.

I don't preach savings to you. I only speak to you of elegance. Buy Rosine perfumes.[1]

Seeking to go beyond the world of clothing, Paul Poiret diversified in 1911 by setting up two companies, one dedicated to interior design (La Maison Martine) and the other to perfumes. Offering his clients an all-encompassing approach to life, he was the first designer to make his own perfumes, a natural extension of designing clothes – like luxury jewelry, perfume is highly aspirational, an indulgence. Poiret was involved in creating the perfumes, which he experimented with like an artist: 'Whatever the nature of the business and whatever area I am working in, I have always put all my personality and my sensibility into everything I have done.'[2]

The company, 'Les Parfums de Rosine', was named after his eldest daughter, who was five years old at the time. The premises, at number 39 Rue du Colisée, in the former stables of the designer's private mansion, on Avenue d'Antin, housed a laboratory. As the company grew, the perfumes and cosmetics were later created with help of Dr Midy in his pharmaceutical laboratory, in Courbevoie, where he made use of developments in organic chemistry to synthetically recreate plant extracts. Around forty employees worked there during this period.[3] The packaging for the small bottles, which was different for each perfume, was created by the packaging workshop, called 'Colin', after Poiret's son – naming his companies after three of his children highlighted the importance of family in his businesses. Poiret often visited the laboratory and was involved in every stage of creating the perfumes, then also in selecting the bottles, stoppers and cases.

'Confessor and adviser to the queens of beauty, the designer seems to know all the secrets of seduction and all the formulas for finery.'[4] As part of his quest for feminine beauty, he came up with descriptive notes and fragrances that allowed the customer to choose the perfume that matched her personality: 'You think you are refined because you do not stand out from others. You are wrong. Be unique.'[5] Some of the very distinctive fragrances and their highly elaborate bottles added a touch of Orientalism to customers' daily lives. The first perfume released by the company, *Nuit persane*, was given to three hundred female guests at the 'Thousand and Second Night' party that Poiret held in 1911 in the gardens of his fashion house. However, the composition of the perfume, which lacked stability, did not win them over. The first success came in 1913 with *Nuit de Chine*, which sealed the alliance between fashion and the world of scents. It was followed by thirty or so perfumes, all with evocative names, that were produced up until 1929, with the perfumiers Maurice Schaller and then Henri Alméras (ILL. 1, 2).

In his memoir *En habillant l'époque*, Poiret recalls his experiments in creating perfumes using plant-based ingredients: 'I wanted to pick the leaves of certain perfume plants that up until then had only been used for their flowers or their roots. I enjoyed working with geranium leaves, which I used to make the perfume Borgia, then with the mastic tree and balsamic plants from the heaths of Provence'.[6] Even as a child, he had wanted to 'borrow the scent from roses', according to a recipe he had made up: 'I put them in bottles of alcohol or sparkling water, as at that age I had no understanding of chemistry, or I crushed them in sealed boxes.'[7] In this way, creating a perfume is similar to coming up with a recipe, where all the ingredients are chosen very carefully. This is the reason why the passages about Les Parfums de Rosine are included in the 'Gastronomy' chapter of his autobiography.

Poiret decorated every bottle and glass atomizer with painted arabesques and flowers, or covered them with a piece of printed fabric designed by the pupils of the Martine School (École Martine). From 1924 onwards, the business was proving unprofitable for the bankers who controlled the fashion house's accounts. Poiret complained about their financial demands, which focused on production costs to the detriment of creativity: 'What is the point of so much useless creativity? Perfumes with leaves? [...] Your bottles, your novelties, we don't want them, it's too expensive,'[8] they told him. In his view, the price was a guarantee of quality: ' [...] the most expensive because it's the best'.[9] In 1925, the designer lost financial control of Les Parfums de Rosine.

At the exhibition 'Les parfums à travers la mode' ('Perfumes throughout fashion'), held in 1945 by Marcel Rochas in his fashion house and dedicated to Poiret, the designer paid tribute to his master, who had died the year before: 'Poiret could only make something beautiful when it was expensive.' In the exhibition catalogue, he wrote a glowing description of Poiret's perfumes that draws on the imagery of *The Thousand and One Nights*: 'Sometimes it's "Aladin" and all the wonders of the grand Moorish palaces, or "Maharadjah", the warm and captivating perfume of an opulent Oriental sovereign, or even "Antinéa", the bitter scent of seaweed at the bottom of the ocean. Sometimes romanticism in "Pierrot", sometimes the influence of Picasso in "Arlequinade" (CAT. 301, 143). Finally, all the childish whims of Rosine, his beloved daughter, in "Le Mouchoir de Rosine" ["Rosine's Handkerchief"], green, blue, yellow, red depending on the weather, or rather depending on the mood, a rainbow of all the qualities, of a true clairvoyant of modern art.'[10]

Mlle Spinelly préfère le " Fruit Défendu "

ILL.1 Delphi, 'Mlle Spinelly prefers le "Fruit Défendu"' in *Les Parfums de Rosine*, advertising catalogue for Maison Paul Poiret's perfumes, c. 1930

ILL.2 Raoul Dufy (illustration), Henri Alméras (perfume), Les Parfums de Rosine, *Le Fruit défendu* and box, 1915, glass, metal, cardboard and paper. Paris, Palais Galliera–Musée de la Mode de la Ville de Paris, inv. 1990.155.1.AB

CAT. 143 Marie Vassilieff, Julien Viard (glass artist), Henri Alméras (perfumier), Les Parfums de Rosine, *Arlequinade*, 1923, glass, bakelite and fabric. Grasse, Musée international de la Parfumerie

CAT. 301 Pierre Delbo, *Arlequinade*, 1925, gelatin silver print. Claude Bernès Collection

ILL.1 Anonymous, portrait of Paul Poiret in the kitchen, 1934, gelatin
silver print. Paris, Librairie Diktats

Marie-Sophie Carron de la Carrière

From couture to gastronomy

1
Louis Roubaud, *Au pays des mannequins. Le roman de la robe*, Paris: Les éditions de France, 1928, p. 62.

2
Ibid., 1930, p. 53.

3
Ibid., p. 288.

4
Ibid.

5
Poiret, *En habillant l'époque*, p. 289.

6
This was the 'Parisian barge', moored near the Place de la Concorde, which had belonged to Marshal Joffre.

7
Paul Poiret, *107 recettes ou curiosités culinaires*, Paris: H. Jonquières, 1928.

8
Paul Poiret, quoted in Palmer White, *Poiret le magnifique. Le destin d'un grand couturier*, Paris: Payot, 1986, p. 257.

9
Poiret, *107 recettes ou curiosités culinaires*, p. 294.

10
Ibid., p. 293.

Here, you are in a restaurant where we offer beautifully presented scrambled eggs with truffles; we don't know how to make chips. But I called you for chips! Monsieur Paul agreed.[1]

In 1901, when Gaston Worth interviewed Paul Poiret for a job, he compared his prestigious fashion house, which dressed Empress Eugénie and the court at the Tuileries Palace, to an upmarket restaurant that served only truffles. Times had changed, the high-society clientele wanted a wardrobe that suited the demands of modern life: 'Princesses sometimes take the bus, and walk down the road.'[2] With this in mind, the Worth fashion house decided to open a 'chips department' and Poiret became its 'chip fryer', before setting up his own fashion house two years later.

Paul Poiret's stout figure, captured standing in front of his oven in a photograph from 1934 (ILL.1), shows his love of good food and haute cuisine. Known by his friends as a 'connoisseur in matters of gastronomy',[3] he defined the word *gourmet*, which he believed applied to him thanks to his knowledge of wine, as follows: 'Being a gourmet means having a special education made up of a lot of happy, or unhappy, experiences. It means trips to the Bordelais region, trips to Champagne and Bourgogne, to sample their classic vintages and develop the palate.'[4] He regularly visited the restaurant La Tour d'Argent, 'this academy of gastronomic traditions', whose head sommelier he held in great esteem. Finally, he argued with great conviction, 'I believe that an artist should only eat good things and should avoid bad meals as much as he should avoid bad sights'.[5]

A member of the Club des Cent, a French society of a hundred gastronomy lovers, founded in 1912, he wrote a humorous account of his misfortunes at a dinner held on Marshal Joffre's barge.[6] That evening he sparked an uproar when, during the dinner, which was exclusively for members of the circle, a winegrower presented a wine that he judged to be mediocre, 'unspeakable cheap plonk'. After this minor incident, he was thrown out of the gastronomic club by its president and, in response to this exclusion, in 1922 he formed a new gastronomic circle, which he called, with a touch of mischief, 'le club des Purs Cent' (the Club of the Pure Hundred).

Three years later, at the International Exhibition of Decorative Arts in Paris, Poiret presented his designs in three barges moored on the Seine and decorated by the Martine workshop (Atelier Martine). One of them, *Délices*, was transformed into a restaurant for the occasion; the guests were welcomed mostly by Poiret himself, who took great care over updating the menu every day (CAT. 331).

In 1928, the designer, who had been elected honorary president of the Pure Hundred by his fellow members, published a book of '107 recipes or culinary curiosities' (CAT. 327), collected from great chefs and illustrated by Marie Alix.[7] The 'salade du nouveau pauvre' ('salad of the new poor man'), made with herring fillets and potato, is placed at the beginning of the book, perhaps a sign of his changed circumstances, as his business's financial situation had deteriorated dramatically. The number of recipes evokes, with a touch of nostalgia, the number of his former fashion house on the Avenue d'Antin, which he was very sad to leave. The book was published the same year that his mother, Louise Poiret, died, and the year he divorced his wife, Denise. Depressed, Poiret entertained himself by cooking ('We are going to live more simply,' he told the children. 'You will make your beds. I will make the food')[8] or by eating at restaurants – while avoiding paying the bill, as he did not have the money. Drawing on his passion for French cuisine, he saw food as a hobby to enjoy, which brought him a number of pleasures: 'To the end of my days, I want to retain a sufficient appetite to appreciate food, which is a passion of mine.'[9] In his memoirs, he wrote with great relish about his favourite recipe, which he made himself: *œuf du pêcheur* ('fisherman's egg'). Simple to make, its description whets the reader's appetite: 'When you eat mussels, keep the juice and use it to poach an egg. Serve it on a well-toasted crust of bread that has been slathered with crème fraiche, and sprinkle it with grated cheese. Put the whole thing in the oven on a high heat. It should crisp up nicely, but the egg should stay soft; the role of the cream is to insulate it from the oven's heat. When you slide a fork into the egg, the yolk should ooze out into the juice of the mussels. It's very good.'[10]

Paul Poiret, a hedonist with a refined palate, was a man who enjoyed life to the full, who relished his pleasures, with flair, humour and a touch of poetry.

LA SALADE DU NOUVEAU PAUVRE

Dois-je avouer que cette salade me doit son existence? Dois-je dire aussi ce qui m'incita à la composer? J'avais remarqué dans une feuille quotidienne, sans doute lue par des personnes fastueuses, la recette d'une salade dans laquelle entraient à la fois, entre autres choses, du caviar et du foie gras. Il y a des incompatibilités que nos grands novateurs semblent ignorer. Nous avons un prince, on parle d'une académie… il nous manque un critique culinaire. Mais voici la recette.

1

1

tourne pendant un quart d'heure en y ajoutant peu à peu la farine et les amandes pilées. Quand la première mixture est refroidie on y ajoute le deuxième contingent en y mettant les blancs d'œufs battus en neige. Prendre alors un moule, le beurrer, y mettre cette pâte et laisser cuire pendant trois quarts d'heure à four chaud.
    Glacer au chocolat.

ROBERT SPA.

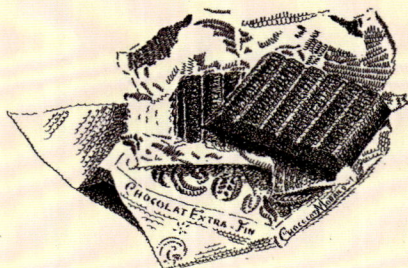

GÂTEAU AU CHOCOLAT

Un quart d'amandes, un quart de beurre, trois cuillerées de farine, quatre œufs frais, une demi-livre de sucre, une demi-livre de chocolat.
    On fait d'abord fondre le chocolat dans un quart de verre d'eau avec un quart de sucre et on laisse cuire le tout pendant une demi-heure. On prend ensuite dans une autre coupe le restant de sucre et quatre jaunes d'œufs que l'on

186

187

CAT. 327 Paul Poiret, Sébastien Voirol (text), Marie Alix (illustrations), 'The salad of the new poor man' and 'Chocolate cake' from *107 recettes ou curiosités culinaires recueillies par Paul Poiret* [*107 recipes or culinary curiosities collected by Paul Poiret*], honorary president of the 'Purs Cent' club, Paris, H. Jonquières, 1928. Paris, library of the Musée des Arts décoratifs

la péniche " délices " est consacrée au
sens de l'odorat " parfums de rosine "
et à celui du goût " restaurant délices ".

elle est aménagée par martine. tous
les éléments qui la constituent: mobilier,
service de table, verrerie, lingerie,
argenterie, décoration intérieure, lumi-
naire, etc., sont mis en vente par la
maison martine.

les commandes peuvent être prises sur
la péniche même.

la cave est composée et contrôlée par des
connaisseurs éclairés (mm. les membres
du club des purs cent) ; les vins sont
mis en vente et livrés en bouteilles.

les commandes peuvent être prises sur
la péniche, par le maître d'hôtel ou le
sommelier.

toutes les sommités de la cuisine française sont invitées à passer un ou plu-
sieurs jours à bord de la péniche
" délices " pour y présenter au public
parisien les spécialités originales qui
ont fait leur célébrité.

menu

hors-d'œuvre

homard armoricaine

riz pilaff

agneau de pauillac poêle

haricots panachés

asperges de cavaillon sauce mousseline

glace délices

fruits de saison

inauguration
de la péniche " délices "
24 avril 1925

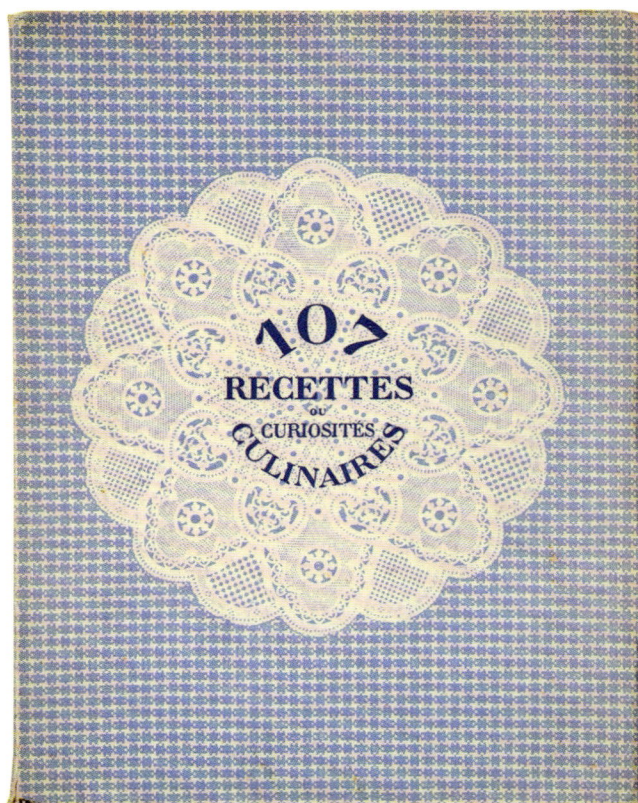

CAT. 331 Menu for the official opening dinner on the barge *Délices*
presented at the International Exhibition of Modern Decorative
and Industrial Arts in 1925, Paris, Imprimerie Coquemer, 24 April
1925. Paris, library of the Musée des Arts décoratifs

CAT. 327 Paul Poiret, Sébastien Voirol (text), Marie Alix (illustration),
cover of *107 recipes or culinary curiosities*, Paris: H. Jonquières,
1928. Paris, library of the Musée des Arts décoratifs

Marie-Sophie Carron de la Carrière

Couturier and art collector

1
'Around 1891 [...] Among his favourite pastimes were visits to the Musée du Louvre, where he admired the portraits of women in all their finery.' (timeline established by Guillaume Garnier (ed.) in *Paul Poiret et Nicole Groult. Maîtres de la mode Art déco*, exh. cat., Paris: Musée de la Mode et du Costume–Palais Galliera, 1986, p. 177).

2
Paul Poiret, *En habillant l'époque*, Paris: Grasset, 1930, p. 20: '[...] my opinions were seen as subversive and shocked my family with their independence of thought.'

3
Ibid., p. 13.

4
Ibid., p. 156.

5
Ibid., p. 9.

6
Ibid., p. 69.

7
Ibid., p. 69.

8
Gustave Babin, 'Une leçon d'élégance', in *L'Illustration*, 9 July 1910, pp. 21–22.

9
François Chapon, *Mystère et splendeurs de Jacques Doucet*, Paris: Jean-Claude Lattès, 1984, p. 14.

10
Poiret, *En habillant l'époque*, p. 26.

The interplay between fashion and art is at the heart of the modern, learned couturier that Paul Poiret embodied in the early years of the 20th century. In his autobiography *En habillant l'époque*, Poiret describes his interest in art, which was fostered very early on by his Parisian education and his visits to the Louvre[1] and to the Universal Exhibitions of 1889 and 1900. A little later, his attendance at the Salons allowed him to stay informed about artistic life and new trends. Much like an art critic, he already showed a certain independence of spirit, offering terse aesthetic judgments on official and society painters. 'Clairin and Bouguereau seem obsolete, Carolus Duran outmoded and Bonnat pretentious.'[2] Keen to be seen as the discoverer of promising talents, he expressed his appreciation of Charles Cottet, symbol of a new approach in painting, who made his debut at the Salon of 1889, and his interest in the new sensibility of Impressionist painters, making no distinction. In the countryside as well, far away from the Salons, he trained his artistic vision on the objects around him, which were often of little value. In his memoirs he recalls that, even as a child, in his family home in Billancourt, he collected pieces of scrap metal in the vegetable garden and the orchard, labelled them 'like a curator' and put together 'a museum of antiquities'. He saw this as the start of 'what would later become the object of my research and my passion'.[3] When describing the originality of his approach, which consisted of 'decorating his mind as you decorate a house and accumulating riches of art borrowed from museums or from all the beauties of nature',[4] he insisted that 'culture cannot be improvised'.[5] The designer shared this desire to expand his knowledge in every way with Denise (CAT. 245 AND ILL. 4), whom he married in 1905, as he recalls in his memoirs: 'We visited antiques dealers, museums, and we worked ceaselessly to enrich our knowledge of culture, to refine our sensibility.'[6] The couple's travels played an important part in this process of enrichment: 'We were familiar with all the museums of Europe'[7] (ILL. 1).

Shaping a vision

In the same article in which he dubbed Paul Poiret an 'artist-couturier', the journalist and art critic Gustave Babin praised his decision to present his designs outdoors, in the gardens of the mansion on the Avenue d'Antin, the premises of his fashion house, which he had bought in 1909.[8] A more traditional choice of setting in which to present his collections to his clients might have been the rooms on the ground floor, decorated by the interior designer Louis Süe. By opening the gates to his garden – 'a genius idea', according to Babin, who cites it as the reason for dedicating an article to the designer in his newspaper *L'Illustration* – he sparked the interest of the press. Photographed by Henri Manuel, the group of eight models walked, like a tableau vivant, through the garden, which had been set up so as to create three places to pose: 'on the steps', 'in front of a trellis arch' and 'in front of the French-style flowerbeds' (ILL. 2). According to the journalist, their way of walking, with slow, small steps, in their narrow skirts, was reminiscent of 'women from the Orient balancing full vases on their heads'. In Babin's view, Poiret had 'imbued the material with a soul, given his dream an existence [...]. He has created a work of art.'

In the 19th century, the connection between fashion and art had already been explored by pioneers such as Jean-Philippe Worth and Jacques Doucet, directors of the two fashion houses where Poiret learned his trade, each in his own way. However, in 1908, the year when Paul Poiret published a book of his designs illustrated by Paul Iribe, a great couturier was still, in the eyes of high society, nothing more than a supplier – to such an extent that Doucet, the first couturier to also be a 'collector of collections',[9] showed great discretion when it came to his passion for art, which followed a parallel trajectory to his work as a designer. He never expressed the desire to translate his interest in avant-garde art into his fashion designs. It would be Poiret, first Doucet's assistant and then his friend, who would succeed in combining these two worlds, an idea he had been contemplating since working alongside his mentor. Fascinated by the interior design of Doucet's Parisian apartment, at 27 Rue de la Ville-l'Evêque in the 8th arrondissement, Poiret described it as characteristic of the refined, classic style of the Belle Époque: 'All Monsieur Doucet's surroundings were made up of old engravings and 18th-century paintings, and rare vintage furniture, which was very modest and chosen with very assured taste.'[10] The young man saw this prince of taste as role model,

ILL.1 Anonymous, Paul Poiret at a museum, November 1925, gelatin silver print from the *Photographic Album of Paul Poiret's visit to Copenhagen*. Paris, Palais Galliera–Musée de la Mode de la Ville de Paris, inv. 1987.1.447

11
Ibid.

12
See Chantal Georgel,
'Qui êtes-vous Monsieur
Doucet ?', in *Jacques Doucet.*
Collectionneur et mécène,
Paris: Les Arts décoratifs–
INHA, 2016, p. 14.

13
André Salmon, 'Pour les
absents', in *L'Europe nouvelle*,
no. 13, 6 April 1918, p. 631.

14
Poiret, *En habillant l'époque*,
p. 54.

15
Ibid., p. 55.

16
Ibid., p. 54.

17
Jean-Philippe Worth,
A Century of Fashion, Boston:
Little, Brown, and Company,
1928, p. 2.

18
Ibid., p. 77.

19
Poiret, *En habillant l'époque*,
p. 93.

20
Ibid.

declaring: 'In my mind, I was already the Doucet of the future.'[11] In 1912, the master parted with almost his entire collection of 18th-century furniture, paintings and sculptures, putting them up for auction, before embracing a radical modernity that would shape his new collection. In February 1924, on the advice of André Breton, Doucet bought *Les Demoiselles d'Avignon*, the 'incredible' painting by Picasso, dating to 1907.[12] Eight years earlier, in July 1916, he had seen the painting exhibited for the first time, at the Salon d'Antin held at the Barbazanges Gallery. Poiret was a regular visitor to this gallery, whose premises, next to his fashion house at 107 Rue du Faubourg-Saint-Honoré, he had rented out to his friend Henri Barbazanges since 1910. According to André Salmon, the organizer of the salon, 'it was the only exhibition, since the war, that was open to revolutionary artists'.[13] After this showing, the painting was returned to Picasso's studio, where it remained until it was bought by Doucet.

After learning his trade under Doucet, Poiret went on to work at the Worth fashion house. After Doucet the collector-couturier, Poiret therefore had a second initiation into the world of haute couture and the importance of art in the form of Worth, the couturier who created innovative new fashions. In 1901 he was hired by Gaston Worth, the son of the father of haute couture, Charles Frederick Worth, to work alongside his brother, Jean-Philippe, who had been artistic director since their father's death in 1895. Still embracing the extravagant luxury that was typical of the fashion house's designs, Jean-Philippe found it difficult to admit the need to adapt to the simpler approach popular with a new generation of clients. To reach this market, Gaston Worth asked Poiret to modernize the fashion house's output by designing coats and tailored dresses with a pared-back structure – innovations that did not find favour with Jean-Philippe, who 'could not understand how it was possible to create a dress stripped of all opulence'.[14] The young Poiret quickly came to understand the fundamental disagreement between himself and Jean-Philippe Worth: 'He didn't like me very much, because in his eyes I represented the new spirit, in which there was a power (he could feel it) that would destroy and carry away his dreams.'[15] This perceptive observation did not stop him from understanding the older man, a complicated character, whom he depicted as an inspired and authentic artist when he described his creative process: 'The dresses that came from Jean's hands were wonders of art and purity. He worked a lot from paintings by the great masters, and I saw him take some magnificent ideas from paintings by Nattier and de Largillière.'[16] At the beginning of Jean-Philippe Worth's memoirs, written in 1926 and published two years later,[17] there is a reproduction of a painting of Elizabeth I of England, dressed as Iris in a velvet ballet costume embroidered with eyes and ears, as if in echo of Poiret's words. In this book, Jean-Philippe Worth recalls Sundays spent with his father, Charles Frederick, and the landscape painter Camille Corot, when he was about fifteen years old, around 1870. Having enjoyed an unparalleled introduction to art, Jean-Philippe recalls a lesson on freedom and sincerity from his conversations with Corot, whom he describes as a spiritual guide: 'You should paint with your heart, with your soul.'[18] In the early 20th century, he put this advice to use in the world of fashion, becoming a gifted designer with his own unique imagination and sensibility – a precursor to the contemporary figure of a fashion designer as a creator of a way of living as much as a way of dressing.

From 1910 onwards, Poiret, in his own way, succeeded in achieving a synthesis of these two personalities and the different aesthetics of his era.

The bohemian life

Poiret felt an 'irrevocable sympathy' with painters. His closeness to a number of artists was fostered by shared areas of interest: 'It seems to me that we have the same vocation and that they are my colleagues.'[19] In 1901, he met André Derain and Maurice de Vlaminck, who shared a studio in Chatou. They became friends, all three being driven by a desire to break away from the French Academy's approach and pursue authenticity, 'in a healthy atmosphere of freedom and carefreeness'.[20] Derain, like Poiret, was a regular visitor to the Louvre, making copies of works by the great masters, and would go on to become a faithful friend. The designer definitely attended the exhibition of the 'cage aux fauves' ('cage of wild beasts') at the Salon d'Automne in 1905, which was an immediate success and sparked an instant scandal. Founded by Derain and Matisse, Fauvism was an art movement characterized by a simplified drawing style, clear craftsmanship, and free and expressive use of colour. It seems to have influenced Poiret in his liberal use of bright, acidic colour palettes, with the couturier reintroducing, violet, royal blue, orange, apple green and bright red into his designs.

During the First World War, Poiret and Derain, who were mobilized in August 1914, found themselves in the same infantry regiment in Lisieux, where they stayed in the Hôtel du Maure. In his letters to his partner, Alice Géry, the painter describes the lack of action during the six first months of the war and mentions Poiret: '[…] he is charming with me and is fundamentally a truly great person. He gets so very bored.'[21] To combat the boredom, Poiret commissioned Derain to paint his portrait, which Derain did in March 1915 (CAT. 158, P. 22), in a bedroom hung with wallpaper in the colours of the French flag (now in the collection of the Musée de Grenoble). Poiret often went off on unauthorized adventures, and he brought the painter back colours from Paris. He told Derain that he did not want to be painted wearing his military uniform, preferring to wear civilian clothes. He was charmed by the result, which he thought was a faithful depiction of his character, 'which, it seems, is despotic and Venetian'.[22] Poiret's money came at an opportune moment for Derain, as he was no longer receiving any income from his exclusive seller, Daniel-Henry Kahnweiler, who was in exile in Switzerland because of the war. In return for this commission in his time of need, the designer could count on the painter's generosity in moments of great hardship. From 1936 onwards, Derain regularly invited him to dine at his property in Chambourcy.[23]

A gift for parties

This is how the painter André Dunoyer de Segonzac remembered his friend: 'Very quickly Poiret was able to surround himself with young artists, most of whom were still almost unknown: Dufy, Vlaminck, Iribe, Boussingault, Bernard Naudin, etc., etc. He knew how to discover the shades of the new in their talents.'[24] Parties were an opportunity to bring them together, while also having fun. By involving his friends in organizing them, Poiret found a pretext to unite them all. He sought to 'create a centre that was the capital of taste and of the Parisian spirit'.[25] Holding a party and hosting friends was a way of showing himself to be an artist. Fernande Olivier, who was Picasso's partner at the time, recalls receiving a few invitations from Poiret in 1905, to visit the apartment on the Rue de Rome where he lived with his wife. 'Poiret immediately started inviting Picasso and his friends to his house. He invited them to dinners and parties.'[26] She recalls evenings that were 'free-and-easy, gay and animated, in pleasant surroundings which he knew how to make intimate'.[27] These dinners gave him an opportunity to engineer meetings between artists, such as Lepape, Luc-Albert Moreau, Süe and Dunoyer de Segonzac, 'a close friend of Poiret, given to doing imitations of the peasants from his part of the world'.[28]

The designer also held costume parties, which he sought to make into society events that were reported on by the press, and sparkling performances that brought together the great and the good of Paris.[29] 'Poiret amuses himself and amuses Paris', as Maurice Sachs remembered. The 'Party of Kings' held in the early 1920s was a true Who's Who of Parisian society.[30] Beneath their costumes as kings or queens, assigned by the designer, were, among others, Poiret as Oedipus, Guy Arnoux as a hunt leader, Baroness Robert de Rothschild as the Queen of Sheba, Madame Jacques Lebel as king of the dance, Damia as queen of Paris's city walls, Princess Lucien Murat as the Queen of Naples, Jean-Gabriel Domergue as François I, Baron de Rothschild as Charles X, and even Kees van Dongen as Neptune, king of the seas (CAT. 249). The spectacle created by the guests was matched by a theatrical performance of Regnard's play Le Divorce by Dullin's company. 'We stayed until seven o'clock in the morning,' Sachs recalls warmly.

A 'pure' artist?

There was one person, however, who did not recognize Poiret as an artist: as Fernande Olivier recalls, the poet Guillaume Apollinaire, a friend of Picasso's since 1905, 'couldn't bear the fact that [Poiret] considered himself a "pure" artist. He wrote an article about it saying that if dress designing was to be considered as an art at all it could never be

21
André Derain, Lettres à Alice, 1914–1919, Paris: Éditions du Centre Pompidou, 2017, p. 56.

22
Poiret, En habillant l'époque, p. 199.

23
According to Geneviève Taillade, André Derain's great-niece and president of the Association des amis de Derain.

24
André Dunoyer de Segonzac, 'Une figure française Paul Poiret', in Comœdia, 13 May 1944, p. 1.

25
Poiret, En habillant l'époque, p. 149.

26
Fernande Olivier, Picasso and His Friends, London: Heinemann, 1964, p. 116.

27
Ibid., p. 116.

28
Ibid., p. 116.

29
See 'Le bal des rois chez Poiret', Femina, March 1924, p. 40.

30
Maurice Sachs, Au temps du Bœuf sur le toit, Paris: Éditions Grasset et Fasquelle, 1987, pp. 167–168.

ILL. 2 Henri Manuel, *A Parade of Models by the French-Style Parterre*, from the article 'Une leçon d'élégance dans un parc' ['A lesson in elegance in a park'] by Gustave Babin, published in *L'Illustration*, no. 3515, 9 July 1910, p. 22. Paris, library of the Musée des Arts décoratifs

CAT. 245 Delphi, Denise Poiret wearing the dress *Mythe* or *Faune* by Paul Poiret, 1919, gelatin silver print. Behind her is the sculpture *Maiastra* by Constantin Brancusi. Paris, Musée des Arts décoratifs

CAT. 249 Kees van Dongen, *Self Portrait as Neptune*, 1922, oil on canvas. Paris, Centre Pompidou–Musée national d'art moderne–Centre de création industrielle

CAT. 256 Raoul Dufy, *The Shepherdess* wall hanging, 1910, painted and block-printed on linen. Private collection

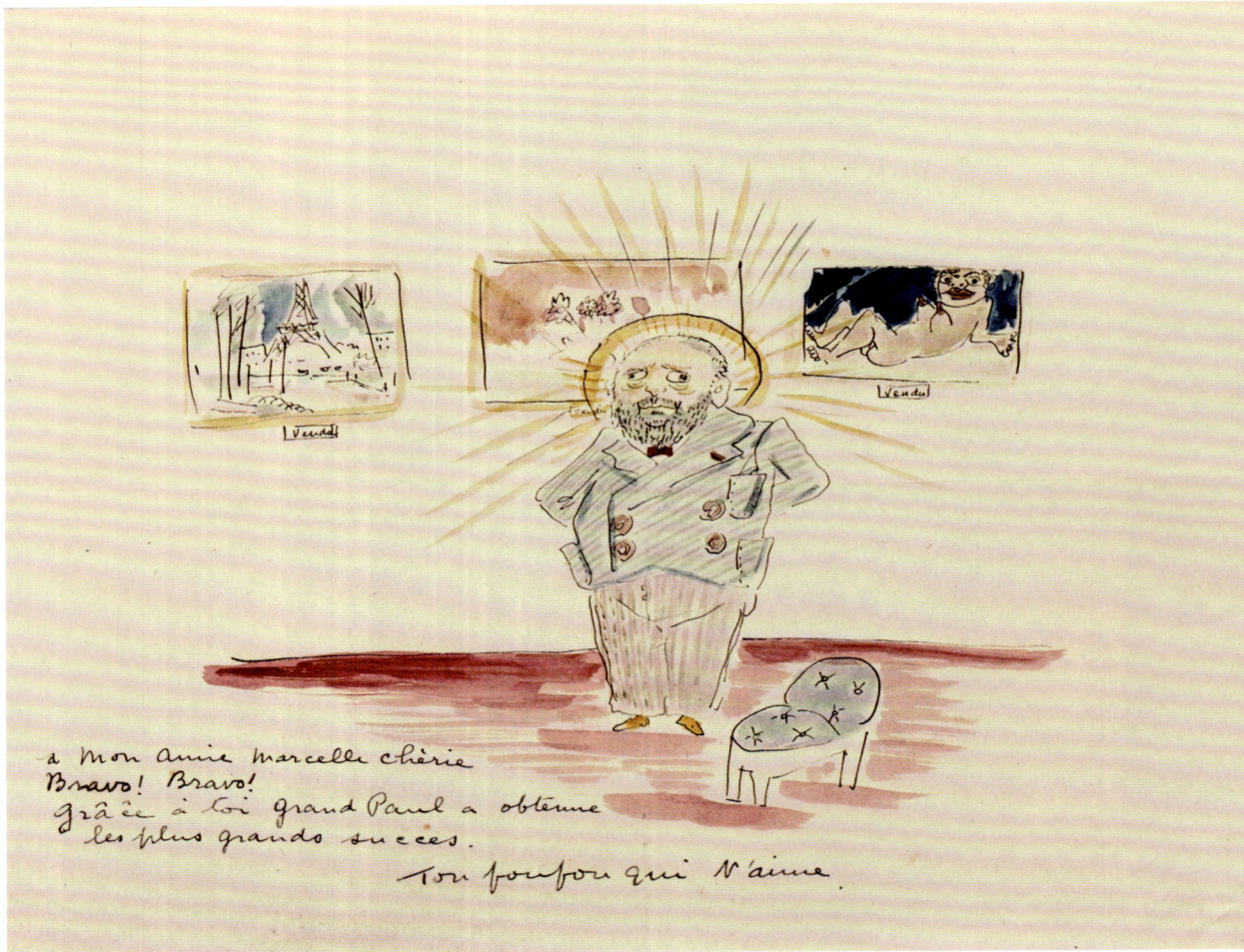

ILL. 3 Tsuguharu Foujita, *Portrait of Paul Poiret*, for Marcelle Houry, undated. Danièle Thompson Collection

CAT. 304 Paul Poiret, *Still Life with Flowers*, 1927, oil on canvas. Paris, Musée des Arts décoratifs

31
Fernande Olivier, *Picasso and His Friends*, p. 116.

32
See Le Wattman, 'Nos échos', *L'Intransigeant*, 9 December 1911, unpaginated.

33
Letter from Guillaume Apollinaire addressed to Raoul Dufy in December 1911, reproduced in Gérard Oury, *Mémoires d'éléphant*, Paris: Olivier Orban, 1988, p. 27.

34
Ibid., p. 27.

35
Poiret, *En habillant l'époque*, p. 151.

36
Jean Cocteau, 'Paul Poiret peint', in a brochure published by the Charpentier gallery, 76 Rue du Faubourg-Saint-Honoré, Paris (8th arrondissement), private view on Saturday 11 March 1944.

anything but an inferior art. Poiret never forgave him this.'[31] In June 1911, Apollinaire turned down Poiret's invitation to attend his Persian costume party the 'Thousand and Second Night'. Well known in avant-garde circles, he was the regular art critic at the newspaper *L'Intransigeant* from 1910 to 1914. This daily paper published a column by '*le Wattman*', which described the designer's latest collections as 'Parisian Persianeries' and 'pitiful masquerades'.[32] Like many others, Raoul Dufy believed that it was Apollinaire hiding behind '*le Wattman*'. The poet was forced to issue a formal denial: he was not the author of the article. He added that he was not conducting a campaign against a businessperson and that he did not write about fashion, as the subject was too commercial. Anxious to clear his name, he insisted to Dufy: 'In my article about the Salon d'Automne, I included a nice sentence about Poiret, I called him the Couturier of the Graces and the sentence was deleted.'[33] As the filmmaker Gérard Oury, whose mother, Marcelle, worked for Poiret, said: 'Dufy will remain loyal to Poiret for all his life and will defend him against the attacks sparked by the designer's success and character'[34] (ILL. 3).

Ironically, in some ways it was Apollinaire who brought about the collaboration between his friend Dufy and Poiret. The publication, in 1911, of his collection *Le Bestiaire ou Cortège d'Orphée* (*The Bestiary or Orpheus' Retinue*), illustrated by Dufy's woodcuts, shortly after the exhibition of four engravings at the Salon des Indépendants in 1910, caught Poiret's attention. He asked the painter to design motifs to be printed on textiles (CAT. 256), following a creative process that Dufy developed and Poiret described as follows: 'Dufy drew and sculpted in wood some of the woodcuts taken from his Bestiary. He turned them into sumptuous fabrics, which I used to make dresses.'[35]

As if in response to Guillaume Apollinaire's words, when he was asked in 1924 by the daily newspaper *Excelsior*, 'Is a dress really a work of art?', Paul Poiret answered: 'If it is made by an artist who imbues it with a fragment of his personal sensibility. The thought, still luminous at the moment when we create, passes into the negative pole that is the worker; when crossing this neutral territory, the creator of a design must ensure it emerges just as brilliant as when it sprang from him […]. I feel, when I am making them, that my dresses are works of art: I project something of my personality into the material.' He added: 'we are artists who do business.'

'Paul Poiret paints'

Towards the end of Poiret's life, the Charpentier gallery held an exhibition of twenty-three of his paintings, which depicted views of Paris or landscapes. The poet Jean Cocteau wrote a short presentation text entitled 'Paul Poiret paints', which included an apt and somewhat grandiloquent description of the designer's various metamorphoses: 'Fashion is a strange religion that transforms its rites but maintains an underlying through-line. Paul Poiret was one of its high priests.'[36] Painting provided him with his final incarnation (CAT. 304). The exhibition was held in occupied France, a few weeks before his death on 28 April 1944. Cocteau's description is a heroic portrait that draws on the historical context: 'He is like the admiral of some ghost ship, painting in the middle of a storm – 1944 – Paul Poiret infuses his city with new colours.'

ILL. 4 Boris Lipnitzki, Denise Poiret in her room, c. 1920, gelatin silver print. In the background, *Quietude* by Kees Van Dongen. Sophie Rang des Adrets collection

CAT. 279 Charles Camoin, *Siesta by an Open Window*, c. 1928, oil on canvas. It shows Perrine Poiret, the designer's daughter, at Paul Poiret's house in Saint-Tropez. Alain Bras Collection

CAT. 39 Natalia Goncharova (artist), Muolle Rossignol (costumer), costume worn by Caryathis in *Danse espagnole*, presented at the Oasis in 1921, dyed silk satin, graphite, hand- and machine-embroidered tulle, ribbon, wood and painted cotton fabric. Paris, Musée des Arts décoratifs

ILLS. 5, 6 & 7 Anonymous, exhibition of Paul Poiret's personal collection at the Galerie Barbazanges, Paris, from 26 April to 12 May 1923, gelatin silver prints. Paris, Musée d'Orsay, inv. ODO 1996 52 1887 to inv. ODO 1996 52 1890

The titles of works identified in these photographs are taken from the exhibition catalogue 'La collection particulière de M. Paul Poiret', Paris, Galerie Barbazanges (26 April–12 May 1923). Corrected titles and additional information have been added after a long dash (—).

[1] Henri Matisse, *Paysage — Collioure in August*, c. 1911, oil on canvas
[2] André Derain, *Portrait de M. P. P. — Portrait de Paul Poiret*, 1915, oil on canvas, Musée de Grenoble
[3] Amedeo Modigliani, *Max Jacob (Portrait) — Portrait of Max Jacob*, 1916, oil on canvas, Musée des Beaux-arts de Quimper
[4] Raoul Dufy, *Noix (Aquarelle) — Still Life with Bowl of Walnuts*, c. 1914, pastel
[5] Raoul Dufy, *Mozart — Hommage à Mozart*, c. 1915, watercolour and ink on paper, Buffalo AKG Art Museum
[6] Raoul Dufy, *Régate (Marine) — Regattas*, 1907
[7] Kees Van Dongen, *Les Colombes —* 1912, oil on canvas
[8] Kees Van Dongen, *Amour — Quietude*, 1918, oil on canvas
[9] Kees Van Dongen, *Trois femmes assises*

[10] Kees Van Dongen, *Comedia — Montparnasse Blues*, oil on canvas
[11] Kees Van Dongen, *Femme au corset — The Antichamber*, c. 1911
[12] Jean-Louis Boussingault, *Grand panneau décoratif*
[13] Chériane (Chérie-Anne Charles), *Maternité*
[14] Georges Kars, *Nègre aux gants jaunes — Portrait*, c. 1912
[15] Vera Rockline, *La Femme en rose (Portrait)*
[16] Marie Vassilieff, *Jeune fille à la rose —* c. 1920
[17] Georges Kars, *Saint-Tropez (Paysage) — Southern Landscape*, c. 1910, oil on canvas
[18] Georges Kars, *Lodge — Das Gespräch (In der Loge)*, 1913, oil on canvas

ILL.1 Giovanni Boldini, *Portrait of Madame Eugène Doyen*, shown wearing a Paul Poiret gown, 1910, oil on canvas. Private collection

Éric Pujalet-Plaà

From Poiret to Dior

1
'He [Dior] is revolutionizing daytime fashions as Poiret did in his day and Chanel in hers. A Paris cab driver remarked to our reporter, "I hear that there is a rival to Balenciaga, at last"', quoted in *Harper's Bazaar*, April 1946.

2
Christian Dior, *Christian Dior & moi*, Paris: Amiot-Dumont, 'Bibliothèque Amiot-Dumont' collection, 1956, p. 26.

3
'Miss O', according to Palmer White, *Poiret le magnifique. Le destin d'un grand couturier*, Paris: Payot, 1986, p. 257.

4
Dior, *Christian Dior & moi*, p. 208.

5
André Salmon, 'Preface', in *La Collection particulière de M. Paul Poiret*, exh. cat., Paris: galerie Barbazanges, Devambez, 1923.

6
Fernande Olivier, *Picasso et ses amis*, Paris: Stock, 1933, p. 140.

7
Paul Poiret, *En habillant l'époque*, Paris: Grasset, 1930, p. 26.

8
Christian Dior, *Christian Dior & moi*, p. 211.

9
Ibid., p. 212.

The idea of comparing Paul Poiret (1879–1944) and Christian Dior (1905–1957) seems obvious when we consider the similarities between their careers; however, there is nothing to suggest that these two designers, trailblazers of their respective eras (Poiret before 1914, Dior from 1947 onwards), knew one another.

It was Carmel Snow, the editor of *Harper's Bazaar*, who, in 1947, first drew a connection between the two men: '[Dior] is revolutionizing daytime fashions as Poiret did in his day.'[1] In terms of style, Poiret's dresses sometimes prefigure Dior's – deliberately Orientalist, historicist or floral (ILL. 1, CAT 107 AND 178). Robert Piguet, also a designer and a disciple of Poiret's, and whom Dior worked for in the early days of his career, functioned as a kind of intermediary between the two designers, providing a through-line from the rose motif designed by Iribe, which was so precious to Poiret, to the flower-woman silhouette created by Dior; all three were also perfumiers.

First, Poiret and Dior are alike in that they are among the few designers who were also writers. Each wrote his autobiography at the age of fifty-one: *En habillant l'époque*, published in 1930, for Poiret, *Christian Dior et moi*, published in 1956, for Dior.

Dior, who had in all likelihood read the older designer's memoir, situates his own career, among other influences, in the context of Poiret's, who 'came and shook everything up'.[2] There are other similarities in their autobiographies, such as their shared love of parties and their vision of America. Their accounts place great importance on destiny, twists of fate and even financial ruin, which Poiret knew in his later years and Dior in his youth.

Their lives are therefore not parallel, but symmetrical, and their stories echo one another: Dior's first memories of fashion are from the early days of Poiret's career, and both men were inspired by the elegance of the Belle Époque, as depicted by the painter Paul Helleu.

They also shared certain personality traits. We might compare their dandyism, their figures, their tastes in matters of interior design, even their interest in fortune telling and gastronomy. Paul and Christian both grew up in bourgeois families during the Third Republic, adoring their mothers and, at different times, even studying under the same English teacher![3]

Collectors and gallerists, they sometimes had works by the same artists hanging on their walls. Dior even mentions a painting by Raoul Dufy, *Plan of Paris* (ILL. 3), that Poiret sold to him and which he resold when in need of money, shortly before he started working as a designer. Both men moved in the same artistic circles, around Max Jacob, whom Dior had been friendly with since before 1927, and whom Poiret was friends with probably from around 1900. The painter Jean Oberlé, a friend of Poiret's,

was also invited twice, in 1931, to exhibit in galleries associated with Dior.

The artistic connections between Poiret and Dior are numerous and indirect, often related to the Ballets Russes, whose collaborators both designers were friendly with, at different times. One of these was Jean Cocteau, mentioned by both in their memoirs. Boris Kochno, the ballet company's manager, and the composer Henri Sauguet were also loyal friends of Dior's who had connections to Poiret's artistic, professional and personal world.

Growing up in environments that embraced poetry, music, dance, painting and fashion, Poiret and Dior developed similar aesthetics, influenced by one major figure, as Dior wrote: 'It is strange that in 1956, people describe the work and the masters that we admired between the ages of fifteen and twenty as avant-garde, as an aesthetic of the future, designers who had already been famous for ten years among the most well-informed of our elders, guided by Guillaume Apollinaire.'[4] A number of artists whom Poiret knew were friends of Apollinaire's. When, in 1923, the art critic André Salmon alluded to the poet and critic's 1916 speech at the 'Salon d'Antin', where Poiret exhibited Pablo Picasso's *Les Demoiselles d'Avignon* for the first time, he described the designer as an 'activist', a defender of 'contemporary art'.[5] Poiret was certainly one of these elders mentioned by Dior, 'guided by Apollinaire'. However, the designer and the poet ended up falling out, as mentioned by Fernande Olivier: 'Apollinaire could not stand the fact that he [Poiret] considered himself to be a "pure" artist. He wrote an article on this subject, saying that if couture was to be considered an art, it would never be anything more than a lesser art form. Poiret could not forgive him.'[6] It was Jacques Doucet that Poiret turned to as his teacher and role model: 'In my mind, I was already the Doucet of the future.'[7]

Finally, of all the arts, it is perhaps music that brings these two great designers together the most strongly.

Paul Poiret played the violin. He was a knowledgeable music lover, as can be seen from the chamber music concerts held 'in the home of Madame Paul Poiret' in 1910–1912, which featured works by Couperin, Rameau, Bach, Gluck, Haydn, Boccherini, Mozart, Beethoven and even Schumann, and for which he asked his friend Bernard Naudin – a painter, illustrator and gifted guitarist – to illustrate the programmes.

Christian Dior was also a musician: 'I had obtained, not without difficulty, my parents' permission to study musical composition. Very soon, I became fascinated by the reaction sparked by Satie and Stravinsky with Les Six, then the Arcueil School'[8] (ILL. 2). And he saw in Henri Sauguet a kindred spirit: 'His music does away with all our differences. It was the music I would have dreamed of writing if heaven had given me the gift of being a true musician.'[9]

"QUE PENSEZ-VOUS DES SIX?"

OU

ON NE PEUT PAS ÊTRE TRANQUILLE

ROBE DU SOIR, DE PAUL POIRET

Nº 10 de la Gazette du Bon Ton.

Année 1921. — Planche 79

ILL. 2 André Édouard Marty, 'What do you think of Les Six? or One Can't Get a Moment of Peace, evening gown by Paul Poiret', Gazette du Bon Ton, no. 10, 1921, plate 79, Paris: Éditions Lucien Vogel, 1921, photogravure and pochoir print. Paris, library of the Musée des Arts décoratifs

Promoters, observers and actors in the world of modern art, Paul Poiret and Christian Dior seem to have shared or continued some of Apollinaire's interests (Poiret's interest in African art, Dior's taste for surrealism).

Their knowledge of music most likely meant that they were aware of the revolutions in harmony during their respective youths, moving away from the classical, romantic heritage towards Eastern inspirations, modernity and the evolution of jazz, along with all the effects that these changes had on the perception of the body.

ILL. 3 Thérèse Bonney, dining room in Paul Poiret's home with *Plan of Paris* by Raoul Dufy on the wall, 1927, gelatin silver print. Paris, Bibliothèque historique de la ville de Paris, number NN-006-02715

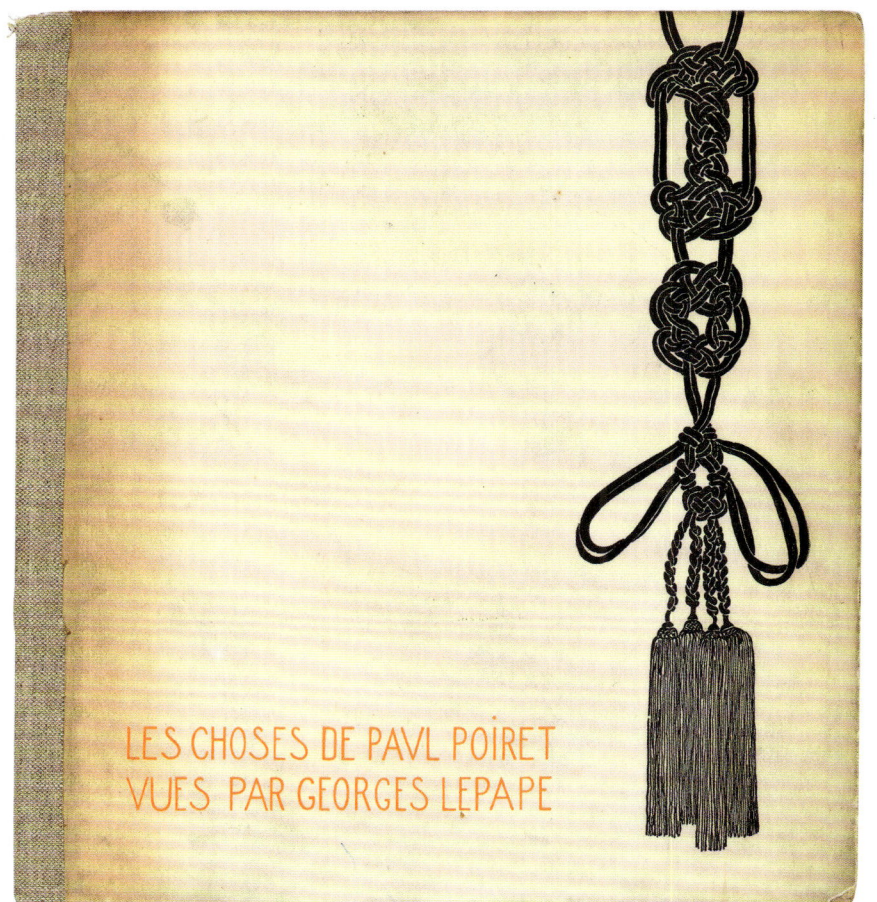

CAT.107 Christian Dior, *Minuit* evening coat, from the Autumn–Winter 1948 haute couture collection, 'Ligne ailée', black silk velvet embroidered with wool passementerie and braid. Paris, Musée des Arts décoratifs, Ufac Collection

CAT.178 Georges Lepape, *Les Choses de Paul Poiret vues par Georges Lepape*, 1911, phototype and pochoir print. Paris, library of the Musée des Arts décoratifs

ILL.1 Jean-Pierre Ronzel, Azzedine Alaïa, rue des Marronniers,
1963, gelatin silver print. Fondction Azzedine Alaïa

Olivier Saillard

Paul Poiret in the collections of the Fondation Azzedine Alaïa

Azzedine Alaïa (ILL. 1) is the only designer who built up a collection of fashion archives with such a broad range of pieces that it covered the entire history of the discipline and celebrated the art and techniques of fashion design. Now conserved by the foundation that he set up and that bears his name, 20,000 items of clothing acquired from the 1960s onwards trace the evolution of clothing and fashion from the 18th century to the contemporary era. Over the course of several decades, Azzedine Alaïa collected original designs, clothes, accessories, photographs and documents. After his death in 2017, those tasked with drawing up an inventory counted almost 700 dresses by Madame Grès, more than 500 designs by Cristóbal Balenciaga and a similar number by Christian Dior, 250 evening gowns by Madeleine Vionnet, and hundreds of pieces by Jeanne Lanvin and Adrian, to mention just a few...

While Alaïa's tastes naturally drew him towards the great masters of pattern cutting, his interest in those who worked on the fringes of the decorative arts and breathed new life into the art of appearances, such as Paul Poiret and Jeanne Lanvin, is less well known. He collected more than fifty major designs by Poiret, from different eras of the 'magnificent couturier's' career, from his time on the Rue Pasquier, where he was based between 1904 and 1909, to his time on the Rue du Faubourg-Saint-Honoré, from 1914 onwards.

On two occasions, Azzedine Alaïa hosted exhibition sales, the first dedicated to the iconoclastic creations of Elsa Schiaparelli, the second to the original designs of Paul Poiret. In 2005, 'La création en liberté' ('Creating with freedom'), a temporary exhibition held on the premises of the Alaïa fashion house itself, displayed the entirety of Denise Poiret's wardrobe, ahead of the auction at which the designer's wife's personal effects were sold for record sums – almost 600 pieces of clothing and accessories were sold by the Drouot auction house. Alaïa wanted to celebrate the creative force who had invented 20th-century fashion and revolutionized the role of the designer, by showcasing a discerning selection of pieces. He took pride in reviving the memory of a man whose work had not been the subject of an exhibition since the one held at the Musée Galliera in 1986, moving heaven and earth to convince designers and journalists to come and admire Poiret's groundbreaking designs.

Then, thanks to two auctions in 2005 and 2008, he acquired a number of rare and precious designs, with stunning linings.

One of these, a coat inspired by North African garments, has a generous cut, a high collar, asymmetrical buttons and a low waist, designed as a 'driving coat' – very fashionable in the 1920s. While the outer fabric, by Rodier, is relatively understated, the lining, designed by the Martine workshop (Atelier Martine), is made of silk pongee printed with colourful geometric motifs. Drawing inspiration from sportswear, this coat brings together cultural traditions and technological innovations in its cut, while the pattern on the lining testifies to Poiret's taste for exoticism.

Another acquisition, the *Moscovite* jacket, made famous by a photograph in which Denise Poiret wears it with pride (CAT. 261), is now in the collections of the Fondation Alaïa. Inspired by Russian traditional costume, it has an asymmetrical row of buttons, fastened with a passementerie button. Braiding and a collar embellished with printed flowers stand out against the blue fabric, dividing up the jacket. The lining boasts an original design by the Martine workshop, on silk in matching colours. An iconic piece that testifies to Poiret's groundbreaking creative vision, this jacket from 1912 breaks with the restrictive 'S-shaped' silhouette of the previous decade and allows its wearer greater freedom of movement. With nothing to constrain the figure, it does not mark the waistline, a challenge to decades of corseted silhouettes.

Dating to 1919, the outfit *Tanger* is another treasure in Alaïa's collection of Poiret designs (CAT. 226). Also from Denise Poiret's personal wardrobe, this two-piece outfit consists of a dress and long traditional coat made of coarse wool, with a hood that is reminiscent of the burnous worn in North Africa. A Westernized version of a Berber garment that could not fail to charm Alaïa, *Tanger* appealed to his tastes as a collector because this outfit represented, for him, a decisive stage in the history of the styles and creative processes of the early 20th century. In drawing directly on 'exotic' inspirations and shapes to design elegant women's clothing, Poiret was decades ahead of creative minds such as Yves Saint Laurent and Kenzo. Boldly, but backed up by historical knowledge, Azzedine Alaïa did not hesitate to compare Paul Poiret to Martin Margiela. They both reimagined historical or traditional garments, as well as combining various ethnic inspirations, and some of Poiret's disarmingly simple white cotton blouses from the 1910s find a surprising echo in the Belgian designer's groundbreaking styles from the 1990s.

The Fondation Alaïa's collection also boasts Empire-style dresses that date to Poiret's early years. Dresses for dancing, embroidered in the 1920s or made of lamé, contrast with tunics inspired by the approach of the Vienna Workshops.

Always a passionate defender of those forgotten by fashion history, Alaïa was tireless on the subject of Poiret's innovations. Not only did Poiret liberate women's bodies in the early 20th century by doing away with corsets, but he was also ahead of his time in embracing contemporary creative ventures for designers, with perfumes, furniture, artistic collaborations, and so on.

The flamboyant designer was one of the first to see fashion as a way of life, although this approach did not bring him financial success, unlike those who emulated him. Despite laying the foundations for the modern luxury industry, towards the end of his life he was alone, financially ruined and soon forgotten by everyone. His fall from notoriety to anonymity, a fate feared by all contemporary couturiers and designers, was doubtless part of what drew Alaïa to try to resurrect his memory. However, it is clear from the archives that the Tunisian-born designer built up in homage to Poiret that he did not want to revive the memory of this media darling's indulgences, but to celebrate a designer who was able to draw inspiration from the past, learn from it and avoid it by steering contemporary fashion in a new direction and coming up with unique and timeless creations.

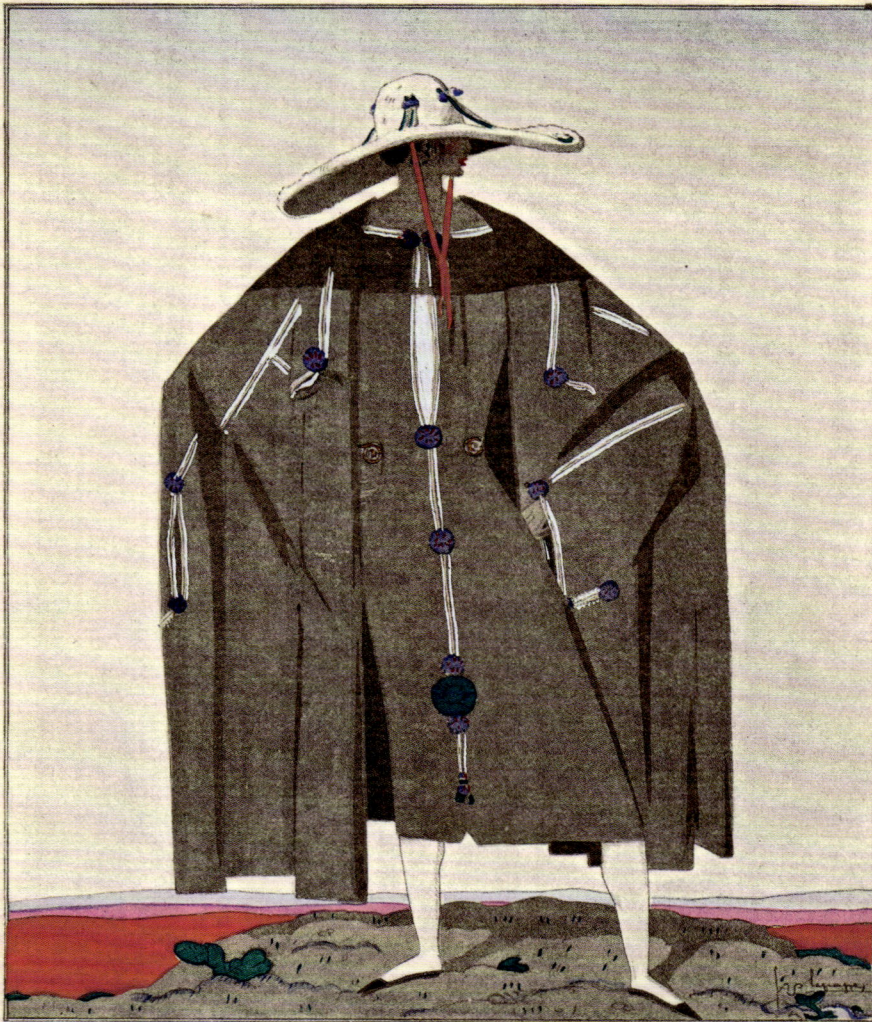

TANGER
ou
LES CHARMES DE L'EXIL
Robe d'après-midi et Cape de Paul Poiret

CAT. 226 Georges Lepape, 'Tanger or The Charms of Exile, afternoon dress and cape by Paul Poiret' in Gazette du Bon Ton, no. 1, 1920, plate 7, Paris, Éditions Lucien Vogel, 1921, photogravure and pochoir print. Paris, library of the Musée des Arts décoratifs

CAT. 261 Geisler & Baumann, Denise Poiret wearing clothes by Paul Poiret at the Plaza Hotel, New York, during their trip to the United States, 1913 (2/3). Paris, library of the Musée des Arts décoratifs

AFTER
PAUL
POIRET

In his autobiography, Paul Poiret speculated about the legacy of his creations: 'People have been good enough to say that I have exercised a powerful influence over my age, and that I have inspired the whole of my generation.'[1]

1
Paul Poiret, *En habillant l'époque*, Paris, Grasset, 1930, p.77.

Since his career began, the couturier has by turns embodied two contradictory faces of fashion: either luxurious and all-conquering, or out of style. In a sketch entitled *Poiret Leaves – Chanel Arrives*, Cocteau was one of the first to grasp this ambivalence, which is also an element of his iconic status.

Couturier, perfumer, interior designer, amateur painter and musician: Poiret walked many paths. Elsa Schiaparelli, whom he met in 1922, was so struck by the range of his talents that she compared him to Leonardo da Vinci. Thirty years later, in the 1950s, Christian Dior lauded him as a great fashion renovator. Subsequently, many generations of couturiers and creators have been inspired by Poiret, reworking his themes without necessarily quoting him directly.

Without any claim to be exhaustive, the examples of connections presented here show the extent of Poiret's legacy in the world of fashion. These examples have been selected from the world of couture over the last fifty years, from Kenzo to Maitrepierre. The 1970s, in fact, were a key moment for Poiret as a source of inspiration. Fashion museums undoubtedly played a role in this, whether right from the moment of their founding or as part of their evolution. They made Poiret's message contemporary by making his legacy part of fashion heritage and exhibiting his work as that of a master.

The pages that follow showcase a selection of museum pieces that share certain features of style with the creations of Paul Poiret, as well as with each other. The folk costume influence on Kenzo is revisited in the work of Christian Lacroix; the *Opéra–Ballets Russes* collection by Yves Saint Laurent, *Le Grand Voyage* by Jean Paul Gaultier, the orientalism of Dries Van Noten and the east-meets-west style of Issey Miyake come together to map an imaginary world; the roses of Paul Iribe are perhaps reborn in the work of Olivier Theyskens for Rochas; the lively prints from the Martine workshop are echoed in the floral fantasies of Rei Kawakubo and Maitrepierre; Karl Lagerfeld designed a dress for Chloé that Poiret might have seen in Vienna when he visited the Wiener Werkstätte in 1910; and John Galliano reinvents the gilded youths of Christian Dior, fascinated by Poiret and his art of living.

Whether in fashion or decor, in styles that range from minimalist to playful, Adeline André, Jean-Charles de Castelbajac, Azzedine Alaïa and Agatha Ruiz de la Prada interpret many forms of inspiration – textiles or paintings, sensual or structural – and evoke memories of the great couturier.

Poiret himself collected fabrics and clothes with many provenances, sometimes as sources of inspiration, sometimes in order to create new designs by transforming them. This approach to working and reworking, foreshadowing that of Martin Margiela, also poses questions about the posterity of fashion history.

Kenzo Jap
Ensemble
Autumn–Winter 1970 ready-to-wear collection
Cotton velvet, quilted printed cotton and
brocade ribbon
Paris, Musée des Arts décoratifs
CAT. 111, P. 202

Chloé by **Karl Lagerfeld**
Evening gown, unique design created for the
singer Régine for the opening of her Paris
nightclub 'Réginskaïa'
1971
Painted taffeta painted by Nicole Lefort,
design inspired by Gustav Klimt
Paris, Musée des Arts décoratifs
CAT. 34, P. 203

Yves Saint Laurent
Evening ensemble
Autumn–Winter 1976 haute couture collection,
'Opéra – Ballets russes'
Silk velvet and chiffon
Paris, Musée des Arts décoratifs
CAT. 112, P. 204

Issey Miyake
Oblate coat, bodice and trousers
Spring–Summer 1979 ready-to-wear collection
Nylon crepe, gold lamé nylon voile
Tokyo, Miyake Design Studio,
Paris, Musée des Arts décoratifs
CAT. 60 & 61, P. 205

Jean Patou by **Christian Lacroix**
Incredible ensemble
Autumn–Winter 1985 haute couture collection
Pekin silk and gold diamanté
Paris, Musée des Arts décoratifs
CAT. 114, P. 206

Jean-Charles de Castelbajac
Hommage à l'art du xxᵉ siècle coat
Autumn–Winter 1988–89 ready-to-wear
collection, 'Le temps a laissé son blanc manteau
à la cour Carrée du Louvre'
Hand-painted cotton and grey faux leopard fur
Jean-Charles de Castelbajac
CAT. 115, P. 207

Maison Martin Margiela
Ensemble
Autumn–Winter 1989 ready-to-wear collection
Wool knit, leather, cotton serge, ceramics
and steel wire
Paris, Musée des Arts décoratifs
CAT. 116, P. 208

Jean Paul Gaultier
Ensemble
Autumn–Winter 1994 ready-to-wear collection,
'Le Grand Voyage'
Shot silk damask and synthetic fur
Paris, Musée des Arts décoratifs
CAT. 63, P. 209

Ágatha Ruiz de la Prada
Tarta dress
1994 ready-to-wear collection, 'Ágatha Ruiz de la
Prada en Paris'
Silk organza and plastic hoopse
Paris, Musée des Arts décoratifs
CAT. 68, P. 210

Christian Dior by **John Galliano**
Stourhead evening coat and dress
Spring–Summer 1998 haute couture collection,
'Hommage poétique à la marquise Casati'
Gold figured silk brocade, hand-painted
and fleece-lined, aged goffered silver lamé,
chiffon embroidered with metallic silver thread
and diamanté
Paris, Musée des Arts décoratifs
CAT. 117, P. 211

Rochas by **Olivier Theyskens**
Evening gown
Spring–Summer 2004 ready-to-wear collection
Synthetic goffered and pleated taffeta, cordonnet
braid, coated taffeta, goffered muslin, lace frill,
satin ribbons and gathered lamé
Paris, Musée des Arts décoratifs
CAT. 35, P. 212

Adeline André
'Poiret' coat
Autumn–Winter 2005 haute couture collection
Wool doeskin
Paris, Musée des Arts décoratifs
CAT. 119, P. 213

Dries Van Noten
Coat
Autumn–Winter 2006 ready-to-wear collection
Wool serge, embroidered with gold thread,
sequins, copper and acetate twill
Paris, Musée des Arts décoratifs
CAT. 64, P. 214

Comme des Garçons
Three-piece ensemble
Autumn–Winter 2013 collection, 'The Infinity of
Tailoring'
Printed velvet and aged leather
Paris, Musée des Arts décoratifs
CAT. 90, P. 215

Azzedine Alaïa
Gilet and skirt ensemble
Autumn–Winter 2016 couture
Gilet made from laser-cut leather with metal
studs, lined with crepe, skirt made from virgin
wool; belt made from leather with silver-coloured
metal eyelets
Fondation Azzedine Alaïa
CAT. 120, P. 216

Maitrepierre
Viktor coat, wearable *Bouquet* sculpture by
Gracelee Lawrence
Autumn–Winter 2024 ready-to-wear collection
Imitation astrakhan and 3D-printed sculpture
made from biodegradable PLA (biodegradable
polymer made from maize, beetroot and wheat
starch)
Alphonse Maitrepierre
CAT. 121, P. 217

REFERENCE

Chronology

Marie-Sophie Carron de la Carrière
and Astrid Novembre

1879

20 April: Alexandre Paul Poiret, known as Paul Poiret, is born at 21 Rue des Deux-Écus (Paris, 1st arrondissement). He has four sisters: Louise Eugénie (1869–1883); Amable Jeanne, known as Jeanne (1871–1959); Jeanne Louise Germaine, known as Germaine (1885–1971); and Pauline Marie, known as Nicole (1887–1966). The eldest sister is born during the Second Empire (1852–1870), while the others are born during the Third Republic (1870–1940). Their father, Denis Auguste Poiret (born in 1845), is a cloth merchant and their mother, Marie Louise Heinrich (born in 1849), does not work.

1886

13 March: Denise Boulet, Paul Poiret's future wife, is born in Elbeuf (Seine-Maritime).

1893

9 January: Jeanne Poiret marries the French jeweller René Boivin (1864–1917).

1896

Spring: After finishing his schooling, Paul Poiret is sent by his father to work for an umbrella manufacturer in order to learn a trade.

1898:

Spring: Paul Poiret sells some designs to the couturier Louise Chéruit (1866–1955), who encourages him to pursue his vocation.
Summer: He is recruited by the couturier Jacques Doucet (1853–1929) to work in his fashion house, where he is head of the tailoring department until April 1900.
Trial of Alfred Dreyfus. Poiret defies his father by openly supporting Dreyfus.

1900–1901

Poiret does his military service in Rouen.

1901

Winter: He starts working for Worth, the fashion house run by Gaston Worth (1853–1924, financial director) and Jean-Philippe Worth (1856–1926, artistic director). His role is to modernize the house's image.
He rents a house in Auvers-sur-Oise and becomes friends with the painters André Derain (1880–1954) and Maurice de Vlaminck (1876–1958).

1903

His father dies.
September: He founds his fashion house, called 'Paul Poiret', with financial support from his mother. It is located at 5 Rue Auber, behind the Paris Opera house.

1904

26 November: Germaine Poiret marries Louis Bongard.

1905

30 September: Paul Poiret marries Denise Boulet (1886-1982) at the 9th arrondissement town hall.
2 October: The couple married religiously at the Madeleine Church. They move into an apartment at 151 Rue de Rome (Paris, 17th arrondissement).
18 October – 25 November: The 'Fauvist' painters exhibit their work at the Salon d'Automne.

1906

March: Paul Poiret's fashion house grows and moves to 37 Rue Pasquier (Paris, 8th arrondissement).
11 October: The Poirets' first child, Rosine, is born.

1907

18 June: Nicole Poiret marries the French interior designer André Groult (1884–1966).

1908

October: Publication of the book *Les Robes de Paul Poiret racontées par Paul Iribe*.
1 October – 8 November: Denise Poiret exhibits eight embroidered cushions at the Salon d'Automne.

1909

Paul Poiret travels to London to present his collection in the home of Lady Asquith (1864–1945), the wife of the British prime minister.
October: Paul Poiret moves his fashion house and family home to an 18th-century mansion. Situated between three streets in Paris's 8th arrondissement (Avenue d'Antin, Rue du Faubourg-Saint-Honoré and Rue du Colisée), the building is at 107 Rue du Faubourg-Saint-Honoré and 26 Avenue d'Antin (now Avenue Franklin D. Roosevelt).

ILL.1 Routhier, Paul Poiret, 1898, gelatin silver print. Sophie Rang des Adrets collection

1910

Poiret goes on a ten-week cruise around the Mediterranean on board a yacht, accompanied by artist friends. He leaves from Marseille and visits Ajaccio, Naples, Amalfi, Paestum, Sicily, Sousse, Kairouan, Tunis, Béjaïa, Constantine, Algiers, Oran, Almería, Alicante, Valencia, Tarragona, Barcelona and Sète.

He rents out part of the ground floor of his mansion to Henri Jean Barbazanges (1875–1944), who sets up an eponymous gallery there. The entrance to the gallery is at 109 Rue du Faubourg-Saint-Honoré (Paris, 8th arrondissement).

4 June: Paul and Denise Poiret attend the premiere of *Shéhérazade* at the Paris Opera. It is performed by Sergei Diaghilev's (1872–1929) Ballets Russes, to music by Nikolai Rimsky-Korsakov (1844–1908). The choreography is by Mikhail Fokin (1880–1942) and the sets and costumes are designed by Léon Bakst (1866–1924).

Autumn: Poiret travels to Berlin, Vienna and Brussels. In Vienna, he visits the studios of the Wiener Werkstätte, led by architect and designer Josef Hoffmann (1870–1956). In Brussels, he visits the Stoclet Palace, one of Hoffmann's masterpieces.

October: Diaghilev and the dancer Vaslav Nijinsky (1889–1950) visit Poiret, who shows them his designs.

1 October – 8 November: Georges Lepape (1887–1971) exhibits his work at the Salon d'Automne. This is when Poiret meets him. Poiret is looking for an artist to put together a book similar to the one illustrated by Paul Iribe.

18 November: Musical performance hosted by Madame Paul Poiret. The programme, illustrated by Bernard Naudin (1876–1946), mentions pieces by Joseph Haydn (1732–1809), Johann Sebastian Bach (1685–1750) and Mozart (1756–1791).

1910–1911

Poiret commissions Raoul Dufy (1877–1953) to design motifs to be used on printed fabrics. He sets him up in a studio, the Little Factory, located at 104 Boulevard de Clichy (Paris, 18th arrondissement).

1911

Paintings by Bernard Boutet de Monvel (1881–1949) and Georges Lepape are exhibited at the Barbazanges Gallery.

January: Poiret designs the costumes worn by Édouard de Max (1869–1924) in Maurice de Faramond's (1862–1923) play *Nabuchodonosor*, which is performed at the Théâtre des Arts. The costumes for this play are exhibited at the Salon d'Automne in the Théâtre des Arts section (1 October – 8 November 1911), where they are shown alongside sets designed by André Dunoyer de Segonzac (1884–1974).

20 January: Musical performance hosted by Madame Paul Poiret. The programme,

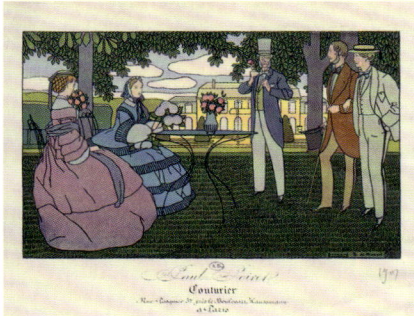

ILL.2 Bernard Boutet de Monvel, invitation from the fashion house on the rue Pasquier, 1907, chromolithograph on paper. Paris, library of the Musée des Arts décoratifs, Maciet 256/15/76

illustrated by Bernard Naudin, mentions pieces by Ludwig van Beethoven (1770–1827).

February: Publication of the book *Les Choses de Paul Poiret vues par Georges Lepape*.

18 February: Musical performance hosted by Madame Paul Poiret. The programme, illustrated by Bernard Naudin, mentions pieces by Robert Schumann (1810–1856).

9 March: The Poirets' second daughter, Martine, is born.

April: Paul Poiret sets up the Martine School (named after his second daughter), based in a room on the first floor of his private mansion. Marguerite Sérusier (1879–1950) is director of this school, which focuses on interior design, until 1912.

April–June: Henri-Pierre Roché (1879–1959) introduces the artist Marie Laurencin (1883–1956) to Nicole Groult at the Salon des Indépendants. The two women become close friends.

May: Poiret attends the Bal des Quat'z'arts (Four Arts Ball) wearing the Nebuchadnezzar costume originally designed for de Max.

16 May: 18th-century chamber music concert hosted by Madame Paul Poiret. The programme, illustrated by Bernard Naudin, mentions pieces by Jean-Philippe Rameau (1683–1764), Louis-Claude Daquin (1694–1772), Federigo Fiorillo (1755–1823), François Couperin (1668–1733), Jean-Marie Leclair (1697–1764) and Luigi Boccherini (1743–1805).

17 June: Concert hosted by Madame Paul Poiret. The programme, illustrated by Bernard Naudin, mentions pieces by Haydn, Beethoven and Mozart.

24 June: The 'Thousand and Second Night' party is held in the gardens of the fashion house.

Autumn:
Poiret founds his perfume business Les Parfums de Rosine, named after his eldest daughter, and sets up his laboratory in the former outbuildings of his home, at 39 Rue du Colisée (Paris, 8th arrondissement).

He opens a Martine boutique at 83 Rue du Faubourg-Saint-Honoré (Paris, 8th arrondissement). It sells pieces created by the Martine workshop, which is directed by Guy-Pierre Fauconnet (1882–1920) from 1911 to 1914, alongside pieces by artists who collaborate with Poiret.

October–November: Accompanied by nine models in uniform, Poiret travels to a number of major European cities (Frankfurt, Berlin, Warsaw, Krakow, Moscow, St Petersburg, Bucharest, Budapest and Vienna).

1912

He rents a hunting lodge in La Celle-Saint-Cloud, the Pavillon du Butard, built by the architect Ange-Jacques Gabriel (1698–1782), which he keeps as a summer home until 1917. He carries out renovations and decoration work, with the help of Raoul Dufy.

4 February: Poiret is one of the founding members of the gastronomic society Le Club des Cent.

28 February – 13 March: Exhibition of paintings by Robert Delaunay (1885–1941) and Marie Laurencin at the Barbazanges Gallery.

20 June: The 'Feast of Bacchus' is held at the Pavillon du Butard. Isadora Duncan (1877–1927) performs an improvised dance wearing a costume inspired by Ancient Greece.

The Martine workshop publishes an edition of Giovanni Giacomo Gastoldi's (c. 1554–1609) *balletti*, illustrated by Bernard Naudin. They are performed at the 'Feast of Bacchus'.

19 September: The Poirets' third child, Colin, is born.

Paul Poiret sets up a packaging workshop called 'Colin', after his son.

1 October – 18 November: Projects by students at the Martine School are exhibited at the Salon d'Automne.

1913

The perfume *Nuit de Chine* is released by Parfums de Rosine. For the first time, Bakelite is used for the rings on the sides of the bottle. This perfume is one of the company's most successful.

Spring: Poiret designs the costumes for Jacques Richepin's (1880–1946) play *Le Minaret*, which is performed at the Théâtre de la Renaissance. He is assisted by Erté (1892–1990) and José de Zamora (1889–1971).

20 September–15 October: The Poirets visit North America, where the designer gives a number of lectures. They go to New York, Philadelphia, Washington, DC, Boston, Chicago, Buffalo, Pittsburgh and Toronto. On his return to Paris, Poiret suggests to those designers who are members of the haute couture trade association that they should have more control over the sales and exports of their designs. This proposal gives rise to the creation of the Syndicate for the Protection of French Couture and Related Industries in June 1914, with Poiret as president.

1914

June: Dinner held for the *Gazette du Bon Ton*, founded by Lucien Vogel (1886–1954), in the gardens of the private mansion on the Avenue d'Antin. This event brings together designers, artists and writers.

June–July: Poiret goes on a business trip to Germany, accompanied by his models. During this trip, he receives an order to attend a period of military training.

31 July: Assassination of Jean Jaurès (1859–1914), a French journalist and politician.

1 August: French president Raymond Poincaré (1860–1934) orders a general mobilization. Poiret closes his fashion house.

14 August: Poiret is sent to Lisieux, where he works with the regimental tailor. He decides to rethink the military uniforms and designs a simple 'horizon-blue' greatcoat that allows the army to save large amounts of fabric.

27–31 August: He presents his design to Alexandre Millerand (1859–1943), Minister of War.

2 September: The government leaves Paris and the Ministry of War moves to Bordeaux. Poiret is transferred to the technical clothing section, which is part of this ministry. His task is to oversee the manufacturing of the military uniforms that he designed. As part of this, he has to write explanatory instructions for French tailors.

19 September: Publication of a memorandum entitled 'Making the articles of clothing, infantry greatcoat and military cap in all military regions', which details Poiret's proposals.

The designer is sent to a number of French cities to explain the manufacturing instructions. He goes to Marseille, Limoges, Rennes and Cherbourg.

9 November: He is expelled from the technical section after a police report during his trip to Cherbourg. He has to return to Lisieux, where he is redeployed.

His greatcoat designs are modified by the army, creating two new 'simplified' designs.

1915

March: Poiret commissions André Derain (1880–1954), who is also deployed to Lisieux, to paint his portrait. Both men are staying in the Hôtel du Maure.

June: His daughter Rosine dies from Spanish flu.

Poiret passes the administration officer exams. He is deployed to the army's general store in Vanves, then to Reims.

1916

5 June: The Poirets' fourth child, Perrine, is born.

16–31 July: The exhibition 'Modern art in France' is held at the Barbazanges Gallery, curated by the art critic André Salmon (1881–1969). It is the first time that Pablo Picasso's (1881–1973) painting *Les Demoiselles d'Avignon* (1907) has been exhibited.

1917

Poiret is transferred to Clermont-Ferrand, where he runs the workshops making uniforms.

The Martine workshop publishes *L'Almanach des lettres et des arts (Almanac of Literature and Arts)*, edited by André Mary (1879–1962) and Raoul Dufy.

March: Exhibition of the work of Kees van Dongen (1877–1968) at the Barbazanges Gallery.

12 April – 12 May: Exhibition of Poiret's personal collection at the Barbazanges Gallery.

24 June: Poiret attends the premiere of the Surrealist play *Les Mamelles de Tirésias (The Breasts of Tiresias)* by Guillaume Apollinaire (1880–1918) at the Théâtre Renée-Maubel.

1918

15 January: The Poirets' fifth child, Gaspard, is born and dies within the year.

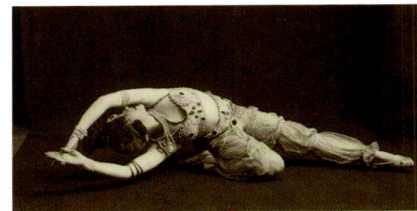

CAT. 205 Talbot studio, Tamara Karsavina as Zobeïde in *Shéhérazade*, 1911–14, gelatin silver print. Paris, Musée des Arts décoratifs

ILL. 4 Bernard Naudin, programme for the concert held on 16 May 1911 by Madame Paul Poiret, 1911, lithograph on paper. Paris, library of the Musée des Arts décoratifs

Poiret sells off the outbuildings of his mansion at 39 Rue du Colisée.

11 November: The Armistice is signed.

1919

After the war, Poiret goes on a trip to Morocco for a few weeks. He visits Casablanca, Marrakesh, Fes and Demnat.

11–28 June: Exhibition of paintings by Natalia Goncharova (1881–1962) and Mikhail Larionov (1881–1964) at the Barbazanges Gallery.

Summer: Poiret sets up an open-air theatre, the Oasis, in the gardens of his mansion on the Avenue d'Antin. He puts on shows and holds café-concerts, dances and parties there. It closes at the end of summer.

1920

The actress Andrée Spinelly (1887–1966) tours the United States wearing designs by Paul Poiret.

Poiret buys some land on the hill of Mézy-sur-Seine (in Yvelines). In 1923, he commissions the architect Robert Mallet-Stevens (1886–1945) to build a villa there: the Château de Mézy, also known as 'Le Gibet' or 'Villa Poiret'. Construction work is abandoned the following year owing to lack of funds. Only the structural works are completed.

Poiret designs costumes for the film *Le Secret de Rosette Lambert*, directed by Raymond Bernard (1891–1977).

Scenes from the film *Irène*, directed by Marcel Dumont (1885–1951), are shot in Poiret's home.

3–14 February: Exhibition of work by students from the Martine School at the Barbazanges Gallery.

16–28 February: After the death of Guy-Pierre Fauconnet in January, a retrospective of his work is held at the Barbazanges Gallery.

October–December: Poiret gives a lecture entitled 'A defence of fashion' at the Salon d'Automne. It is published in issue 8 of the *Gazette du Bon Ton*.

1921

Shoes by the shoe designer André Perugia (1893–1977) are shown in the rooms of Paul Poiret's fashion house.

The perfume *Maharadjah* is released by Parfums de Rosine. Its name is a reference to the role of the maharajah played by Édouard de Max in the play *Le Prince d'Aurec*, for which Poiret designed the costumes.

Spring: Poiret designs the costumes worn by the actress Arletty (1898–1992) in the revue show *Si que je s'rai roi* by Rip (1884–1941) and Régis Gignoux (1878–1931), which is performed at the Théâtre des Capucines.

8–26 March: Exhibition of etchings, engravings, lithographs and drawings by Bernard Naudin at the Barbazanges Gallery.

8–30 April: Exhibition of work by students from the Martine School at the Barbazanges Gallery.

9 June: Reopening of the Oasis theatre. Poiret installs an inflatable dome in his garden, developed by Gabriel Voisin (1880–1973), an aviation pioneer and car manufacturer.

Summer: The Opera's annual ball is hosted by its president, Princess Lucien Murat. Paul Poiret is asked to choose the theme of the ball and oversee the decoration. He suggests 'Bal des perroquets' ('parrots'), with costumes in red and purple.

June–July: The dancers Caryathis (1888–1971) and Nyota Inyoka (1896–1971) perform at the Oasis.

1922

On the advice of Gabriële Buffet-Picabia (1881–1985), the American photographer Man Ray (1890–1976) approaches Paul Poiret to offer his services. Poiret buys two of his prints and asks him to photograph his designs.

Poiret hires Robert Piguet (1898–1953) as his assistant and tasks him with modernizing his fashion house's image. He works there until 1923.

Late August – 13 September: Poiret takes a second trip to the United States.

15 November: He gives a lecture at the Théâtre de Lausanne, accompanied by a runway show of models wearing Martine designs.

December: He gives a lecture at the Salon d'Automne, which is published in the journal *L'Art et la mode* on 16 December.

11 December: Poiret is kicked out of the Club des Cent.

1923

He designs the costumes for the actress Marthe Ferrare (1899–?) in the film *L'Autre Aile*, directed by Henri Andréani (1877–1936).

He designs evening gowns for the film *La Garçonne*, directed by Armand Du Plessy (1883–1924), based on the novel of the same name by Victor Margueritte (1866–1942). This film, which is now lost, was censored when it was released in France.

6 February: Poiret founds the Club des Purs Cent, of which he is president. A group of rebels from the Club des Cent, the society is based at 68 Rue Bayen (Paris, 17th arrondissement) and aims to 'promote the development of tourism in France'.

26 April – 18 May: Exhibition of Poiret's personal art collection at the Barbazanges Gallery. André Salmon writes the introduction to the catalogue.

16 August: The journal *Comœdia* reports on the arrival in Paris of the American actor Rudolph Valentino (1895–1926) and his wife, the artist Natacha Rambova (1897–1966). Rambova's 'many fittings' at a 'great couturier's' are mentioned in an article published in the same journal on 28 September. The January 1924 issue of *Photoplay* mentions that Natacha made the most of this trip to purchase some designs from Paul Poiret. Poiret provided the artist's clothes throughout autumn 1923, while she was staying in the South of France.

ILL.5 Henri Manuel, Paul and Denise Poiret in their costumes for the 'Feast of Bacchus', a party held at the Pavillon du Butard on 20 June 1912, gelatin silver print. Paris, Bibliothèque nationale de France, Prints and Photography department

1 November – 16 December: Date of the Salon d'Automne, which features a 'regional gastronomic section'. It was set up by the writer Austin de Croze (1866–1937) and Poiret is on the patron committee.

1923–1924

Poiret takes another trip around Central Europe with his models. They visit Vienna, Prague and Budapest. In Vienna, he hires the Kammerspiele der Josefstadt theatre to present his designs.

1924

The Poiret family moves to 45, avenue Montaigne (Paris, 8th arrondissement).
Poiret designs the costumes for the actress Sarah Bernhardt (1844–1923) in the film *La Voyante*, directed by Leon Abrams (1895–1977) and Louis Mercanton (1879–1932).

He designs the costumes for the actress Natalya Lisenko (1884–1969) in the film *Les Ombres qui passent*, directed by Alexandre Volkoff (1885–1942).

He designs the costumes for the actress Arlette Marchal (1902–1984) in the film *Das Bildnis* (*The Portrait*), directed by Jacques Feyder (1885–1948).

February: He invites the members of the Club des Purs Cent to dine at his home on the Rue du Faubourg-Saint-Honoré.

March: He sells the mansion on the Avenue d'Antin, Rue du Faubourg-Saint-Honoré.

Spring: Exhibition of the works of André Dunoyer de Segonzac at the Barbazanges Gallery.

Winter: Poiret is awarded the Légion d'honneur.

November: Release of the film *L'Inhumaine*, directed by Marcel L'Herbier (1888–1979). The actress Georgette Leblanc (1869–1941) wears costumes designed by Poiret. The sets feature furniture and fabrics by the Martine workshop.

26 November: Paul Poiret's fashion house is sold to the Aubert finance group. Poiret refuses to give up the Rosine and Martine companies. This financial transaction leads to the creation of a limited company, called Maison Paul Poiret, which is incorporated on December 1924. Poiret remains artistic director of the fashion house but can no longer use his name, which now belongs to the finance group. As well as the boutique in Paris, this group now also owns the branches that Poiret opened elsewhere in France and abroad. In France, these are in Deauville (21 Rue Gontaut-Biron), La Baule (Boulevard du Casino) and Biarritz (Villa Casablanca).

December: Poiret offers signed, life-sized, full colour 'cut-out patterns' for sale. Sold in a luxurious pouch, these patterns are accompanied by technical explanations and advice from the designer.

24 December: The fashion house moves to 1 Rond-point des Champs-Élysées (Paris, 8th arrondissement). The occasion is marked by a nighttime celebration.

1925

Poiret designs the costumes for the actresses Sandra Milowanoff (1892–1957) and Madeleine Rodrigue in the film *Le Fantôme du Moulin-Rouge*, directed by René Clair (1898–1981).

He designs the costumes for Natalya Lisenko in the film *Le Double Amour*, directed by Jean Epstein (1897–1953).

He designs the costumes for the actress Lili Damita (1904–1994) in the film *Das Spielzeug von Paris* (*The Toy of Paris*), directed by Michael Curtiz (1886–1962).

8 February: He gives a lecture on 'great couture' in his fashion house.

28 April – 30 November: At his own cost, he takes part in the International Exhibition of Modern Decorative and Industrial Arts, mooring three barges near the Pont Alexandre-III: *Amours* (presenting designs by the Martine workshop), *Orgues* (for fashion shows) and *Délices* (for the Rosine perfumes and a restaurant). Raoul Dufy paints 14 wall hangings for *Orgues*. The barges are officially opened on 24 April by Fernand David (1869–1935), the exhibition's head curator, and Paul Léon (1874–1962), his second in command, during a luncheon held on *Délices*. Poiret installs a carousel on a terrace overlooking the Seine: the Carousel of Parisian life. He commissions the sculptor Pierre Vigoureux (1884–1965) to create 47 carousel figures. The venture is a financial failure for the designer.

3–23 May: The exhibition 'Le Maroc: peintures et bas-reliefs de Bernard Boutet de Monvel' ('Morocco: paintings and bas-reliefs by Bernard Boutet de Monvel') is held at the Barbazanges Gallery.

22 June: The company Maison Paul Poiret is floated on the stock market and shares begin to be sold.

2 September: Together with Ambroise Ruhle (born in 1877) and Léon Schulmann (born in 1871), Poiret sets up the public limited company Martine, L'Art appliqué ('Martine Applied Arts'), which aims to 'make, sell and display everything that has anything at all to do with furniture and interior design, both in France and in all other countries'. Poiret is the company's president and its head office is at 40 Rue des Petites-Écuries (Paris, 10th arrondissement). After the second general meeting, on 15 September, the company's name is changed to Martine, Choses à la mode ('Martine, Fashionable things').

4 September: Together with Roger Julien Bloch (b. 1879) and René Marcel Bloch (b. 1887), Poiret sets up the public limited company Les Parfums de Rosine, which will carry out 'all activities to do with the manufacturing and sale of perfumes and all products to do with perfumery, soaps and accessories, in France and the French colonies and […] in foreign countries'. Poiret is the company's president and its head office is at 43 Avenue Victor-Emmanuel-III (now Avenue Franklin D. Roosevelt, Paris, 8th arrondissement). René Bloch, Roger Bloch, Édouard Pereire, Gaston Fossey, Georges Blum and Roger Schwab are the shareholders.

CAT. 264 Anonymous, Denise Poiret and her children, c. 1914, gelatin silver print. Paris, Musée des Arts décoratifs

CAT. 269 Denise Poiret, Paul Poiret and his children at the Pavillon du Butard when he was on leave, 1915–16, gelatin silver print. Paris, Musée des Arts décoratifs

November: Poiret visits Denmark, accompanied by Reine, his salesperson, and Christian, his Danish tailor, as well as five models.

18 November: He puts 110 paintings, pastels, watercolours and drawings from his collection up for sale by the auctioneer Bellier at the Hôtel Drouot. These include works by some of the greatest artists of his time: Matisse, Modigliani, Picasso, Marquet, van Dongen, Dufy, Utrillo, Derain and Dunoyer de Segonzac.

3–19 December: Exhibition of works by a 'group of French women painters' at the Barbazanges Gallery, which features work by Marie Laurencin.

1926

Poiret travels to Spain and Morocco with Dufy.

1927

He designs the costumes for the actress Edna Purviance (1895–1958) in *Éducation de prince*, directed by Henri Diamant-Berger (1895–1972).

January: *La Vagabonde*, a comedy in four acts by Colette (1873–1954), is performed at the Théâtre de l'Avenue. Poiret plays the role of Brague, a mime teacher, appearing alongside Colette.

October–November: He takes his third trip to the United States.

December: He publishes a collection of calligrams entitled *Popolôrepô, morceaux choisis par un imbécile et illustrés par un autre* (*Popolorepo, pieces chosen by one idiot and illustrated by another*, Paris: Jonquières). The illustrations are by Pierre Fau (1888–1960).

1928

His mother dies.

He designs the costumes for Lili Damita in the film *The Golden Butterfly*, directed by Michael Curtiz (based on the novel by P. G. Wodehouse).

He publishes two books: *107 recettes ou curiosités culinaires* (*107 recipes or culinary curiosities*, Paris: Jonquières), illustrated by Marie Alix, and *Pan. Annuaire du luxe à Paris* (*Pan: A Directory of Luxury in Paris*, Paris: Devambez), illustrated by a number of artists including Dufy, Jean Cocteau (1889–1963) and Tsuguharu Foujita (1886–1968).

March: The Aubert group, which owns Maison Paul Poiret, asks the designer to leave.

29 March: Paul and Denise Poiret divorce.

April: The Aubert group launches a civil suit against the designer, asking for the ten-year contract between the two parties to be annulled. The group accuses Poiret of breaking the terms of the contract by using the name 'Paul Poiret' in France and the United States.

CAT.166 Delphi, St Catherine's Day celebration at Poiret's home, c. 1920, gelatin silver print. Paris, Musée des Arts décoratifs

1929

Easter: Poiret buys a sardine boat on the Île d'Yeu, fits it out with bunks and names it *Monsieur Dumollet*. He sails along the southern coast of Brittany with his children.

1–15 May: He takes part in a group exhibition at the Th. Briant Gallery at 32 Rue de Berri (Paris, 8th arrondissement).

24 October: Stock market crash in New York, known as 'Black Thursday'. The crisis impacts the French luxury industries, which lose their American customers.

Winter 1929–1930: Paul Poiret moves into the caretaker's cottage at his villa in Mézy-sur-Seine, where he writes the first volume of his memoirs, *En habillant l'époque*, which he finishes in August 1930.

1930

January: The legal battle with the Aubert group reaches its end. An agreement is negotiated between the two parties. Poiret is replaced.

May: He exhibits 24 paintings from his 'Mézy period' at the Gallery of the Renaissance, 11 Rue Royale (Paris, 8th arrondissement).

15 June – 15 July: He takes part in the exhibition 'Visage de Paris' ('Face of Paris') at the Gilbert Gallery, 1 Rue Madame (Paris, 6th arrondissement).

He sells his villa in Mézy-sur-Seine to the French-Romanian actress Elvira Popescu (1894–1993). He uses the proceeds from the sale to pay off his debts.

December: Publication of *En habillant l'époque* (Paris: Bernard Grasset), which he dedicates to his mother. It is later published in Spanish: *Vistiendo la época (Recuerdos)* (Madrid: Ediciones literarias).

1–15 December: Poiret takes part in a group exhibition at the Gilbert Gallery.

1931

Publication of the English translations of *En habillant l'époque*:

My First Fifty Years, the Autobiography of Paul Poiret (London: Victor Gollancz Ltd) – English version.

King of Fashion, the Autobiography of Paul Poiret (Philadelphia and London: J. B. Lippincott Company) – American version.

Publication of the book *Deauville* (Paris: M-P. Trémois). Text by Paul Poiret and illustrations by van Dongen.

15–30 January: Poiret takes part in a group exhibition at the Gilbert Gallery.

May: He is named artistic director of the fashion house Passy 10-17, located at 12 Rue de Presbourg (Paris, 8th arrondissement).

28 August: Maison Paul Poiret, which belongs to the Aubert group, is officially liquidated by the courts.

December: Poiret leaves Passy 10-17.

1932

January: He opens a new fashion house, Elle, on Place Possoz (Paris, 16th arrondissement).

8 April: A judgement from the commercial court of the Seine declares the limited company Maison Paul Poiret bankrupt.

May: Poiret publishes the second volume of his memoirs, *Revenez-y* (Paris: NRF-Librairie Gallimard), which he dedicates to his son, Colin.

12 August: The limited company Maison Paul Poiret is dissolved.

November: Release of the film *Panurge*, directed by Michel Bernheim (1908–1985), in which Poiret plays the role of a cobbler.

c. 1932–1933

Poiret moves into a large apartment above the Salle Pleyel, at 252 Rue du Faubourg-Saint-Honoré (Paris, 8th arrondissement). He moves out in 1935.

1933

He exhibits his work at the Zak Gallery, at 16 Rue de l'Abbaye (Paris, 6th arrondissement).

28 February: He presents his first collection for the Printemps department store. The collaboration between the department store and the designer lasts only one year.

March: He presents a collection designed for the shop Liberty in London.

1934

He publishes the third volume of his memoirs, *Art et phynance* (Lutetia), which he dedicates to 'my enemies'. The preface is written by Dr Joseph-Charles Mardrus (1868–1949).

11 August: An article published in the weekly newspaper *Aux Écoutes* reveals that Poiret has 'applied for and been granted unemployment benefit'.

18 August: An article published in *La Revue de Lausanne* reveals that he receives 10 francs a day and takes his meals in a restaurant for 'poor intellectuals'.

1935

2 January: Publication of an article in *La Revue de Lausanne* in which Poiret announces that he bought back the rights to his name for 5,000 francs a few weeks earlier.

1 February: The company Les Croisières de la mode is founded. It is intended to support Paul Poiret in returning to work as a designer. Lucien Vogel and Maurice Dufrène (1876–1955) are among the company's founders.

27 February: Poiret gives a lecture at the Club de la publicité entitled 'La mode, la meilleure publicité pour la France' ('Fashion, the best advert for France'), followed by a runway show.

28 February: He goes on a promotional trip around France and abroad, accompanied by his models.

1936

4 April: The company Les Croisières de la mode goes bankrupt.

1937

25 May – 25 November: Poiret takes part in a project by the Théâtre de Marionnettes, which is presented at the International Exhibition of Arts and Techniques Applied to Modern Life (class 4).

1938

27 January: Release of the film *L'Île étrange*, directed by Robert Mariaud, in which Poiret appears. This short film appears in contemporary press under the title *En mer* and is classed as a 'documentary'.

1939–1941

Poiret moves to Saint-Tropez, then to Cannes, where he recites fables by La Fontaine in a music hall.

20 May: An article published in *La Dépêche algérienne* reports on his idea to create an academy of luxury and fashion in Cannes.

1942

He moves to Gouzon (Creuse), where he paints.

1943

He moves to Paris, where he lives with his sister Jeanne Boivin.

June: He exhibits his work at the Caumartin art studio, at 19a Rue Caumartin (Paris, 9th arrondissement).

1944

11 March: Private view of his exhibition at the Charpentier Gallery, 76 Rue du Faubourg-Saint-Honoré (Paris, 8th arrondissement). Cocteau writes the preface to the exhibition catalogue.

27 April: Publication of an article entitled 'Va-t-on laisser Poiret le Magnifique finir sa vie dans la misère?' ('Will we allow Poiret the Magnificent to end his life in poverty?') in *Les Nouveaux Temps*.

28 April: Paul Poiret dies at home at 15 Rue Henri-Rochefort (Paris, 17th arrondissement). He is buried in Montmartre Cemetery.

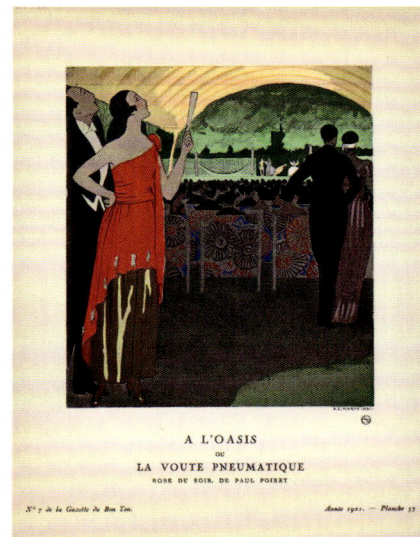

CAT. 247 André Édouard Marty, 'À l'Oasis ou la voûte pneumatique, evening gown by Paul Poiret', *Gazette du Bon Ton*, no. 7, 1921, plate 53, Paris: Éditions Lucien Vogel, 1921, photogravure and pochoir print. Paris, library of the Musée des Arts décoratifs

CAT. 203 Studio Talbot, Michelle Frondaie wearing a design by
Paul Poiret, 1911–14, gelatin silver print. Paris, Musée des Arts
décoratifs

Complete catalogue of works by Paul Poiret in the collection of the Musée des Arts décoratifs

Works that are not illustrated were too fragile or damaged to be photographed. Works with no catalogue number are not included in the exhibition.

CAT. 11
Évêque **skirt and blouse ensemble**
1906
Pleated lawn, woodblock-printed cotton and mother-of-pearl
Purchased with funds from the Fonds du Patrimoine—Ministère de la Culture and thanks to financial support from Michel and Hélène David-Weill, 2005

Inv. 2005.37.3.1-2

CAT. 12
Gavarni **day dress**
1906
Linen
Purchased with funds from the Fonds du Patrimoine—Ministère de la Culture and thanks to financial support from Michel and Hélène David-Weill, 2005

Inv. 2005.37.4

CAT. 47
Ispahan **coat**
1907
Embroidered silk velvet and appliquéd cordonnet braid
Ufac Collection, 1995
Gift of Denise Boulet-Poiret

Inv. UF 63-18-2

CAT. 1
Evening gown (back)
1907
Silk tulle hand-embroidered with beads, sequins, copper rings, metallic strips and cabochons
Ufac Collection, 1995
Gift of Denise Boulet-Poiret

Inv. UF 64-46-9

CAT. 13
1811 **evening gown**
1907
Pekin silk, metallic lace and chiffon
Ufac Collection, 1995
Gift of Denise Boulet-Poiret

Inv. UF 64-46-1

CAT. 14
Eugénie evening gown
1907
Figured cotton gauze, tulle
and taffeta
Ufac Collection, 1995
Gift of Denise Boulet-Poiret

Inv. UF 64-46-2

CAT. 2
Joséphine evening gown
1907
Silk satin, silk netting and
metallic braid embroidered
with satin stitch
Ufac Collection 1995
Gift of Marcel Piccioni

Inv. UF 70-38-10

CAT. 48
Cairo tunic
1907
Silk ottoman fabric
embroidered with silk thread
and metallic thread, appliquéd
braid and gold-coloured metal
Ufac Collection, 1995
Gift of Denise Boulet-Poiret

Inv. UF 64-46-16

CAT. 15
Evening gown
1908
Shot silk satin, passementerie
and lawn
Ufac Collection, 1995
Gift of Denise Boulet-Poiret

Inv. UF 64-46-3

CAT. 16
Evening coat
c. 1910
Trimmed gros de Tours
with brocade design in gold
thread and silver strips,
shot taffeta, passementerie
and silver-coloured metal
Ufac Collection, 1995
Gift of Marcel Piccioni

Inv. UF 70-38-45

CAT. 17
Evening coat
c. 1910
Silk satin, guipure lace
made from silk thread
and metallic thread
Ufac Collection, 1995
Purchase

Inv. UF 61-40-2

CAT. 70
Image evening coat
c. 1910
Shot satin, lace made of gold
thread and passementerie
Ufac Collection, 1995
Gift of Denise Boulet-Poiret

Inv. UF 69-20-2

CAT. 3
Lavallière evening gown
c. 1910
Silk satin embroidered
with cylindrical glass beads
Ufac Collection, 1995
Gift of Denise Boulet-Poiret

Inv. UF 63-18-7

CAT. 26
Mosaïque evening gown
c. 1910
Chiffon embroidered with silk
thread and beads, gold braid,
mink fur and silk satin
Ufac Collection, 1995
Gift of Mr Veysset

Inv. UF 61-37-1

CAT. 18
Handbag
c. 1910
Silk embroidered with
glass beads
Ufac Collection, 1995
Purchase

Inv. UF 75-19-9

CAT. 36
Evening gown
1910
Silk satin, chiffon embroidered
with cylindrical glass beads
and silk velvet
Ufac collection, 1995
Don M. Bienvenu

Inv. UF 52-6-1

Coat
1910-14
Silk satin brocade with gold
strips and gold thread
and silk velvet
Ufac Collection, 1995
Gift of Madame Pergusson

Inv. UF 75-16-1

Evening gown
1910-14
Shot silk satin, chiffon
and gold braid
Ufac Collection, 1995
Gift of Marcel Piccioni

Inv. UF 70-38-9

CAT. 19
Coat
c. 1911
Silk velvet embroidered with
gold cordonnet braid
and mink fur
Ufac Collection, 1995
Gift of Denise Boulet-Poiret

Inv. UF 64-46-17

CAT. 50
Flammes shawl and
culotte-dress
1911

Shawl made from hand-
embroidered silk crepe (cut
into Manila shawl style);
culotte-dress made from
silk velvet, chiffon and
passementerie
Purchased with funds from
the Fonds du Patrimoine–
Ministère de la Culture and
thanks to financial support
from Michel and Hélène
David-Weill, 2005

Inv. 2005.37.9.1-2

CAT. 20
Hat
1911
Ribbed silk, silk velvet, feather;
braid embroideredwith
metallic thread, diamanté
and artificial gems
Ufac Collection, 1995
Gift of Andrée Lhuer

Inv. UF 52-21-7

CAT. 21
Child's hat
1911
Silk velvet and metallic netting
Ufac Collection, 1995
Gift of Andrée Lhuer

Inv. UF 52-21-36

CAT. 22
Nénuphar coat
1911
Silk, embroidered silk tulle
and passementerie
Ufac Collection, 1995
Gift of Denise Boulet-Poiret

Inv. UF 63-18-4

CAT. 84
Beach ensemble
c. 1912
Block-printed linen with
the design *Les Artichauts
[Artichokes]* by the
Martine workshop
Purchased with support from
Louis Vuitton, 2014

Inv. 2014.45.1.1-2

CAT. 85
Parasol
c. 1912
Block-printed cotton
in the design *Les Anémones*
by the Martine Workshop
and varnished bamboo
Ufac Collection, 1995

Inv. UF 2003-05-3

CAT. 71
**Dress that belonged to
Rosine Poiret**
c. 1912
Silk crepe
and silk cordonnet
Purchased with funds from
the Fonds du Patrimoine–
Ministère de la Culture and
thanks to financial support
from Michel and Hélène
David-Weill, 2005

Inv. 2005.37.10.1-2

CAT. 86
Les Anémones **fabric**
1912
Roller-printed linen
with a design by the
Martine Workshop
Gift of Manuel Canovas,
1986

Inv. 58345

Evening coat
1912
Shot taffeta, embroidery, fur
and taffeta lining
Ufac Collection, 1995
Gift of Stanislas Lami

Inv. UF 53-33-1

CAT. 51
Fleurie **summer dress**
1912
Embroidered cotton muslin,
appliquéd braid and
bronze buttons from the
Directory period
Ufac Collection, 1995
Gift of Denise Boulet-Poiret

Inv. UF 64-46-11

CAT. 37
Mélodie **dress**
1912
Silk damask, silk velvet,
galalith and piping
Ufac Collection, 1995
Gift of Denise Boulet-Poiret

Inv. UF 63-18-8

CAT. 28
Coat
c. 1913
Cotton crêpe with chain stitch
embroidery, lace and glass
Ufac Collection, 1995
Gift of Madame Le Bec

Inv. UF 69-26-38

CAT. 94
Coat
c. 1914
Silk ottoman fabric, silk satin,
embroidered cotton netting,
silk bias binding and
gold-coloured metal
Ufac Collection, 1995
Purchase

Inv. UF 61-40-1

CAT. 73
Wig
c. 1914
Dyed horsehair and
metallic gold tulle
Purchased with funds from
the Fonds du Patrimoine–
Ministère de la Culture and
thanks to financial support
from Michel and Hélène
David-Weill, 2005

Inv. 2005.37.5

CAT. 23
Headpiece
1914
Chiffon embroidered with
diamanté, cellulose fibre
and silk taffeta
Musée des Arts décoratifs

Inv. 987.112

Coat
c. 1918
Wool jersey
Purchased with funds from
the Fonds du Patrimoine–
Ministère de la Culture and
thanks to financial support
from Michel and Hélène
David-Weill, 2005

Inv. 2005.37.7

CAT. 52
**Printemps shawl
and summer dress**
1919
Handwoven silk, braided wool
and ribbed cotton
Purchased with funds from
the Fonds du Patrimoine—
Ministère de la Culture
and thanks to financial
suport from Michel and
Hélène David-Weill, 2005

Inv. 2005.37.8.1-3

Caucase culotte-skirt
1919
Silk satin, appliquéd braid
and passementerie
Ufac Collection, 1995
Gift of Denise Boulet-Poiret

Inv. UF 63-18-10

Evening coat
1919
Silk velvet embroidered
with metallic strips
and passementerie
Ufac Collection, 1995
Gift of Madame Edmond
de Galéa

Inv. UF 50-16-4

CAT. 53
Bretonne dress
1919
Embroidered silk velvet,
silk crepe and silk netting
Ufac Collection, 1995
Gift of Denise Boulet-Poiret

Inv. UF 64-46-5

CAT. 74
Malgré moi dress
1919
Silk velvet, silk satin
and silk tulle embroidered
with sequins
Ufac Collection, 1995
Gift of Denise Boulet-Poiret

Inv. UF 63-18-6 AB

CAT. 75
Tout de suite dress
1919
Silk velvet, printed cotton,
silk passementerie
and metallic thread
Ufac Collection, 1995
Gift of Denise Boulet-Poiret

Inv. UF 63-18-5

Pierrot costume
c. 1920
Silk crepe and chiffon
Ufac Collection, 1995
Purchase

Inv. UF 57-55-1 ABC

Coat
c. 1920
Silk velvet, shot taffeta
and passementerie
Ufac Collection, 1995
Gift of Madame Julliard

Inv. UF 54-9-1

Coat
c. 1920
Silk velvet and silk satin
Ufac Collection, 1995
Gift of Alice Natter

Inv. UF 64-6-1

CAT. 95
Evening coat
c. 1920
Printed silk velvet
embroidered with
metallic thread
Ufac Collection, 1995
Gift of Madame Edmond
de Galéa

Inv. UF 50-16-6

CAT. 76
Ice Cream-Soda **evening coat**
c. 1920
Silk panne velvet
and shot taffeta
Ufac Collection, 1995
Gift of Denise Boulet-Poiret

Inv. UF 63-18-3

CAT. 77
Abbesse **dress**
c. 1920
Silk velvet, taffeta
and figured silk satin
lamé lining
Ufac Collection, 1995
Gift of Denise Boulet-Poiret

Inv. UF 64-46-6

CAT. 88
**Summer dress
that belonged to
Martine Poiret**
c. 1920
Block-printed silk satin
to a design by the
Martine Workshop
and cordonnet braid
Purchased with funds from
the Fonds du Patrimoine–
Ministère de la Culture
and thanks to financial
support from Michel and
Hélène David-Weill, 2005

Inv. 2005.37.2

Pea jacket
c. 1920
Wool, embroidery
with woollen thread
and appliquéd braid
Ufac Collection, 1995
Gift of Denise Boulet-Poiret

Inv. UF 69-20-1

CAT. 93
**Jacket that belonged
to Paul Poiret**
c. 1920
Woodblock-printed linen
with a design by the
Martine Workshop, figured
silk crepe and braided leather
Ufac Collection, 1995
Gift of Denise Boulet-Poiret

Inv. UF 64-46-4

CAT. 79
Dress
1920
Silk ottoman fabric, silk satin
lamé and glass paste
Ufac Collection, 1995
Gift of Denise Boulet-Poiret

Inv. 64-46-13

CAT. 54
Skirt-suit
1920
Ribbed silk, printed cotton
and appliquéd braid
Ufac Collection, 1995
Gift of Madame E. Grandperrin

Inv. UF 78-20-1 AB

Laitue **day dress**
1921
Ribbed silk and taffeta
Ufac Collection, 1995
Gift of the Comtesse
d'Hinnisdäl

Inv. UF 56-47-1

CAT. 81
**Sailor suit that belonged
to Colin Poiret**
1922
Linen and mother-of-pearl
Purchased with funds from
the Fonds du Patrimoine–
Ministère de la Culture
and thanks to financial
support from Michel and
Hélène David-Weill, 2005

Inv. 2005.37.1.1-2

CAT. 55
Han Kéou **evening gown**
1922
Trimmed figured silk,
velvet and silk plush
Ufac Collection, 1995
Gift of Denise Boulet-Poiret

Inv. UF 63-18-9

CAT. 41
Spi **evening gown**
1922
Embroidered silk velvet
Ufac Collection, 1995
Gift of Madame Couvreur,
via Denise Boulet-Poiret

Inv. UF 56-44-1

CAT. 56
Exotique **dress**
1922
Printed crepe de chine,
chiffon, passementerie
and jet beads
Ufac Collection, 1995
Gift of Denise Boulet-Poiret

Inv. UF 63-18-11 AB

CAT. 96
Manège **dress**
1922
Panne velvet, embroidered
with sequins and metallic
thread and gold lamé silk
Ufac Collection, 1995
Gift of Denise Boulet-Poiret

Inv. UF 63-18-12

CAT. 57
Martinique **dress**
1922
Crepe marocain and
printed crepe de chine
Ufac Collection, 1995
Gift of Louise Janin

Inv. UF 53-14-1

CAT. 43
Ballon **travel coat**
Vers 1923
Peau de tortue fabric,
silk velvet and silk pongee
lining by Dagobert Peche
(textile designer)
Ufac Collection, 1995
Gift of Denise Boulet-Poiret

Inv. UF 64-46-18

Dress
1923
Silk taffeta, silk velvet,
appliquéd embroidered
ribbon and gold braid
Ufac Collection, 1995
Purchase

Inv. UF 86-70-9

CAT. 58
Mandchoue **two-piece dress**
1923
Silk lamé and silk velvet
Ufac Collection, 1995
Purchase

Inv. UF 86-70-10 AB

CAT. 97
Fils du ciel **dress**
1923
Silk velvet embroidered
with metallic thread
and silk satin bias binding
Ufac Collection, 1995
Gift of Madame Feuillatte

Inv. UF 60-17-1

Gondole **dress**
1923
Silk satin, appliquéd
grey chenille and silk crepe
Ufac Collection, 1995
Gift of Denise Boulet-Poiret

Inv. UF 64-46-10

CAT. 59
La Source **coat**
1924
Roumécla fleuri fabric
by Rodier (cotton, machine
embroidery in gold thread
and cotton thread), buckle
by Paul Kiss (metalworker)
Ufac Collection, 1995
Gift of Louisa Boucard

Inv. UF 61-32-1

Day dress
1924
Silk damask
Purchased with support
from Louis Vuitton, 2015

Inv. 2015.140.1

CAT. 4
Marrakech evening gown
1924
Silk satin, silver strip
embroidery in Tsel stitch,
chinchilla fur and silk velvet
Ufac Collection, 1995
Gift of Madame Couvreur,
via Denise Boulet-Poiret

Inv. UF 56-44-2

CAT. 98
Mistigri coat
c. 1925
Figured wool jersey
and silk velvet
Ufac Collection, 1995
Purchase

Inv. UF 77-8-14

CAT. 99
Evening gown
1925
Silk velvet embroidered
with jet beads
Ufac Collection, 1995
Gift of Alice Natter

Inv. UF 56-46-1

CAT. 100
Saltimbanque dress
1925
Perforated leather
embroidered with
metallic thread, beads
and metal, satin and
silk crepe and wool serge
Ufac Collection, 1995
Gift of Denise Boulet-Poiret

Inv. UF 64-46-14

CAT. 101
Sailor top and trousers
Ensemble worn by the staff
on one of Paul Poiret's
three barges
1925
Ivory cotton satin painted with
black ink, cotton and brass
Gift of Bernadette Caille,
2009

Inv. 2009.127.1.1-2

CAT. 104
Reine reflets evening dress
1926
Sequin embroidery
and silk gauz
Gift of Krystyna Campbell-
Pretty, 2024

Inv. 2024.74.1

CAT. 105
Evening shawl
c. 1928
Silk satin and silk bias binding
Bequest of Dolly van Dongen,
1987

Inv. 987.946

Long dress
c. 1932
Moire, silk crepe
and silver braid
Ufac Collection, 1995
Gift of the Comtesse
d'Hinnisdäl

Inv. UF 56-47-2

Exhibited works

Fashion, textiles and accessories

Statement

CAT. 1 [REPR. P. 228]
Paul Poiret
Evening gown (back)
1907
Silk tulle hand-embroidered with beads, sequins, copper rings, metallic strips and cabochons
Paris, Musée des Arts décoratifs, UFAC Collection, 1995, gift of Denise Boulet-Poiret, inv. UF 64-46-9

CAT. 2 [REPR. PP. 71 & 229]
Paul Poiret
Joséphine evening gown
1907
Silk satin, silk netting, metallic braid embroidered with satin stitch
Paris, Musée des Arts décoratifs, UFAC Collection, 1995, gift of Marcel Piccioni, inv. UF 70-38-10

CAT. 3 [REPR. PP. 83 & 229]
Paul Poiret
Lavallière evening gown
c. 1910
Silk satin embroidered with cylindrical glass beads
Paris, Musée des Arts décoratifs, UFAC Collection, 1995, gift of Denise Boulet-Poiret, inv. UF 63-18-7

CAT. 4 [REPR. PP. 127 & 235]
Paul Poiret
Marrakech evening gown
1924
Silk satin, embroidery of silver strips with Tsel stitch, chinchilla fur and silk velvet
Paris, Musée des Arts décoratifs, UFAC Collection, 1995, gift of Madame Couvreur, via Denise Boulet-Poiret, inv. UF 56-44-2

An artistic education

CAT. 5
Worth
House dress that belonged to Élisabeth de Caraman-Chimay, Countess Greffulhe
c. 1895
Silk velvet on satin ground
Paris, Musée des Arts décoratifs, UFAC Collection, 1995, gift of the Duke of Gramont, inv. UF 60-1-1

CAT. 6
Doucet
Transformation gown with day blouse
1900–05
Chiffon, appliqué embroidery, chenille and silk thread, diamanté and needle lace
Paris, Musée des Arts décoratifs, UFAC Collection, 1995, purchase, inv. UF 54-64 bis-26 AB

CAT. 7
Anonymous
Dance shoe that belonged to Cléo de Mérode
c. 1900
Silk satin
Paris, Musée des Arts décoratifs, UFAC Collection, 1995, gift of Ghislaine Fairweather-Lauwick, in memory of Cléo de Mérode, inv. UF 67-9–195

CAT. 8
Anonymous
Corset with suspenders that belonged to Cléo de Mérode
c. 1900
Figured trimmed taffeta, appliquéd bobbin lace, silk satin ribbon and silk fastening
Paris, Musée des Arts décoratifs, UFAC Collection, 1995, gift of Ghislaine Fairweather-Lauwick, in memory of Cléo de Mérode, inv. UF 67-9-91

CAT. 9
Chéruit
Evening gown
c. 1900
Silk tulle embroidered with sequins
Paris, Musée des Arts décoratifs, UFAC Collection, 1995, gift of Mr and Mrs Wormser, inv. UF 72-10-1

CAT. 10
Doucet
First Empire hussar costume that belonged to Cléo de Mérode
c. 1900
Wool, appliquéd woollen braid, silver-coloured metal, cotton and Mongolian lambswool frogging
Paris, Musée des Arts décoratifs, UFAC Collection, 1995, gift of Ghislaine Fairweather-Lauwick, in memory of Cléo de Mérod, inv. UF 67-9-170 ABCDEF

The couturier's early years

CAT. 11 [REPR. P. 228]
Paul Poiret
Évêque skirt and blouse ensemble
1906
Pleated lawn, woodblock-printed cotton and mother-of-pearl
Paris, Musée des Arts décoratifs, purchased with funds from the Fonds du patrimoine–Ministère de la Culture and thanks to financial support from Michel and Hélène David-Weill, 2005, inv. 2005.37.3.1-2

CAT. 12 [REPR. P. 228]
Paul Poiret
Gavarni day dress
1906
Linen
Paris, Musée des Arts décoratifs, purchased with funds from the Fonds du patrimoine–Ministère de la Culture and thanks to financial support from Michel and Hélène David-Weill, 2005, inv. 2005-37-4

CAT. 13 [REPR. PP. 67 & 228]
Paul Poiret
1811 evening gown
1907
Pekin silk, metallic lace and chiffon
Paris, Musée des Arts décoratifs, UFAC Collection, 1995, gift of Denise Boulet-Poiret, inv. UF 64-46-1

CAT. 14 [REPR. P. 229]
Paul Poiret
Eugénie evening gown
1907
Figured cotton gauze, tulle and taffeta
Paris, Musée des Arts décoratifs, UFAC Collection, 1995, gift of Denise Boulet-Poiret, inv. UF 64-46-2

CAT. 15 [REPR. P. 229]
Paul Poiret
Evening gown
1908
Shot silk satin, passementerie and lawn
Paris, Musée des Arts décoratifs, UFAC Collection, 1995, gift of Denise Boulet-Poiret, inv. UF 64-46-3

CAT. 16 [REPR. P. 229]
Paul Poiret
Evening coat
c. 1910
Trimmed gros de Tours with brocade design in gold thread and silver strips, shot taffeta, passementerie and silver-coloured metal
Paris, Musée des Arts décoratifs, UFAC Collection, 1995, gift of Marcel Piccioni, inv. UF 70-38-45

CAT. 17 [REPR. P. 229]
Paul Poiret
Evening coat
c. 1910
Silk satin, guipure lace made from silk thread and metallic thread
Paris, Musée des Arts décoratifs, UFAC Collection, 1995, purchase, inv. UF 61-40-2

CAT. 18 [REPR. P. 229]
Paul Poiret
Handbag
c. 1910
Silk embroidered with glass beads
Paris, Musée des Arts décoratifs, UFAC Collection, 1995, purchase, inv. UF 75–19-9

CAT. 19 [REPR. P. 230]
Paul Poiret
Coat
c. 1911
Silk velvet embroidered with gold cordonnet braid and mink fur
Paris, Musée des Arts décoratifs, UFAC Collection, 1995, gift of Denise Boulet-Poiret, inv. UF 64-46-17

CAT. 20 [REPR. P. 230]
Paul Poiret
Hat
1911
Ribbed silk, silk velvet, feather; braid embroidered with metallic thread, diamanté and artificial gems
Paris, Musée des Arts décoratifs, UFAC Collection, 1995, gift of Andrée Lhuer, inv. UF 52-21-7

CAT. 21 [REPR. P. 230]
Paul Poiret
Child's hat
1911
Silk velvet and metallic netting
Paris, Musée des Arts décoratifs, UFAC Collection, 1995, gift of Andrée Lhuer, inv. UF 52-21-36

CAT. 22 [REPR. P. 230]
Paul Poiret
Nénuphar coat
1911
Silk, embroidered silk tulle and passementerie
Paris, Musée des Arts décoratifs, UFAC Collection, 1995, gift of Denise Boulet-Poiret, inv. UF 63-18-4

CAT. 23 [REPR. P. 231]
Paul Poiret
Headpiece
1914
Chiffon embroidered with diamanté, cellulose fibre and silk taffeta
Paris, Musée des Arts décoratifs, inv. 987.112

Artistic collaborations

CAT. 24
Maurice de Vlaminck (1876–1958)
André Metthey (1871–1920)
Buttons
c. 1906–1910
Tin-glazed ceramic (10 buttons)

Paris, Musée du Louvre, bequest from Solange Prével-Vlaminck, daughter of Maurice de Vlaminck, to the state, 1978, on loan to the Musée des Beaux-Arts in Chartres, inv. D.78.2.5.2, inv. D.78.2.5.3, inv. D.78.2.5.6, inv. D.78.2.5.7, inv. D.78.2.5.10 to inv. D.78.2.5.12, inv. D.78.2.5.16, inv. D.78.2.5.20 and inv. D.78.2.5.21

CAT. 25
Maurice de Vlaminck (1876–1958)
Buttons
c. 1910
Painted and varnished terracotta (3 buttons)
Paris, Musée des Arts décoratifs, former collection of Loïc Allo, purchased with funds from the Fonds du patrimoine–Ministère de la Culture and thanks to financial support from Hermès Sellier, Solanet et Fibelage, Ancelle et Associés, 2012, inv. 2012.48.606 to inv. 2012.48.608

CAT. 26 [REPR. PP. 79 & 229]
Paul Poiret
Mosaïque evening gown
c. 1910
Chiffon embroidered with silk thread and beads, gold braid, mink fur and silk satin
Paris, Musée des Arts décoratifs, UFAC Collection, 1995, gift of Mr Veysset, inv. UF 61-37-1

CAT. 27
Paul Poiret
Raoul Dufy (1877–1953), textile designer
La Perse coat
1911
Block-printed cotton velvet, silk satin, grey fox fur and metallic netting
The Metropolitan Museum of Art, purchased by the Friends of the Costume Institute, inv. 2005.199a–d

CAT. 28 [REPR. P. 231]
Paul Poiret
Coat
c. 1913
Cotton crepe embroidered with chain stitch, lace and glass
Paris, Musée des Arts décoratifs, UFAC Collection, 1995, gift of Madame Le Bec, inv. UF 69-26-38

CAT. 29
Raoul Dufy (1877–1953)
Les Alliés purse
1915
Silk pongee printed in 5 colours
Paris, Musée des Arts décoratifs, gift of Louis Metman, 1920, inv. 22193

CAT. 30
Paul Poiret
Raoul Dufy (1877–1953) for Bianchini-Férier
Bois de Boulogne dinner dress
1919
Printed silk charmeuse satin, silk tulle and crepe de chine
The Metropolitan Museum of Art, Millia Davenport and Zipporah Fleisher Fund, inv. 2005.197a–c

CAT. 31
Raoul Dufy (1877–1953) for Bianchini-Férier
Les Arums fabric
1919
Woodblock-printed on cotton and linen
Paris, Musée des Arts décoratifs, gift of Bianchini-Férier, 1927, inv. 25986

CAT. 32
Raoul Dufy (1877–1953) for Bianchini-Férier
Tulipes fabric
1914
Printed silk satin
Paris, Musée des Arts décoratifs, purchased thanks to the patronage of Mrs Jayne Wrightsman, 2001, inv. 2002.53.1

CAT. 33
Paul Poiret
Les Fruits dressing gown
c. 1924
Figured silk
Palais Galliera–Musée de la Mode de la Ville de Paris, inv. 1985.173.4

CAT. 34 [REPR. P. 201]
Chloé by Karl Lagerfeld (1933–2019)
Evening gown
1971
Silk crepe painted by Nicole Lefort, design inspired by Gustav Klimt
Unique design created for the singer Régine for the opening of her Paris nightclub 'Réginskaïa'
Paris, Musée des Arts décoratifs, gift of Régine, 1988, inv. 988.1029

CAT. 35 [REPR. P. 201]
Rochas by Olivier Theyskens (born 1977)
Evening gown
Spring–Summer 2004 ready-to-wear collection
Synthetic goffered and pleated taffeta, cordonnet braid, coated taffeta, goffered muslin, lace frill, satin ribbons and gathered lamé
Paris, Musée des Arts décoratifs, gift of Rochas, 2007, inv. 2007.104.3

Dressing dancers and actresses for the city and the stage

CAT. 36 [REPR. PP. 91 & 230]
Paul Poiret
Evening gown
1910
Silk satin, chiffon embroidered with cylindrical glass beads and silk velvet
Paris, Musée des Arts décoratifs, UFAC Collection, 1995, gift of Mr Bienvenu, inv. UF 52-6-1

CAT. 37 [REPR. PP. 99 & 231]
Paul Poiret
Mélodie dress
1912
Silk damask, silk velvet, galalith and piping
Paris, Musée des Arts décoratifs, UFAC Collection, 1995, gift of Denise Boulet-Poiret, inv. UF 63-18-8

CAT. 38
Paul Poiret
Bolero that belonged to the dancer Nyota Inyoka
1920–1930
Silk, appliqué of gold and metallic cordonnet braid, tulle and passementerie
Bibliothèque nationale de France, Performing Arts department, inv. COS-2001/00208/01

CAT. 39 [REPR. P. 185]
Natalia Goncharova (1881–1962)
Muolle Rossignol, costume designer
Dance costume
1921
Dyed silk satin, graphite, hand- and machine-embroidered tulle, ribbon, wood and painted cotton
Paris, Musée des Arts décoratifs, UFAC Collection, 1995, gift of Michel Hogg, inv. UF 67-15-1 ABCDEF

CAT. 40
Paul Poiret
Tolède evening gown that belonged to Andrée Spinelly
1921–22
Silk crepe, embroidery with metallic thread, passementerie and fur
Palais Galliera–Musée de la Mode de la Ville de Paris, inv. 1983.126.2

CAT. 41 [REPR. P. 234]
Paul Poiret
Spi evening gown
1922
Embroidered silk velvet
Paris, Musée des Arts décoratifs, UFAC Collection, 1995, gift of Madame Couvreur, via Denise Boulet-Poiret, inv. UF 56-44-1

Travel for business and inspiration

CAT. 42 [REPR. P. 121]
Louis Vuitton
Hat box in Monogram fabric, formerly belonging to Paul Poiret
1911
Coated canvas, wood, brass and iron
Louis Vuitton Collection, inv. 2008.002.003628

CAT. 43 [REPR. PP. 119 & 234]
Paul Poiret
Ballon travel coat
c. 1923
Peau de tortue fabric, silk velvet and silk pongee lining by Dagobert Peche (1887–1923), textile designer
Paris, Musée des Arts décoratifs, UFAC Collection, 1995, gift of Denise Boulet-Poiret, inv. UF 64-46-18

CAT. 44
Louis Vuitton
Garment bag that belonged to Paul Poiret
1923
Cowhide
Paris, Musée des Arts décoratifs, donated by Gaston-Louis Vuitton, 1989, inv. 987.61

Expanding the mind through travel

CAT. 45
Anonymous
Fabric swatch
Egypt, 19th century
Embroidered cotton
Paris, Musée des Arts décoratifs, gift of Marie Joly, 1891, inv. 7009

CAT. 46
Anonymous
Fabric swatch
Persian, Qajar period – 19th century
Lampas on serge ground
Paris, Musée des Arts décoratifs, purchased in 1901, inv. 9706

CAT. 47 [REPR. PP. 75 & 228]
Paul Poiret
Ispahan coat
1907
Embroidered silk velvet and appliquéd cordonnet braid
Paris, Musée des Arts décoratifs, UFAC Collection, 1995, gift of Denise Boulet-Poiret, inv. UF 63-18-2

CAT. 48 [REPR. P. 229]
Paul Poiret
Cairo tunic
1907
Silk ottoman fabric embroidered with silk thread and metallic thread, appliquéd braid and gold-coloured metal
Paris, Musée des Arts décoratifs, UFAC Collection, 1995, gift of Denise Boulet-Poiret, inv. UF 64-46-16

CAT. 49
Henri Espagnat, illustrator
André Groult (1884–1966), designer
Rambouillet fabric factory
Swatch of upholstery fabric
c. 1910
Woodblock-printed on linen
Paris, Musée des Arts décoratifs, inv. 29778

CAT. 50 [REPR. PP. 95 & 230]
Paul Poiret
Flammes shawl and culotte-dress
1911
Shawl made from hand-embroidered silk crepe (cut into Manila shawl style); culotte-dress made from silk velvet, chiffon and passementerie
Paris, Musée des Arts décoratifs, purchased with funds from the Fonds du patrimoine–Ministère de la Culture and thanks to financial support from Michel and Hélène David-Weill, 2005, inv. 2005.37.9.1-2

CAT. 51 [REPR. P. 231]
Paul Poiret
Fleurie summer dress
1912
Embroidered cotton muslin, appliquéd braid and bronze buttons from the Directory period
Paris, Musée des Arts décoratifs, UFAC Collection, 1995, gift of Denise Boulet-Poiret, inv. UF 64-46-11

CAT. 52 [REPR. P. 232]
Paul Poiret
Printemps shawl and summer dress
1919
Handwoven silk, braided wool and ribbed cotton
Paris, Musée des Arts décoratifs, purchased with funds from the Fonds du patrimoine–Ministère de la Culture and thanks to financial support from Michel and Hélène David-Weill, 2005, inv. 2005.37.8.1-3

CAT. 53 [REPR. PP. 103 & 232]
Paul Poiret
Bretonne dress
1919
Embroidered silk velvet, silk crepe and silk netting
Paris, Musée des Arts décoratifs, UFAC Collection, 1995, gift of Denise Boulet-Poiret, inv. UF 64-46-5

CAT. 54 [REPR. P. 233]
Paul Poiret
Skirt suit
1920
Ribbed silk, printed cotton and appliquéd braid
Paris, Musée des Arts décoratifs, UFAC Collection, 1995, gift of Madame E. Grandperrin, inv. UF 78-20-1 AB

CAT. 55 [REPR. P. 233]
Paul Poiret
Han Kéou evening gown
1922
Trimmed figured silk, velvet and silk plush
Paris, Musée des Arts décoratifs, UFAC Collection, 1995, gift of Denise Boulet-Poiret, inv. UF 63-18-9

CAT. 56 [REPR. P. 234]
Paul Poiret
Exotique dress
1922
Printed crepe de chine, chiffon, passementerie and jet beads
Paris, Musée des Arts décoratifs, UFAC Collection, 1995, gift of Denise Boulet-Poiret, inv. UF 63-18-11 AB

CAT. 57 [REPR. PP. 115 & 234]
Paul Poiret
Martinique dress
1922
Crepe marocain and printed
crepe de chine
Paris, Musée des Arts
décoratifs, UFAC Collection,
1995, gift of Louise Janin,
inv. UF 53-14-1

CAT. 58 [REPR. P. 234]
Paul Poiret
Mandchoue two-piece dress
1923
Silk lamé and silk velvet
Paris, Musée des Arts
décoratifs, UFAC Collection,
1995, purchase, inv. UF 86-
70-10 AB

CAT. 59 [REPR. PP. 123 & 234]
Paul Poiret
La Source coat
1924
Roumécla fleuri fabric by
Rodier (cotton, machine
embroidery in gold thread
and cotton thread), buckle by
Paul Kiss (metalworker)
Paris, Musée des Arts
décoratifs, UFAC Collection,
1995, gift of Louisa Boucard,
inv. UF 61-32-1

CAT. 60 [REPR. P. 205]
Issey Miyake
Bodice and trousers
Spring–Summer 1979 ready-
to-wear collection
Gold lamé nylon voile
Paris, Musée des Arts
décoratifs, purchased with
support from Louis Vuitton,
2014, inv. 2014.2.5.1-3

CAT. 61 [REPR. P. 205]
Issey Miyake
Oblate coat
Spring–Summer 1979 ready-
to-wear collection
Nylon crepe
Tokyo, Miyake Design Studio

CAT. 62
Jean Patou by Christian
Lacroix (born 1951)
Fleur des pois ensemble
Spring–Summer 1987 haute
couture collection
Blouse made from silk
embroidered with cutout
sequins, glass beads and
silk thread; skirt made from
taffeta, broderie anglaise and
tulle; belt made from silk satin
with leather lining
Paris, Musée des Arts
décoratifs, gift of São
Schlumberger, 1994,
inv. 994.112.3 ABC

CAT. 63 [REPR. P. 209]
Jean Paul Gaultier
Ensemble
Autumn–Winter 1994 ready-
to-wear collection, 'Le Grand
Voyage'
Shot silk damask and
synthetic fur
Paris, Musée des Arts
décoratifs, inv. PR 2011.24.2 (1)

CAT. 64 [REPR. P. 214]
Dries Van Noten
Coat
Autumn–Winter 2006 ready-
to-wear collection
Wool serge, embroidered with
gold thread, sequins, copper
and acetate twill
Paris, Musée des Arts
décoratifs, gift of Dries Van
Noten, 2011, inv. 2011.138.1

Organizing parties and performances

CAT. 65
Paul Poiret
Minaret ensemble
1911
Turban made from draped
silk satin, cotton, feather and
beads; lampshade tunic made
from silk satin with appliquéd
braid and metallic fringe;
lorgnette made from feathers,
ribbon of metallic thread,
taffeta and wood; shoe made
from leather and silver fabric
with diamanté
Fundación Museo de la Moda,
Santiago de Chile, inv. Pre-
Ad Nº 11853

CAT. 66
Paul Poiret
Bacchus
Tunic and wig
1912
Tunic made from cotton
crepe, braid in metallic
gold thread; wig made from
cannetille in metallic gold
thread
Palais Galliera–Musée de
la Mode de la Ville de Paris,
inv. GAL1985.148.1-2

CAT. 67
Paul Poiret
Mariano Fortuny (1871–1949),
textile designer
Bacchante ensemble
1912
Tunic made from
printed filigree chiffon,
passementerie tassels, taffeta
embellishments; crown made
from leaves of taffeta, gold-
plated glass beads, gold lamé
thread, silk cordonnet braid;
sandals made from leather
Palais Galliera–Musée de
la Mode de la Ville de Paris,
inv. GAL1985.148.1

CAT. 68 [REPR. P. 210]
Ágatha Ruiz de la Prada
Tarta dress
1994 ready-to-wear
collection, 'Agatha Ruiz de la
Prada en Paris'
Silk organza and plastic
hoops
Paris, Musée des Arts
décoratifs, gift of Ágatha
Ruiz de la Prada, 2024,
inv. 2024.13.5

Family portraits

CAT. 69
André Groult (1884–1966)
Swatch of upholstery fabric
c. 1910
Woodblock-printed on linen
Paris, Musée des Arts
décoratifs
Inv. 29751

CAT. 70 [REPR. P. 229]
Paul Poiret
Image evening coat
c. 1910
Shot satin, lace made of gold
thread and passementerie
Paris, Musée des Arts
décoratifs, UFAC Collection,
1995, gift of Denise Boulet-
Poiret, inv. UF 69-20-2

CAT. 71 [REPR. P. 231]
Paul Poiret
Dress that belonged to Rosine
Poiret
c. 1912
Cashmere, silk crepe and silk
cordonnet braid
Paris, Musée des Arts
décoratifs, purchased with
funds from the Fonds du
patrimoine–Ministère de
la Culture and thanks to
financial support from Michel
and Hélène David-Weill,
2005, inv. 2005.37.10.1-2

CAT. 72 [REPR. P. 56]
André Groult
Dress
1912
Silk crepe, silk satin,
embroidered netting and
taffeta
Paris, Musée des Arts
décoratifs, UFAC Collection,
1995, gift of Marcel Piccioni,
inv. UF 70-38-17

CAT. 73 [REPR. P. 231]
Paul Poiret
Wig
c. 1914
Dyed horsehair and metallic
gold tulle
Paris, Musée des Arts
décoratifs, purchased with
funds from the Fonds du
patrimoine–Ministère de
la Culture and thanks to
financial support from Michel
and Hélène David-Weill,
2005, inv. 2005.37.5

CAT. 74 [REPR. P. 232]
Paul Poiret
Malgré moi dress
1919
Silk velvet, silk satin and
silk tulle embroidered with
sequins
Paris, Musée des Arts
décoratifs, UFAC Collection,
1995, gift of Denise Boulet-
Poiret, inv. UF 63-18-6 AB

CAT. 75 [REPR. P. 232]
Paul Poiret
Tout de suite dress
1919
Silk velvet, printed cotton, silk
passementerie and metallic
thread
Paris, Musée des Arts
décoratifs, UFAC Collection,
1995, gift of Denise Boulet-
Poiret, inv. UF 63-18-5

CAT. 76 [REPR. PP. 47 & 233]
Paul Poiret
Ice Cream Soda evening coat
c. 1920
Silk panne velvet and shot
taffeta
Paris, Musée des Arts
décoratifs, UFAC Collection,
1995, gift of Denise Boulet-
Poiret, inv. UF 63-18-3

CAT. 77 [REPR. P. 233]
Paul Poiret
Abbesse dress
c. 1920
Silk velvet, taffeta and figured
silk satin lamé lining
Paris, Musée des Arts
décoratifs, UFAC Collection,
1995, gift of Denise Boulet-
Poiret, inv. UF 64-46-6

CAT. 78
Favereau
Pair of shoes
1920
Rust-coloured Russian leather
embroidered with metallic
thread
Paris, Musée des Arts
décoratifs, purchased with
financial support from the
museum's International
Council, 2023, inv. 2023.2.1.1-2

CAT. 79 [REPR. P. 233]
Paul Poiret
Dress
1920
Silk ottoman fabric, silk satin
lamé and glass paste
Paris, Musée des Arts
décoratifs, UFAC Collection,
1995, gift of Denise Boulet-
Poiret, inv. 64-46-13

CAT. 80
Nicole Groult
Dress
c. 1921
Embroidered crepe marocain,
crepe de chine and silk satin
Paris, Musée des Arts
décoratifs, UFAC Collection,
1995, gift of Madame
Margaritis, inv. UF 68-17-1

CAT. 81 [REPR. P. 233]
Paul Poiret
Sailor suit that belonged to
Colin Poiret
1922
Linen and mother-of-pearl
Paris, Musée des Arts
décoratifs, purchased with
funds from the Fonds du
patrimoine–Ministère de
la Culture and thanks to
financial support from Michel
and Hélène David-Weill,
2005, inv. 2005.37.1.1-2

Reinventing the decorative arts

CAT. 82
Paul Poiret
Pendant
c. 1911
Tortoiseshell
Paris, Centre Pompidou–
Musée national d'art
moderne–Centre de
création industrielle, gift
of Madame Guillot, 1952,
on loan to the Musée des Arts
décoratifs in Paris since 1985,
inv. MNAM AM 1084 OA

CAT. 83
Paul Poiret
Pillbox hat
1911
Silk cordonnet braid
embellished with wool and
silk thread, with a design by
the Martine Workshop, and
taffeta
Palais Galliera–Musée de
la Mode de la Ville de Paris,
inv. GAL1986.125.6

CAT. 84 [REPR. PP. 153 & 230]
Paul Poiret
Beach ensemble
c. 1912
Block-printed linen with the
design *Les Artichauts* by the
Martine Workshop
Paris, Musée des Arts
décoratifs, purchased with
support from Louis Vuitton,
2014, inv. 2014.45.1.1-2

CAT. 85 [REPR. P. 230]
Paul Poiret
Parasol
c. 1912
Block-printed cotton with
the design *Les Anémones* by
the Martine Workshop, and
varnished bamboo
Paris, Musée des Arts
décoratifs, UFAC Collection,
1995, inv. UF 2003-05-3

CAT. 86 [REPR. PP. 112 & 231]
Martine Workshop
Les Anémones fabric
1912
Roller-printed on linen
Paris, Musée des Arts
décoratifs, gift of Manuel
Canovas, 1986, inv. 58345

CAT. 87 [REPR. P. 152]
Kees Van Dongen (1877–1968)
Martine Workshop
Rug
c. 1919
Wool and lockstitch
Paris, Musée des Arts
décoratifs, bequest of
Dolly Van Dongen, 1987,
inv. 987.945

CAT. 88 [REPR. PP. 111 & 233]
Paul Poiret
Summer dress that belonged
to Martine Poiret
c. 1920
Block-printed silk satin to
a design by the Martine
Workshop and cordonnet
braid
Paris, Musée des Arts
décoratifs, purchased with
funds from the Fonds du
patrimoine–Ministère de
la Culture and thanks to
financial support from Michel
and Hélène David-Weill,
2005, inv. 2005.37.2

CAT. 89
Paul Poiret
Perugia, shoemaker
Pair of Charles IX shoes, *Les
Roses*
1924
Silk velvet and embroidery in
silk chenille with a design by
the Martine Workshop
Palais Galliera–Musée de
la Mode de la Ville de Paris,
inv. GAL2005.8.26.0

CAT. 90 [REPR. P. 215]
Comme des Garçons
Skirt suit
Autumn–Winter 2013
collection, 'The Infinity of
Tailoring'
Printed velvet and aged
leather
Paris, Musée des Arts
décoratifs, purchased with
support from Louis Vuitton,
2013, inv. 2013.60.4.1-5

The couturier and perfumier

CAT. 91
Louis Vuitton
London garment bag
purchased for Les Parfums de
Rosine
1924
Leather and brass
Louis Vuitton Collection,
inv. 2012.002.005174

A designer with many passions

CAT. 92
Paul Poiret
Jacket that belonged to Paul Poiret
1915–1925
Silk damask crepe
Palais Galliera–Musée de la Mode de la Ville de Paris, inv. GAL1985.148.3

CAT. 93 [REPR. PP. 107 & 233]
Paul Poiret
Jacket that belonged to Paul Poiret
c. 1920
Woodblock-printed linen with a design by the Martine Workshop, figured silk crepe and braided leather
Paris, Musée des Arts décoratifs, UFAC Collection, 1995, gift of Denise Boulet-Poiret, inv. UF 64-46-4

The barges of 1925: a synthesis of style

CAT. 94 [REPR. P. 231]
Paul Poiret
Coat
c. 1914
Silk ottoman fabric, silk satin, embroidered cotton netting, silk bias binding and gold-coloured metal
Paris, Musée des Arts décoratifs, UFAC Collection, 1995, purchase, inv. UF 61-40-1

CAT. 95 [REPR. P. 232]
Paul Poiret
Evening coat
c. 1920
Printed silk velvet embroidered with metallic thread
Paris, Musée des Arts décoratifs, UFAC Collection, 1995, gift of Madame Edmond de Galéa, inv. UF 50-16-6

CAT. 96 [REPR. P. 234]
Paul Poiret
Manège dress
1922
Panne velvet, embroidered with sequins and metallic thread and gold lamé silk
Paris, Musée des Arts décoratifs, UFAC Collection, 1995, gift of Denise Boulet-Poiret, inv. UF 63-18-12

CAT. 97 [REPR. P. 234]
Paul Poiret
Fils du ciel dress
1923
Silk velvet embroidered with metallic thread and silk satin bias binding
Paris, Musée des Arts décoratifs, UFAC Collection, 1995, gift of Madame Feuillatte, inv. UF 60-17-1

CAT. 98 [REPR. P. 235]
Paul Poiret
Mistigri coat
c. 1925
Figured wool jersey and silk velvet
Paris, Musée des Arts décoratifs, UFAC Collection, 1995, purchase, inv. UF 77-8-14

CAT. 99 [REPR. P. 235]
Paul Poiret
Evening gown
1925
Silk velvet embroidered with jet beads
Paris, Musée des Arts décoratifs, UFAC Collection, 1995, gift of Alice Natter, inv. UF 56-46-1

CAT. 100 [REPR. P. 235]
Paul Poiret
Saltimbanque dress
1925
Perforated leather embroidered with metallic thread, beads and metal, satin and silk crepe and wool serge
Paris, Musée des Arts décoratifs, UFAC Collection, 1995, gift of Denise Boulet-Poiret, inv. UF 64-46-14

CAT. 101 [REPR. P. 235]
Paul Poiret
Pea jacket and trousers
Ensemble worn by the staff on one of Paul Poiret's three barges
1925
Ivory cotton satin painted with black ink, cotton and brass
Paris, Musée des Arts décoratifs, gift of Bernadette Caille, 2009, inv. 2009.127.1.1-2

CAT. 102
Raoul Dufy (1877–1953)
Presenting models at Poiret's wall hanging
Delivered by the artist to Paul Poiret for the barge Orgues Tournon, 1925
Painted and printed cotton
Paris, Centre Pompidou–Musée national d'art moderne–Centre de création industrielle, purchase, 1937, on loan to the Musée des Arts décoratifs in Paris since 1985, inv. MNAM AM 2144.P

CAT. 103
Paul Poiret
Evening coat
c. 1926
Ermine; inlays of trimmed faux fur with appliqué of gold lamé with plant motifs embroidered in metallic thread, sequins and faceted metal beads; lining in figured silk satin with floral motifs
Fondation Azzedine Alaïa, inv. FAA_POI_0011

CAT. 104 [REPR. P. 235]
Paul Poiret
Reine reflets evening gown
1926
Sequin embroidery and silk gauze
Paris, Musée des Arts décoratifs, gift of Krystyna Campbell-Pretty, 2024, inv. 2024.74.1

CAT. 105 [REPR. P. 235]
Paul Poiret
Evening shawl
c. 1928
Silk satin and silk bias binding
Paris, Musée des Arts décoratifs, bequest of Dolly van Dongen, 1987, inv. 987.946

CAT. 106
Jean-Paul Gaultier
Jumpsuit worn during a performance of Façade, un divertissement by the Ballet Atlantique – Régine Chopinot, 1993
1985
Hessian and cotton jersey, hand-painted stretch tulle, plastic and overstitched hessian
Paris, Musée des Arts décoratifs, gift of the Ballet Atlantique – Régine Chopinot, 2006, inv. 2006.131.61

Paul Poiret's stylistic legacy

CAT. 107 [REPR. P. 193]
Christian Dior
Minuit evening coat
Autumn–Winter 1948 haute couture collection, 'Winged' line
Black silk velvet embroidered with braid and wool passementerie
Paris, Musée des Arts décoratifs, UFAC Collection, 1995
Gift of Elinor Brodie
Inv. UF 69-28-22

CAT. 108 [REPR. P. 51]
Elsa Schiaparelli
Evening gown
Winter 1950–51 haute couture collection, 'Ligne de face'
Silk satin, silk velvet, embroidery by Lesage in metallic thread, cordonnet braid, beads and diamanté
Paris, Musée des Arts décoratifs, UFAC Collection, 1995, gift of Elsa Schiaparelli, inv. UF 73-21-30

CAT. 109
Elsa Schiaparelli
Evening shawl
Winter 1952–53 haute couture collection, 'Cigale'
Figured taffeta, silk velvet and quilted silk satin
Paris, Musée des Arts décoratifs, UFAC Collection, 1995, gift of Elsa Schiaprelli, inv. UF 73-21-21

CAT. 110
Christian Dior by Yves Saint Laurent (1936–2008)
Nuit d'Ispahan reception dress
Spring–Summer 1960 haute couture collection, 'Silhouette de demain'
Printed taffeta on Burg
Paris, Musée des Arts décoratifs, gift of Fina Gomez, 1988, inv. 988.458.A-B

CAT. 111 [REPR. P. 202]
Kenzo Jap
Ensemble
Autumn–Winter 1970 ready-to-wear collection
Cotton velvet, quilted printed cotton and brocade ribbon
Paris, Musée des Arts décoratifs, gift of Maurice Bokanowski, 1988, inv. 988.922.A-C

CAT. 112 [REPR. P. 204]
Yves Saint Laurent
Evening ensemble
Autumn–Winter 1976 haute couture collection, 'Opéra – Ballets russes'
Silk velvet and chiffon
Paris, Musée des Arts décoratifs, gift of Yves Saint Laurent, 1998, inv. 998.39.2.1-4

CAT. 113
Chloé by Karl Lagerfeld (1933–2019)
Pompéi evening gown
Autumn–Winter 1980 collection
Gold lamé silk and Diochon polyester
Paris, Musée des Arts décoratifs, UFAC Collection, 1995, gift of Maison Chloé, inv. UF 80-24-1

CAT. 114 [REPR. P. 206]
Jean Patou by Christian Lacroix (born 1951)
Incredible ensemble
Autumn–Winter 1985 haute couture collection
Pekin silk and gold diamanté
Paris, Musée des Arts décoratifs, purchased with support from Louis Vuitton, 2012, inv. 2012.121.2.1-3

CAT. 116 [REPR. P. 208]
Maison Martin Margiela
Ensemble
Autumn–Winter 1989 ready-to-wear collection
Wool knit, leather, cotton serge, ceramics and steel wire
Paris, Musée des Arts décoratifs, gift of Martin Margiela, inv. 2006.51.1.1-5

CAT. 117 [REPR. P. 211]
Christian Dior by John Galliano (born 1960)
Juliet evening gown
Autumn–Winter 1997 ready-to-wear collection
Embroidered silk satin crepe, patchwork of paper cut-outs, varnish, bamboo
Paris, Musée des Arts décoratifs, gift of Christian Dior Couture, 1998, inv. 998.43.1

CAT. 118
Christian Dior by John Galliano (born 1960)
Stourhead evening coat and dress
Spring–Summer 1998 haute couture collection, 'Hommage poétique à la marquise Casati'
Gold figured silk brocade, hand-painted and fleece-lined, aged goffered silver lamé, chiffon embroidered with metallic silver threads and diamanté
Paris, Musée des Arts décoratifs, gift of Christian Dior, 2006, inv. 2005.159.1.1-2

CAT. 119 [REPR. P. 213]
Adeline André
'Poiret' coat
Autumn–Winter 2005 haute couture collection
Wool doeskin
Paris, Musée des Arts décoratifs, purchased with financial support from the Friends of the Musée des Arts décoratifs, 2023, inv. 2023.98.1.1-4

CAT. 120 [REPR. P. 216]
Azzedine Alaïa
Gilet and skirt ensemble
Autumn–Winter 2016 couture
Gilet made from laser-cut leather with metal studs, lined with crepe, skirt made from virgin wool; belt made from leather with silver-coloured metal eyelets
Fondation Azzedine Alaïa, inv. FAA.AA.02900, inv. FAA.AA.02956 and inv. FAA.AA.02902

CAT. 121 [REPR. P. 217]
Maitrepierre
Viktor coat, Bouquet wearable sculpture by Gracelee Lawrence
Autumn–Winter 2024 ready-to-wear collection
Imitation astrakhan and 3D-printed sculpture made from biodegradable PLA (biodegradable polymer made from maize, beetroot and wheat starch)
Alphonse Maitrepierre

Decorative arts

An artistic education

CAT. 122
François-Honoré-Georges Jacob-Desmalter (1770-1841)
After Louis Delanois (1731-1792)
Chair
1803-1814
Sculpted, painted walnut
Paris, Musée des Arts décoratifs, bequest of Jean-Édouard Dubrujeaud in memory of his brother André, 1970, inv. 42881.B

Artistic collaborations

CAT. 123
Maurice de Vlaminck (1876–1958)
Vase
1906–10
Tin-glazed ceramic
Chartres, Musée des Beaux-Arts, inv. 99.2.1

CAT. 124
Maurice de Vlaminck (1876–1958)
André Metthey (1871–1920), ceramicist
Plates
c. 1908
Tin-glazed ceramic (2 plates)
Paris, Musée des Arts décoratifs, inv. 29485 and inv. 29486

CAT. 125
Raoul Dufy (1877–1953)
Panorama of Paris screen
1933
Wood, wool and silk
Mobilier National, inv. GMT 24695

Travel for business and inspiration

CAT. 126
George Barbier (1882–1932), illustrator
André Groult (1884–1966), designer
The Chinese screen
1911–12
Woodblock-printed on continuous paper, hand-brushed varnished background, wooden frame
Paris, Musée des Arts décoratifs, purchased with financial support from the Friends of the Musée des Arts décoratifs, 2013, inv. 2013.56.1

Reinventing the decorative arts

CAT. 127
Martine Workshop
Cambodian armchair
c. 1912
Painted wood
Paris, Musée des Arts décoratifs, purchased with funds from the Fonds du patrimoine–Ministère de la Culture and thanks to financial support from Michel and Hélène David-Weill, 2005, inv. 2005.37.16

CAT. 128
Martine Workshop
Side table
c. 1912
Painted wood
Paris, Musée des Arts
décoratifs, purchased with
funds from the Fonds du
patrimoine–Ministère de
la Culture and thanks to
financial support from Michel
and Hélène David-Weill,
2005, inv. 2005.37.17

CAT. 129
Martine Workshop
Three-part screen
c. 1912–13
Appliqué and embroidery
on silk background and
painted wood
Paris, Musée d'Orsay,
inv. OAO 1692

CAT. 130
Martine Workshop
The Scotsman
c. 1915
Body made from silk serge,
jacket and gaiters made from
wool, buttons made from
mother-of-pearl, silk thread,
wool, patent leather and silk
taffeta
Paris, Musée des Arts
décoratifs, purchased with
financial support from the
Naja association, 2005,
inv. 2005.42.1

CAT. 131
Georges Lepape (1887–1971)
Paul Poiret (1879–1944)
Marionette
1916
Body made from painted wood
and leather, dress fabric made
from metallic gold netting
with swansdown and silk, glass
beads, metallic cordonnet
braid, ring made from
celluloid, trousers made from
silk organza, belt made from
silk thread and glass beads
Paris, Musée des Arts
décoratifs, purchase, 1987,
inv. 987.266

The couturier and perfumier

CAT. 132
Les Parfums de Rosine
Spray bottle for the perfume
Hahna, l'étrange fleur
1912–20
Painted blown glass
Fragonard Parfumeur,
inv. M299

CAT. 133
Martine Workshop
Les Parfums de Rosine
Rosine spray bottle
After 1912
Painted blown glass
Fragonard Parfumeur,
inv. M016

CAT. 134
Martine Workshop
Les Parfums de Rosine
Rosine spray bottle
After 1912
Painted blown glass
Fragonard Parfumeur,
inv. M011

CAT. 135
Martine Workshop
Les Parfums de Rosine
Rosine spray bottle
After 1912
Painted blown glass
Fragonard Parfumeur,
inv. M015

CAT. 136
Raoul Dufy (1877–1953)
Henri Alméras (1892–1965),
perfumier
Les Parfums de Rosine
Le Fruit défendu perfume
and box
1915
Glass, metal, cardboard and
paper
Palais Galliera–Musée de
la Mode de la Ville de Paris,
inv. GAL1990.155.1.AB

CAT. 137
Henri Alméras (1892–1965),
perfumier
Les Parfums de Rosine
Pierrot perfume and box
1919
Translucent glass, satin and
paper
Grasse, Musée international
de la Parfumerie,
inv. 2012.39.1.1 and
inv. 2012.39.1.2

CAT. 138
Mario Simon
Henri Alméras (1892–1965),
perfumier
Les Parfums de Rosine
Aladin perfume and box
1919
Glass, metal, cardboard and
paper
Palais Galliera–Musée de
la Mode de la Ville de Paris,
inv. GAL2004.846.1

CAT. 139
Martine Workshop
Colin Workshop
Les Parfums de Rosine
Powder compact, *Ocre*
powder scented with *Hahna,
l'étrange fleur*
c. 1920
Cardboard, printed fabric and
passementerie
Agnès Mulon

CAT. 140
Martine Workshop
Colin Workshop
Les Parfums de Rosine
Powder compact, *Rachel*
powder scented with *Le Fruit
défendu*
c. 1920
Cardboard, printed fabric and
passementerie
Agnès Mulon

CAT. 141
Martine Workshop
Maurice Schaller, perfumier
Les Parfums de Rosine
La Coupe d'or spray bottle
1920–25
Hand-painted blown glass,
gold thread and rubber
Grasse, Musée international
de la Parfumerie, inv. Z 980

CAT. 142
Julien Viard (1883–1938),
sculptor-glassmaker
Henri Alméras (1892–1965),
perfumier
Les Parfums de Rosine
Le Bosquet d'Apollon perfume
1922
Glass and metal
Palais Galliera–Musée de la
Mode de la Ville de Paris
Inv. GAL1986.209.1

CAT. 143 [REPR. P. 169]
Marie Vassilieff (1884–1957)
Julien Viard (1883–1938),
sculptor-glassmaker
Henri Alméras (1892–1965),
perfumier
Les Parfums de Rosine
Arlequinade perfume
1923
Glass, bakelite and fabric
Grasse, Musée international
de la Parfumerie, inv. 82.9

CAT. 144
Julien Viard (1883–1938),
sculptor-glassmaker
Henri Alméras (1892–1965),
perfumier
Les Parfums de Rosine
1925 perfume
Created for the International
Exhibition of Modern
Decorative and Industrial Arts
1925
Pressed and moulded glass,
fabric
Fragonard Parfumeur,
inv. FF094

CAT. 145
Les Parfums de Rosine
1925 eau de toilette
1925
Glass
Palais Galliera–Musée de
la Mode de la Ville de Paris,
inv. GAL2025.E.12.1

CAT. 146
Mario Simon
Henri Alméras (1892–1965),
perfumier
Les Parfums de Rosine
Hahna, l'étrange fleur
perfume and box
1928
Glass, metal, cardboard and
paper
Palais Galliera–Musée de
la Mode de la Ville de Paris,
inv. GAL2004.845.1

Fine art

An artistic education

CAT. 147
Charles Reutlinger (1816–88)
Charles Frederick Worth with
Scrubs
After 1881
Albumen print
Paris, Musée des Arts
décoratifs, gift of Pierre
and Anne Gugliemi, 2005,
inv. Ac WORT 15

CAT. 148
F. Camel
Gaston Worth
After 1883
Albumen print
Paris, Musée des Arts
décoratifs, gift of Pierre
and Anne Gugliemi, 2005,
inv. Ac WORT 29-2

CAT. 149
Jules Chéret (1836–1932)
Paris Exposition of 1889
1889
Lithograph
Paris, Musée des Arts
décoratifs, inv. 10691.3

CAT. 150
Leonetto Cappiello (1875–
1942)
*The couturier Worth with
beard and sideburns, wearing
a top hat*
1896–1905
Graphite
Paris, Musée d'Orsay
On long-term loan to the
Graphic Arts department at
the Musée du Louvre
Inv. RF 37825, Recto

CAT. 151
René Péan (1875–1955)
Paris Exposition of 1900
1898
Lithograph
Paris, Musée des Arts
décoratifs, inv. 19167.1

CAT. 152
Paul Poiret (1879–1944)
First Empire hussar costume
c. 1900
Graphite, black ink and
gouache on vellum paper
Paris, Musée des Arts
décoratifs, UFAC Collection,
1995

CAT. 153
Reutlinger
Cléo de Mérode
c. 1900
Gelatin silver print
Paris, Musée des Arts
décoratifs, UFAC Collection,
1995

CAT. 154
Reutlinger
Cléo de Mérode
c. 1900
Gelatin silver print
Paris, Musée des Arts
décoratifs, UFAC Collection,
1995

CAT. 155
Paul Helleu (1859–1927)
*Louise Chéruit wearing a fur
collar*
c. 1901
Drypoint on vellum paper
Musée Bonnat-Helleu, musée
des Beaux-Arts de Bayonne,
inv. 2017.4.3

CAT. 156
Leonetto Cappiello (1875–
1942)
*Full-length portrait of Jacques
Doucet*
1903
Graphite, charcoal and
gouache on paper
Avignon, Musée Angladon–
Jacques Doucet Collection,
inv. 1996-K-78

CAT. 157
Henry Tenré (1854–1926)
*Small reception room, known
as 'Fragonard', in Jacques
Doucet's home, rue Spontini*
1911
Oil on wood
Avignon, Musée Angladon–
Jacques Doucet Collection,
inv. 1996-K-83

CAT. 158 [REPR. P. 20]
André Derain (1880–1954)
Portrait of Paul Poiret
1915
Oil on canvas
Grenoble, Musée de
Grenoble, inv. MG 2756

CAT. 159
Man Ray (Emmanuel
Radnitsky) (1890–1976)
Jacques Doucet
1926
Gelatin silver print
Paris, Musée des Arts
décoratifs, UFAC Collection,
1995

The couturier's early years

CAT. 160 [REPR. PP. 69, 73 & 77]
Paul Iribe (1883-1935)
*Les Robes de Paul Poiret
racontées par Paul Iribe*,
Paris: Paul Poiret, 1908
Copy no. 78/250
Photogravure and pochoir
print
Paris, library of the Musée des
Arts décoratifs

CAT. 161
Delphi
Paul Poiret in the fitting room
of his couture house, 107 rue
du Faubourg-Saint-Honoré
c. 1909
Gelatin silver print [March
1973], from a positive
Paris, Bibliothèque nationale
de France, Prints and
Photography department,
inv. OA-702-FOL

CAT. 162
Culver Pictures
Paul Poiret in the garden of
the private mansion on the
avenue d'Antin
c. 1910
Gelatin silver print
Private collection

CAT. 163
Georges Lepape (1887–1971)
*The private mansion on the
avenue d'Antin, home of
M Paul Poiret*
1910
Print with watercolour
Palais Galliera–Musée de
la Mode de la Ville de Paris,
gift of Madame Cabarrus,
inv. GAL2008.26.01

CAT. 164
Henri Manuel (1874–1947)
Paul Poiret
c. 1913
Gelatin silver print
Bibliothèque nationale de
France, Performing Arts
department, inv. 4-ICO-
PER-21189

CAT. 165
Jean-Joseph Crotti (1878–
1958)
Portrait of Paul Poiret
c. 1914
Pencil on paper
Palais Galliera–Musée de
la Mode de la Ville de Paris,
inv. GALK1293

CAT. 166 [REPR. P. 225]
Delphi
St Catherine's Day
celebration at Poiret's home
c. 1920
Gelatin silver print
Paris, Musée des Arts
décoratifs, UFAC Collection,
1995

CAT. 167
Séeberger brothers
Paul Poiret
1927
Gelatin silver print [1975],
printed from the negative
Paris, Bibliothèque nationale
de France, Prints and
Photography department,
inv. OA-38 (181)-4

CAT. 168
Thérèse Bonney (1894–1978)
Paul Poiret and the model
Renée in his fashion house
at 1 rond-point des Champs-
Élysées
1927
Gelatin silver bromide print
by the ARCP [198.], printed
from the negative
Bibliothèque historique
de la ville,
inv. 4C-EPF-006-00933

Artistic collaborations

CAT. 169
André Derain (1880–1954)
*Portrait of Maurice de
Vlaminck*
1905
Oil on card
Maison Vlaminck Endowment
Fund Collection

CAT. 170
Paul Iribe (1883–1935)
Paul Poiret (1879–1944)
Book of 34 preparatory
sketches for *Les Robes de
Paul Poiret racontées par
Paul Iribe*
1908
Graphite and colour pencil
on textured paper
Binding made from blue
Nattier suede
Palais Galliera–Musée de la
Mode de la Ville de Paris, gift
of the Vogue Paris Foundation
2016, inv. GAL2018.01.80

CAT. 171 [REPR. P. 6]
Paul Iribe (1883–1935)
Studies of a rose
c. 1910
Graphite and gouache
on vellum paper (3 sheets)
Paris, Musée des Arts
décoratifs, purchased with
financial support from
Johannes Huth, via the
museum's International
Council, 2018, inv. 2018.66.1,
inv. 2018.66.4 and
inv. 2018.66.8

CAT. 172 [REPR. P. 80]
Victor Lhuer (1876–1952)
Sketch of a dress for Paul
Poiret
c. 1910
Graphite and watercolour
on vellum paper
Paris, Musée des Arts
décoratifs, gift of the artist,
1943–50, inv. RI 2019.8.3.58

CAT. 173
Victor Lhuer (1876–1952)
Designs for Paul Poiret
c. 1910–25
Graphite pencil, watercolour,
gouache, black ink, brown ink,
white highlights and fabric
swatches on vellum paper (8
sheets)
Paris, Musée des Arts
décoratifs, gift of the artist,
1943–50, inv. RI 2019.8.3.1,
inv. RI 2019.8.3.11,
inv. RI 2019.8.3.16,
inv. RI 2019.8.3.24,
inv. RI 2019.8.3.34,
inv. RI 2019.8.3.35,
inv. RI 2019.8.3.54 and
inv. RI 2019.8.3.66

CAT. 174
André Édouard Marty (1882–
1974)
Fashion illustration
1910
Graphite, ink and white
gouache on vellum paper
Paris, Musée des Arts
décoratifs, inv. PR 2019.7.20

CAT. 175
Paul Iribe (1883–1935)
The 'Iribe Rose'
1910
Graphite, colour pencil,
gouache, Indian ink and
fabric swatches on paper
Grenoble, Musée de
Grenoble, inv. MG 2553 to
inv. MG 2557

CAT. 176
Georges Lepape (1887–1971)
Book of sketches for Paul
Poiret, *Battick* coat
c. 1911
Graphite on vellum paper
Paris, Musée des Arts
décoratifs, UFAC Collection,
1995

CAT. 177
Raoul Dufy (1877–1953)
The Little Factory
1911
Indian ink on paper
Paris, Centre Pompidou–
Musée national d'art
moderne–Centre de création
industrielle, bequest of
Madame Raoul Dufy, 1963,
inv. AM 2923 D (301 V)

CAT. 178 [REPR. PP. 35 & 196]
Georges Lepape (1887–1971)
*Les Choses de Paul Poiret
vues par Georges Lepape*
Paris, Paul Poiret, 1911
Copy no. 176/300
Phototype and pochoir print
Paris, library of the Musée des
Arts décoratifs

CAT. 179
Raoul Dufy (1877–1953)
The Little Factory
1911
Indian ink on paper
Paris, Centre Pompidou–
Musée national d'art
moderne–Centre de création
industrielle, bequest of
Madame Raoul Dufy, 1963,
inv. AM 2923 D (301 R)

CAT. 180
Raoul Dufy (1877–1953)
Semainier
1911
Pochoir print (7 pages)
Paris, library of the Musée des
Arts décoratifs

CAT. 181
José de Zamora (1889–1971)
Designs for Paul Poiret
c. 1913
Watercolour and pencil
on tracing paper (3 sheets)
Diktats Bookstore

CAT. 182
Erté (Romain de Tirtoff)
(1892–1990)
Designs for Paul Poiret
c. 1913–14
Graphite pencil, black ink,
gouache, grease pencil and
fabric swatches on vellum
paper (4 sheets)
Paris, Musée des Arts
décoratifs, inv. PR 2021.7.3
to inv. PR 2021.7.5 and
inv. PR 2021.7.9

CAT. 183
Georges Lepape (1887–1971)
'*L'Arbre en fleurs*, summer
dress by Paul Poiret'
Gazette du Bon Ton, no. 5,
March 1913, plate 4
Paris, Librairie centrale des
Beaux-Arts, 1913
Photogravure and pochoir
print
Paris, library of the Musée des
Arts décoratifs

CAT. 184
Georges Lepape (1887–1971)
'*Les Cerises*, countryside
ensemble by Paul Poiret'
Gazette du Bon Ton, no. 7,
May 1913, plate 9
Paris, Librairie centrale des
Beaux-Arts, 1913
Photogravure and pochoir
print
Paris, library of the Musée des
Arts décoratifs

CAT. 185
Georges Lepape (1887–1971)
'*Les Citrons*, summer dress by
Paul Poiret'
Gazette du Bon Ton, no. 8,
June 1913, plate 8
Paris, Librairie centrale des
Beaux-Arts, 1913
Photogravure and pochoir
print
Paris, library of the Musée des
Arts décoratifs

CAT. 186
Georges Lepape (1887–1971)
'*Au clair de la lune*, coat by
Paul Poiret'
Gazette du Bon Ton, no. 9,
July 1913, plate 6
Paris, Librairie centrale des
Beaux-Arts, 1913
Photogravure and pochoir
print
Paris, library of the Musée des
Arts décoratifs

CAT. 187
Georges Lepape (1887–1971)
'*Il fait trop chaud*, summer hat
by Paul Poiret'
Gazette du Bon Ton, no. 10,
August 1913, plate 6
Paris, Librairie centrale des
Beaux-Arts, 1913
Photogravure and pochoir
print
Paris, library of the Musée des
Arts décoratifs

CAT. 188
Georges Lepape (1887–1971)
'*Dieu! Qu'il fait froid…*, winter
coat by Paul Poiret'
Gazette du Bon Ton, no. 12,
October 1913, plate 4
Paris, Librairie centrale des
Beaux-Arts, 1913
Photogravure and pochoir
print
Paris, library of the Musée des
Arts décoratifs

CAT. 189 [REPR. P. 43]
Anonymous
Paul Poiret in military uniform
c. 1914
Gelatin silver print
Paris, Musée des Arts
décoratifs

CAT. 190
Georges Lepape (1887–1971)
'*Voici l'orage*, afternoon dress
by Paul Poiret'
Gazette du Bon Ton, no. 6,
July 1920, plate 45
Paris, Librairie centrale des
Beaux-Arts, 1920
Photogravure and pochoir
print
Paris, library of the Musée des
Arts décoratifs

CAT. 191 [REPR. P. 38]
Anonymous
Photograph of Paul Poiret
design *Tulipes stylisées* for
the legal registry
Motif by Raoul Dufy (1877–
1953) for Bianchini-Férier
c. 1921
Gelatin silver print
Paris, Musée des Arts
décoratifs, c. 1945

CAT. 192
Delphi
Photograph of Paul Poiret
design *Ténacité* for the legal
registry
Motif by Raoul Dufy (1877–
1953) for Bianchini-Férier
1921
Gelatin silver print
Paris, Musée des Arts
décoratifs, c. 1945

CAT. 193
Delphi
Photograph of Paul Poiret
design *Valmer* for the legal
registry
Motif by Raoul Dufy (1877–
1953) for Bianchini-Férier
1921
Gelatin silver print
Paris, Musée des Arts
décoratifs, c. 1945

CAT. 194
Gilbert René
Photograph of Paul Poiret
design *Tournoi* for the legal
registry
Motif by Raoul Dufy (1877–
1953) for Bianchini-Férier
1921
Gelatin silver print
Paris, Musée des Arts
décoratifs, c. 1945

CAT. 195
André Édouard Marty (1882–
1974)
'*C'est moi*, coat by Paul Poiret'
Gazette du Bon Ton, no. 5,
1922, plate 39
Paris, Publications Lucien
Vogel, Condé Nast, 1922
Photogravure and pochoir
print
Paris, library of the Musée des
Arts décoratifs

CAT. 196
Gilbert René
Photograph of Paul Poiret
design *Flou-Tchéou* for the
legal registry
Motif by Raoul Dufy (1877–
1953) for Bianchini-Férier
1922
Gelatin silver print
Paris, Musée des Arts
décoratifs, c. 1945

CAT. 197
Gilbert René
Photograph of Paul Poiret
design *Fraise à la crème* for
the legal registry
Motif by Raoul Dufy (1877–
1953) for Bianchini-Férier
1922
Gelatin silver print
Paris, Musée des Arts
décoratifs, c. 1945

CAT. 198 [REPR. P. 27]
Germaine Krull (1897–1985)
Publicity shot for Paul Poiret
1926
Gelatin silver print
Paris, Centre Pompidou–
Musée national d'art
moderne–Centre de création
industrielle, purchased with
financial support from Yves
Rocher, 2011, inv. AM2012-
3875

**Dressing dancers and
actresses for the city
and the stage**

CAT. 199 [REPR. P. 30]
Léon Bakst (1866–1924)
Set design for the ballet
Shéhérazade
1910
Graphite, watercolour,
gouache and gold highlights
on vellum paper
Paris, Musée des Arts
décoratifs, purchased
by the state; given to
Les Arts Décoratifs in 2008,
inv. 2008.56.122

CAT. 200
Talbot studio
Jane Renouardt wearing
a design by Paul Poiret
1911–14
Gelatin silver print
Paris, Musée des Arts
décoratifs, donated by
Jas Hennessy & Co, 2007,
inv. 2007.38.576

CAT. 201
Talbot studio
Mademoiselle de Lignac
wearing a design by Paul
Poiret
1911–14
Gelatin silver print
Paris, Musée des Arts
décoratifs, donated by
Jas Hennessy & Co, 2007,
inv. 2007.38.1992

CAT. 202
Talbot studio
Mademoiselle Landry wearing
a design by Paul Poiret
1911–14
Gelatin silver print
Paris, Musée des Arts
décoratifs, donated by
Jas Hennessy & Co, 2007,
inv. 2007.38.1991

CAT. 203 [REPR. PP. 63 & 227]
Talbot studio
Michelle Frondaie wearing
a design by Paul Poiret
1911–14
Gelatin silver print
Paris, Musée des Arts
décoratifs, donated by
Jas Hennessy & Co, 2007,
inv. 2007.38.1994

CAT. 204
Talbot studio
Tamara Karsavina as Zobeïde
in *Shéhérazade*
1911–14
Gelatin silver print
Paris, Musée des Arts
décoratifs, donated by
Jas Hennessy & Co, 2007,
inv. 2007.38.1369

CAT. 205 [REPR. P. 222]
Talbot studio
Tamara Karsavina as Zobeïde
in *Shéhérazade*
1911–14
Gelatin silver print
Paris, Musée des Arts
décoratifs, donated by
Jas Hennessy & Co, 2007,
inv. 2007.38.1368

CAT. 206
André Dunoyer de Segonzac
(1884–1974)
Isadora Duncan's students
c. 1911
Ink on vellum paper
Paris, Musée des Arts
décoratifs, gift of André Vera,
1959, inv. 38288

CAT. 207
André Dunoyer de Segonzac
(1884–1974)
Isadora Duncan
1911
Indian ink on vellum paper
Paris, Musée d'Art moderne,
inv. AMD 352

CAT. 208
André Dunoyer de Segonzac
(1884–1974)
Isadora Duncan
1911
Indian ink on vellum paper
Paris, Musée d'Art modern,
inv. AMD 353

CAT. 209
Léon Bakst (1866–1924)
Bacchante
1911
Graphite pencil, charcoal and
gouache on paper
Paris, Centre Pompidou–
Musée national d'art
moderne–Centre de création
industrielle, gift of Mr and
Mrs Léon Baratz in memory of
Mr and Mrs A. Dobry, inv. AM
2561 D

CAT. 210
Erté (Romain de Tirtoff)
(1892–1990)
Dancers
Ink, watercolour and gold
highlights on vellum paper
Paris, Musée des Arts
décoratifs, purchased with
financial support from the
Friends of the Musée des Arts
décoratifs, 2021, inv. 2021.55.1

CAT. 211 [REPR. P. 136]
Georges Lepape (1887–1971)
'*Lassitude*, dinner dress by
Paul Poiret'
Gazette du Bon Ton, no. 1,
1912, plate 8
Paris, Librairie centrale des
Beau-Arts, 1912
Photogravure and pochoir
print
Paris, library of the Musée des
Arts décoratifs

CAT. 212
Jean Cocteau (1889–1963)
Diaghilev and Nijinsky
backstage during
Shéhérazade
1912
Pen and ink on paper
Bibliothèque nationale de
France, Performing Arts
department, inv. FOL-O ICO-
124

CAT. 213
Léon Bakst (1866–1924)
Sacred dance
1912
Watercolour, graphite and
gold paint on paper
Paris, Centre Pompidou–
Musée national d'art
moderne–Centre de création
industrielle, purchase, 1982,
inv. AM 1982-427

CAT. 214
Georges Lepape (1887–1971)
'*Serais-je en avance?*, theatre
coat by Paul Poiret'
Gazette du Bon Ton, no. 2,
December 1912, plate 6
Paris, Librairie centrale des
Beaux-Arts, 1912
Photogravure and pochoir
print
Paris, library of the Musée des
Arts décoratifs

CAT. 215
Max Jacob (1876–1944)
*Two elegant women (Le
Minaret* by Paul Poiret)
c. 1913
Pen and brown ink on paper
Paris, Musée d'Orsay, gift
of Jean Cahen-Salvador
in memory of Marie-Paule
Fontenelle-Pomaret, 1976,
on loan to the Musée des
Beaux-Arts, Quimper,
inv. D.76-2-1-1

CAT. 216
Edward Steichen (1879–1973)
Isadora Duncan
1913
Photogravure
Paris, Musée d'Orsay,
inv. PHO 1981 32 11

CAT. 217
Georges Lepape (1887–1971)
'*Laquelle?*, evening gown by
Paul Poiret'
Gazette du Bon Ton, no. 11,
September 1913, plate 5
Paris, Librairie centrale des
Beaux-Arts, 1913
Photogravure and pochoir
print
Paris, library of the Musée des
Arts décoratifs

CAT. 218
Delphi
Mademoiselle Spinelly
wearing a design by Paul
Poiret
1919–20
Gelatin silver print
Paris, Musée des Arts
décoratifs, UFAC Collection,
1995, gift of Andrée Spinelly

CAT. 219 [REPR. P. 65]
Lumière NY
Mademoiselle Spinelly
wearing a design by Paul
Poiret
1920
Gelatin silver print
Paris, Musée des Arts
décoratifs, UFAC Collection,
1995, gift of Andrée Spinelly

CAT. 220
Natalia Goncharova (1881–
1962)
Spanish Woman with a Fan
c. 1920
Oil on canvas
Paris, Centre Pompidou–
Musée national d'art
moderne–Centre de création
industrielle, purchase, 1951,
inv. AM 3111 P

CAT. 221
Léon Bakst (1866–1924)
Caryathis
1920
Lithograph
Paris, Musée des Arts
décoratifs, gift of Suzanne
Léon-Tézenas, 1978, inv. 17907

CAT. 222
Séeberger brothers
Mademoiselle Spinelly
wearing a dress by Paul Poiret,
with print by Raoul Dufy, at
the Deauville Grand Prix
15 August 1920
Gelatin silver print
Bibliothèque nationale
de France, Prints and
Photography department,
inv. OA-38 (5)-4 (20706)

Travel for business and inspiration

CAT. 223
Armand-Albert Rateau
(1882–1938)
Le Nomade barge design
1913
Black print with watercolour
on vellum paper
Paris, Musée des Arts
décoratifs, gift of François
Rateau, 1996, inv. 995.129.2.7

CAT. 224
Charles Martin (1884–1934)
'*Hindoustan*, coat-dress by
Paul Poiret'
Gazette du Bon Ton, no. 8.
1920, plate 59
Paris, Éditions Lucien Vogel,
1920
Photogravure and pochoir
print
Paris, library of the Musée des
Arts décoratifs

CAT. 225
Georges Lepape (1887–1971)
Paul Poiret, poster for his 'Tour
of Europe'
1920
Lithograph on paper mounted
on card
Boulogne-Billancourt, Musée
des Années Trente / MA-30,
inv. 1998.1.11

CAT. 226 [REPR. P. 196]
Charles Martin (1884–1934)
'*Tanger or The Charms of
Exile*, afternoon dress and
shawl by Paul Poiret'
Gazette du Bon Ton, no. 1,
January–February 1920,
plate 7
Paris, Éditions Lucien Vogel,
1920
Photogravure and pochoir
print
Paris, library of the Musée des
Arts décoratifs

CAT. 227
Charles Martin (1884–1934)
'*Relation*, sports coat by Paul
Poiret'
Gazette du Bon Ton, no. 1,
1921, plate 6
Paris, Éditions Lucien Vogel,
1921
Photogravure and pochoir
print
Paris, library of the Musée des
Arts décoratifs

CAT. 228
Erté (Romain de Tirtoff)
(1892–1990)
Dream Voyage
1923
Gouache on card
Paris, Musée des Arts
décoratifs, purchased with
financial support from the
Friends of the Musée des Arts
décoratifs, 2019, inv. 2019.40.1

CAT. 229
Marianne Breslauer (1909–
2001)
Paul Poiret
1929
Gelatin silver print
Paris, Musée des Arts
décoratifs, purchased with
financial support from the
Partners of the Musée des
Arts décoratifs, particularly
Arkhenum, 2023, inv. 2023.97.1

Expanding the mind through travel

CAT. 230
Victor Lhuer (1876–1952)
Culotte-dress designs for Paul
Poiret
c. 1911
Graphite, watercolour and
gouache on vellum paper
Paris, Musée des Arts
décoratifs, gift of the artist,
1943–50, inv. RI 2019.8.3.7

CAT. 231
Victor Lhuer (1876–1952)
Culotte-dress designs for Paul
Poiret
c. 1911
Graphite, watercolour and
gouache on vellum paper
Paris, Musée des Arts
décoratifs, gift of the artist,
1943–50, inv. RI 2019.8.3.20

Organizing parties and performances

CAT. 232
Hélène Perdriat (1889–1969)
Mademoiselle Tirka, dancer
Undated
Oil on canvas
Paris, Centre Pompidou–
Musée national d'art
moderne–Centre de création
industrielle, donated by
Mr Charles Wakefield-Mori,
1939, on loan to the Musée
des Beaux-Arts de Menton
since 1961, inv. AM 3806 P

CAT. 233
Victor Lhuer (1876–1952)
Portrait of Kees van Dongen
Undated
Graphite on vellum paper
Paris, Musée des Arts
décoratifs, gift of the artist,
1943–50, inv. RI 2019.8.18.50

CAT. 234 [REPR. P. 35]
Georges Lepape (1887–1971)
Denise Poiret at the 'Thousand
and Second Night'
1911
Graphite, gouache, black ink
and silver highlights on vellum
paper
Private collection

CAT. 235
Georges Lepape (1887–1971)
Invitation to the 'Thousand
and Second Night' party,
addressed to the Boutreux
1911
Photomechanical process
Musée Carnavalet–
Histoire de Paris,
inv. CARGMOE017425

CAT. 236 [REPR. P. 34]
Raoul Dufy (1877–1953)
Combined invitation and
programme for the 'Thousand
and Second Night'
1911
Woodcut with gouache
Bibliothèque nationale de
France, Performing Arts
department, inv. APLAT FOL-
ED-88(3)

CAT. 237
Victor Lhuer (1876–1952)
Victor Lhuer at the 'Thousand
and Second Night' party
1911
Graphite and watercolour
on vellum paper
Paris, Musée des Arts
décoratifs, gift of the artist,
1943–50, inv. RI 2019.8.3.29

CAT. 238
Guy-Pierre Fauconnet (1882–
1920)
Poster for the 'Feast of
Bacchus'
1912
Ink on paper
Chelles, Musée archéologique
de Chelles Alfred-Bonno,
inv. 63-5-2

CAT. 239
Guy-Pierre Fauconnet (1882–
1920)
Programme for the 'Feast of
Bacchus'
1912
Ink on paper
Chelles, Musée archéologique
de Chelles Alfred-Bonno,
inv. 63-5-1

CAT. 240
Kees Van Dongen (1877–1968)
Two women
c. 1913
Oil on canvas
Paris, Musée d'Art modern,
inv. AMVP 1904

CAT. 241
Georges Lepape (1887–1971)
'*Les Jardins de Versailles*,
costume by Paul Poiret in the
style of Louis XIV'
Gazette du Bon Ton, no. 4,
February 1913, plate 5
Paris, Librairie centrale des
Beaux-Arts, 1913
Photogravure and pochoir
print
Paris, library of the Musée des
Arts décoratifs

CAT. 242
Bernard Boutet de Monvel
(1881–1949)
*Boussingault painting and
Dunoyer de Segonzac*
1914
Oil on canvas
Pau, Musée des Beaux-Arts,
inv. 79.5.1

CAT. 243
Guy Arnoux (1886–1951)
Paul Poiret, 'The new dancer
at the Oasis'
c. 1919–1920
Watercolour on paper
Diktats Bookstore

CAT. 244
André Édouard Marty (1882–
1974)
'*À l'Oasis*, la jupe lumineuse'
*Modes et manières
d'aujourd'hui*, 1919
Paris, Pierre Corrard
collection, 1919
Phototype and pochoir print
Copy no. 168
Paris, library of the Musée des
Arts décoratifs

CAT. 245 [REPR. PP. 139 & 180]
Delphi
Denise Poiret wearing the
dress *Mythe* or *Faune* by Paul
Poiret
She is standing in front of
Maiastra by Constantin
Brancusi (1876–1957)
1919
Gelatin silver print
Paris, Musée des Arts
décoratifs, UFAC Collection,
1995

CAT. 246
Georges Lepape (1887–1971)
'Dancing, evening coat by
Paul Poiret'
Gazette du Bon Ton, no. 2,
March 1920, plate 12
Paris, Éditions Lucien Vogel,
1920
Photogravure and pochoir
print
Paris, library of the Musée des
Arts décoratifs

CAT. 247 [REPR. P. 226]
André Édouard Marty (1882–
1974)
'*À l'Oasis ou la voûte
pneumatique*, evening gown
by Paul Poiret'
Gazette du Bon Ton, no. 7,
1921, plate 53
Paris, Éditions Lucien Vogel,
1921
Photogravure and pochoir
print
Paris, library of the Musée des
Arts décoratifs

CAT. 248
Jacqueline Marval (1866–
1932)
The Dancer of Notre-Dame
1921
Oil on canvas
Private collection, courtesy
of the Comité Jacqueline
Marval, Paris

CAT. 249 [REPR. P. 181]
Kees Van Dongen (1877–1968)
Self-Portrait as Neptune
1922
Oil on canvas
Paris, Centre Pompidou–
Musée national d'art
moderne–Centre de création
industrielle, gift of the artist
or purchased from the artist,
1924–1927, inv. LUX.0.182 P

CAT. 250
Maurice Crozet (1896–1978)
Portrait of Paul Poiret
27 June 1922
Graphite pencil and black
pencil on Chinese paper
mounted on cardstock
Palais Galliera–Musée de
la Mode de la Ville de Paris,
inv. GAL2024.0.006

CAT. 251
Hans Bendix (1898–1984)
Paul Poiret
1925
Charcoal, pen and black ink
on vellum paper
Paris, Musée des Arts
décoratifs, gift of the artist,
1984, inv. 55475

CAT. 252
Paul Guillaume (1891–1934)
Paul Poiret
1927
Oil on card
Paris, Musée Carnavalet –
Histoire de Paris, inv. P1992

CAT. 253
Pierre de Belay (1890–1947)
Portrait of Paul Poiret
1937
Charcoal on paper mounted
on card
Quimper, collection of the
Musée des Beaux-Arts,
France, nv. 74-42-1

CAT. 254
Marie Vassilieff (1884–1957)
Portrait of Paul Poiret
1950
Gouache on paper and card
Claude Bernès collection

Family portraits

CAT. 255
Henri Manuel (1874–1947)
Denise Poiret wearing the
dress *Sagesse* by Paul Poiret
1910
Gelatin silver print
Paris, Musée des Arts décoratifs,
UFAC Collection, 1995

CAT. 256 [REPR. P. 181]
Raoul Dufy (1877–1953)
The Shepherdess wall
hanging
1910
Painted and block-printed
on linen
Private collection

CAT. 257
Talbot studio
Photograph of Nicole Groult
design for the legal registry
1911–14
Gelatin silver print
Paris, Musée des Arts
décoratifs, donated by
Jas Hennessy & Co, 2007,
inv. 2007.38.1816

CAT. 258
Talbot studio
Photograph of Nicole Groult
design for the legal registry
1911–14
Gelatin silver print
Paris, Musée des Arts
décoratifs, donated by
Jas Hennessy & Co, 2007,
inv. 2007.38.1817

CAT. 259
Talbot studio
Photograph of Nicole Groult
design for the legal registry
1911–14
Gelatin silver print
Paris, Musée des Arts
décoratifs, donated by
Jas Hennessy & Co, 2007,
inv. 2007.38.2709

CAT. 260
Anonymous
Denise Poiret wearing
a design by Paul Poiret
1912
Gelatin silver print
Paris, Musée des Arts décoratifs,
UFAC Collection, 1995

CAT. 261 [REPR. PP. 43 & 197]
Geisler & Baumann
Denise Poiret wearing an
ensemble by Paul Poiret at the
Plaza Hotel, New York
1913
Gelatin silver prints (3
photographs)
Paris, Musée des Arts
décoratifs, UFAC Collection,
1995

CAT. 262
Georges Lepape (1887–1971)
Le Jaloux, evening gown by
Paul Poiret
1913
Gouache on paper
Thomas Fritsch Collection, Paris

CAT. 263
Anonymous
Denise Poiret
c. 1914
Gelatin silver print
Paris, Musée des Arts
décoratifs, UFAC Collection,
1995

CAT. 264 [REPR. P. 224]
Anonymous
Denise Poiret and her children
c. 1914
Gelatin silver print
Paris, Musée des Arts décoratifs,
UFAC Collection, 1995

CAT. 265
Anonymous
Denise Poiret and her children
Martine and Colin, in the
garden of the Pavillon d'Antin
Denise is wearing the dress
Reine de Saba by Paul Poiret
c. 1914
Gelatin silver prints
(4 photographs)
Paris, Musée des Arts
décoratifs, UFAC Collection,
1995

CAT. 266
Anonymous
Denise Poiret wearing the dress
Reine Isabelle by Paul Poiret
in front of the Pavillon d'Antin.
She wore this ensemble for
the 'Party of Kings' (10 January
1914)
c. 1914
Gelatin silver print
Paris, Musée des Arts
décoratifs, UFAC Collection,
1995

CAT. 267
Anonymous
Paul Poiret and his children
c. 1914
Gelatin silver print
Paris, Musée des Arts
décoratifs, UFAC Collection,
1995

CAT. 268
Delphi
Denise Poiret wearing the
dress *Delphinium*, also known
as *Robe Bonheur*, by Paul
Poiret in the garden of the
Pavillon d'Antin
1915
Gelatin silver print
Paris, Musée des Arts
décoratifs, UFAC Collection,
1995

CAT. 269 [REPR. P. 224]
Denise Poiret (1886–1982)
Paul Poiret and his children at
the Pavillon du Butard while
he was on leave
1915–16
Gelatin silver print
Paris, Musée des Arts
décoratifs, UFAC Collection,
1995

CAT. 270
Delphi
Denise Poiret wearing the
dress *Mythe* or *Faune* by Paul
Poiret
1919
Gelatin silver print
Paris, Musée des Arts
décoratifs, UFAC Collection,
1995

CAT. 271 [REPR. P. 57]
Marie Laurencin (1883–1956)
Women with a Dove (self-
portrait of the artist with
Nicole Groult)
1919
Oil on canvas
Paris, Centre Pompidou–
Musée national d'art
moderne–Centre de création
industrielle, gift of Lord
Joseph Duveen, 1931
On loan to the Musée des
Arts décoratifs since 1985,
inv. LUX 104 P

CAT. 272 [REPR. P. 59]
Delphi
Denise Poiret wearing the
Paul Poiret dress *Linzeler*,
which she wore to a party
at the Oasis
1919–20
Gelatin silver print
Paris, Musée des Arts
décoratifs, UFAC Collection,
1995

CAT. 273
Delphi
Denise Poiret
c. 1920
Gelatin silver print
Paris, Musée des Arts
décoratifs, gift of Mr Alain
Charlemagne, son of Paul
Charlemagne and Agnès
Jallat, 2019, inv. 2019.116.45

CAT. 274
Delphi
Denise Poiret wearing
a design by Paul Poiret
c. 1920
Gelatin silver print
Paris, Musée des Arts
décoratifs, UFAC Collection,
1995

CAT. 275
Laure Albin-Guillot (Laure
Meifredy) (1879–1962)
André Groult
1925
Fresson print, mounted
on card
Paris, Centre Pompidou–
Musée national d'art
moderne–Centre de création
industrielle, purchase, 1981,
inv. AM 1988-677

CAT. 276
Man Ray (Emmanuel
Radnitsky) (1890–1976)
Marie Laurencin
1925
Gelatin silver print
Paris, Centre Pompidou–
Musée national d'art
moderne–Centre de création
industrielle, gift, 1994,
inv. AM 1994-394 (3762)

CAT. 277
Man Ray (Emmanuel
Radnitsky) (1890–1976)
Nicole Groult
1925
Gelatin silver print, contact
Paris, Centre Pompidou–
Musée national d'art
moderne–Centre de création
industrielle, gift, 1994,
inv. AM 1994-394 (3997)

CAT. 278
Thérèse Bonney (1894–1978)
Nicole Groult in her home at
29–31 rue d'Anjou
On the wall is *L'Ambassadrice*
by Marie Laurencin
1927
Gelatin silver bromide print
by the ARCP [198.], printed
from the negative
Bibliothèque historique
de la ville de Paris,
inv. 4C-EPF-006-00504

CAT. 279 [REPR. P. 184]
Charles Camoin (1879–1965)
Siesta by an Open Window
c. 1928
Oil on canvas
Alain Bras Collection

**Reinventing the decorative
arts**

CAT. 280
Agnès Jallat (1897–1988)
Sketchbook
Undated
Graphite and gouache
on vellum paper
Paris, Musée des Arts
décoratifs, gift of Mr Alain
Charlemagne, son of Paul
Charlemagne and Agnès
Jallat, 2023, inv. 2023.65.1.1-44

CAT. 281
Martiale Constantini
Martine Workshop
Portrait of Paul Poiret
Undated
Graphite on tracing paper
Paris, library of the Musée des
Arts décoratifs

CAT. 282
Martiale Constantini
Martine Workshop
Study
Undated
Graphite, ink and gouache
on vellum paper
Paris, Musée des Arts
décoratifs, UFAC Collection,
1995

CAT. 283 [REPR. P. 148]
Martiale Constantini
Sketchbook
Undated
Gouache on vellum paper
Paris, library of the Musée des
Arts décoratifs

CAT. 284 [REPR. P. 151]
Agnès Jallat (1897–1988)
Study for the Martine
Workshop
1911–1929
Graphite, gouache and gold
highlights on vellum paper
Paris, Musée des Arts
décoratifs, gift of Mr Alain
Charlemagne, son of Paul
Charlemagne and Agnès
Jallat, 2019, inv. 2019.116.7

CAT. 285 [REPR. P. 147]
Anonymous
Students from the Martine
School
1911–1929
Gelatin silver print
Bibliothèque nationale de
France, Performing Arts
department, inv. 4-ED-88(20)

CAT. 286
Guy-Pierre Fauconnet (1882–
1920)
Interior design projects
1912–1914
Ink and gouache on paper (3
sheets)
Chelles, Musée archéologique
de Chelles Alfred-Bonno,
inv. 70-7-2263, inv. 70-7-2202
and inv. 70-7-2376

CAT. 287
Paul Sérusier (1864–1927)
*Madame Sérusier with
a parasol*
1912
Various techniques on paper
mounted on canvas
Saint-Germain-en-Laye,
Musée départemental
Maurice-Denis,
inv. PMD 979.21.1

CAT. 288 [REPR. P. 151]
Agnès Jallat (1897–1988)
Study for the Martine
Workshops
1913
Gouache on vellum paper
Paris, Musée des Arts
décoratifs, gift of Mr Alain
Charlemagne, son of Paul
Charlemagne and Agnès
Jallat, 2019, inv. 2019.116.3

CAT. 289 [REPR. P. 150]
Agnès Jallat (1897–1988)
Study for the Martine
Workshops
1913
Gouache with silver highlights
on vellum paper
Paris, Musée des Arts
décoratifs, gift of Mr Alain
Charlemagne, son of Paul
Charlemagne and Agnès
Jallat, 2019, inv. 2019.116.2

CAT. 290 [REPR. P. 148]
Gabrielle Drapier, née
Rousselin
Martine Workshop
Les Radis wallpaper and linen
design
1913
Gouache on cardstock
Paris, Musée des Arts
décoratifs, purchased with
funds from the Fonds du
patrimoine–Ministère de
la Culture and thanks to
financial support from Michel
and Hélène David-Weill,
2005, inv. 2005.37.11

CAT. 291
Octave Lepage
Agnès Jallat
1914
Gelatin silver print
Paris, Musée des Arts
décoratifs, gift of Mr Alain
Charlemagne, son of Paul
Charlemagne and Agnès
Jallat, 2019, inv. 2019.116.34

CAT. 292
Martine Workshop
Société anonyme des Anciens
Établissements Desfossé &
Karth
Soleils, *Vases* and *Jacinthes*
wallpaper designs
1919–24
Gouache on continuous paper
Paris, Musée des Arts
décoratifs, former
collection of the I. Leroy
factory, purchase, 1982,
inv. RI 2022.3.772,
inv. RI 2022.3.781 and
inv. RI 2022.3.788

CAT. 293
Martine Workshop
Société anonyme des Anciens
Établissements Desfossé &
Karth
Soleils wallpaper
1919
Brushed texture background
and cylinder-printed
on continuous paper
Paris, Musée des Arts
décoratifs, former
collection of the I. Leroy
factory, purchase, 1982,
inv. 52391.10890.Z

CAT. 294
Martine Workshop
Société anonyme des Anciens
Établissements Desfossé &
Karth
Iris wallpaper
1924
Brushed texture background
and cylinder-printed
on continuous paper
Paris, Musée des Arts
décoratifs, purchased with
funds from the Fonds du
patrimoine–Ministère de
la Culture and thanks to
financial support from Michel
and Hélène David-Weill,
2005, inv. 2005.37.12

CAT. 295
Lipnitzki studio
Paul Poiret
1924
Gelatin silver print
Galerie Jacques Lacoste

Couturier and perfumier

CAT. 296
Guy-Pierre Fauconnet (1882–
1920)
Les Parfums de Rosine
Perfume bottles
1912–14
Ink on tracing paper
Chelles, Musée archéologique
de Chelles Alfred-Bonno,
inv. 70-2388

CAT. 297
Georges Lepape (1887–1971)
Les Parfums de Rosine
Poster design for the perfume
Mam'zelle Victoire
1916
Gouache and Indian ink
on paper
Grasse, Musée international
de la Parfumerie, inv. 93 24

CAT. 298
Georges Lepape (1887–1971)
'*Antinéa*, evening coat by
Paul Poiret'
Gazette du Bon Ton, no. 3,
April 1920, plate 19
Paris, Éditions Lucien Vogel
Photogravure and pochoir
print
Paris, library of the Musée des
Arts décoratifs

CAT. 299
Pierre Delbo (1894–1970)
Marie Vassilieff wearing
a Harlequin costume for the
'Bal banal'
1924
Gelatin silver print
Claude Bernès collection

CAT. 300
Marie Vassilieff (1884–1957)
Les Parfums de Rosine
Test print for an advert for the
perfume *Arlequin*
c. 1925
Print on paper
Claude Bernès collection

CAT. 301 [REPR. P. 169]
Pierre Delbo (1894–1970)
Arlequinade
1925
Gelatin silver print
Claude Bernès collection

A designer with many passions

CAT. 302
Paul Poiret (1879–1944)
Fish
Undated
Oil on canvas
Private collection, Paris

CAT. 303
Paul Poiret (1879–1944)
Landscape
1922
Oil on canvas
Private collection, Paris

CAT. 304 [REPR. P. 182]
Paul Poiret (1879–1944)
Still Life with Flowers
1927
Oil on canvas
Paris, Musée des Arts
décoratifs, purchased with
financial support from
the Friends of the Musée
des Arts décoratifs, 2024,
inv. 2024.76.1

CAT. 305
Paul Poiret (1879–1944)
Woman with puppet
1930
Oil on canvas
Private collection

CAT. 306
Paul Poiret (1879–1944)
Self-portrait
c. 1940
Oil on strip of wood
Sabine Rang des Adrets
collection

CAT. 307
Paul Poiret (1879–1944)
*Self-portrait dedicated to
Robert Piguet*
1944
Oil on canvas
Palais Galliera–Musée de
la Mode de la Ville de Paris,
gift of Mr Georges Marny,
inv. GAL1979.104.14.8

The barges of 1925: a synthesis of style

CAT. 308
André Édouard Marty (1882–
1974)
'*Le Dîner au château*, evening
coat by Paul Poiret'
Gazette du Bon Ton, no. 6,
1921, plate 46
Paris, Éditions Lucien Vogel,
1921
Photogravure and pochoir
print
Paris, library of the Musée des
Arts décoratifs

CAT. 309
André Édouard Marty (1882–
1974)
'*Un peu d'air*, evening gown
by Paul Poiret'
Gazette du Bon Ton, no. 3,
1921, plate 21
Paris, Éditions Lucien Vogel,
1921
Photogravure and pochoir
print
Paris, library of the Musée des
Arts décoratifs

CAT. 310
André Édouard Marty (1882–
1974)
'*En plein cœur*, evening gown
by Paul Poiret'
Gazette du Bon Ton, no. 2,
1922, plate 12
Paris, Publications Lucien
Vogel, Condé Nast, 1922
Photogravure and pochoir
print
Paris, library of the Musée des
Arts décoratifs

CAT. 311
André Édouard Marty (1882–
1974)
'*La Cendre de la cigarette*,
evening gown by Paul Poiret'
Gazette du Bon Ton, no. 10,
1922, plate 77
Paris, Publications Lucien
Vogel, Condé Nast, 1922
Photogravure and pochoir
print
Paris, library of the Musée des
Arts décoratifs

CAT. 312
André Édouard Marty (1882–
1974)
'*Après le diner, dans le parc*,
evening gown by Paul Poiret'
Gazette du Bon Ton, no. 9,
May 1924, plate 52
Paris, 1924
Photogravure and pochoir
print
Paris, library of the Musée des
Arts décoratifs

CAT. 313 [REPR. P. 112]
Auguste Léon (1857–1942)
Paul Poiret's barges for the
International Exhibition of
Modern Decorative and
Industrial Arts in 1925:
Amours, *Orgues* and *Délices*
Interior and exteriors of the
barge *Amours*, decorated
by Ronsin and Laverdet.
The fabrics and decorative
elements are by the Martine
Workshop
1925
Autochrome (4 images)
Collection Archives
de la Planète, Musée
départemental Albert-Kahn/
Département des Hauts-
de-Seine, inv. A47156S,
inv. A47159XS, inv. A 47 160
and inv. A45420S

Cinema: the art of modernity

CAT. 314
Fernand Léger (1881–1955)
Mechanical composition
(preparatory drawing for the
credits of *L'Inhumaine*)
c. 1920–23
Gouache and Indian ink
on paper
Biot, Musée national Fernand-
Léger, inv. MNFL 96033

CAT. 315
Fernand Léger (1881–1955)
Design for the credits of
L'Inhumaine
1923
Gouache, ink and pencil
on paper
Biot, Musée national Fernand-
Léger, inv. MNFL 96001

CAT. 316
Erik Aaes (1899–1966)
L'Inhumaine
1924
Lithograph
Cinémathèque Française,
inv. A001-019 / E700

Films

Cinema: the art of modernity

CAT. 317
L'Autre Aile (Henri Andréani,
1923, digitized to 2K from
the original nitrate negative).
Paris, Cinémathèque
Française

CAT. 318
Les Ombres qui passent
(Alexandre Volkoff, 1924).
Paris, Cinémathèque
Française

CAT. 319
L'Inhumaine (Marcel L'Herbier,
1924). FPA Classics Collection

CAT. 320
Le Fantôme du Moulin Rouge
(René Clair, 1925). FPA Classics
Collection

Bound documents

The couturier's early years

CAT. 321
George Barbier (1882–1932)
Cover of *Les Modes*
magazine, April 1912
Paris, Manzi, Joyant and Cie,
1912
Photogravure
Paris, library of the Musée des
Arts décoratifs

Artistic collaborations

CAT. 322
Guillaume Apollinaire
(1880–1918)
Raoul Dufy (1877–1953)
*Le Bestiaire ou Cortège
d'Orphée*
Woodcut
Paris, library of the Musée des
Arts décoratifs

Dressing dancers and actresses for the city and the stage

CAT. 323
Official programmes from the
Ballets Russes
Paris, M. de Brunhoff, 1910–12
Photogravure
Paris, library of the Musée des
Arts décoratifs

REINVENTING THE DECORATIVE ARTS

CAT. 324
Exhibition catalogue 'Tapis,
paravents et travaux de
l'École Martine' at the Galerie
Barbazanges (18–30 April
1921)
The catalogue is scented
with *Le Fruit défendu* by Les
Parfums de Rosine.
Paris, Musée des Arts
décoratifs, UFAC Collection,
1995

A designer with many passions

CAT. 325
Paul Poiret (1879–1944)
*Pan. Annuaire du luxe à Paris,
an 1928*
Paris, Devambez, 1927
Photogravure
Paris, library of the Musée des
Arts décoratifs

CAT. 326
Paul Poiret (1879–1944)
Pierre Fau (1888–1960),
illustrator
*Popolôrepô. Morceaux choisis
par un imbécile et illustrés
par un autre*
Paris, Éditions Jonquières,
1927
Diktats Bookstore

CAT. 327 [REPR. PP. 172 & 173]
Paul Poiret (1879–1944)
Sébastien Voirol (1870–1930)
Marie Alix, illustrator
*107 recettes ou curiosités
culinaires recueillies par Paul
Poiret, président honoraire
du club des 'Purs Cent',
suivies de quelques pages de
publicité gratuite*
Paris, H. Jonquières, 1928
Paris, library of the Musée des
Arts décoratifs

CAT. 328
Paul Poiret (1879–1944)
En habillant l'époque
Paris, Bernard Grasset, 1930
Typography
Paris, library of the Musée des
Arts décoratifs

CAT. 329
Paul Poiret (1879–1944)
Revenez-y
Third edition
Paris, Librairie Gallimard, 1932
Paris, library of the Musée des
Arts décoratifs

CAT. 330
Paul Poiret (1879–1944)
Art et Phynance
Paris, Éditions Lutetia, 1934
Paris, library of the Musée des
Arts décoratifs

**The barges of 1925:
a synthesis of style**

CAT. 331 [REPR. P. 173]
Menu for the opening dinner
on the barge *Délices*
24 April 1925
Imprimerie Coquemer
Typography
Paris, library of the Musée des
Arts décoratifs

Publicity
material

The couturier's early years

CAT. 332
Bernard Naudin (1876–1946)
Advertising card for Paul
Poiret
c. 1906
Woodcut
Paris, library of the Musée des
Arts décoratifs

**Reinventing the decorative
arts**

CAT. 333
Raoul Dufy (1877–1953)
Label for the Martine
boutique
c. 1920
Ink on paper
Paris, Musée des Arts
décoratifs, UFAC Collection,
1995

The couturier and perfumier

CAT. 334 [REPR. P. 4]
Mario Simon
Les Parfums de Rosine
Scented card
Undated
Bibliothèque nationale de
France, Performing Arts
department, inv. 4-ED-88(17)

CAT. 335
Georges Lepape (1887–1971)
Les Parfums de Rosine
Promotional fan
1910
Paper, wood and metal
Ville de Paris / Bibliothèque
Forney, inv. RES ICO 8008 3
Plano

CAT. 336
Mario Simon
Les Parfums de Rosine
Advertisement for the
perfume *La Rose de Rosine*
c. 1912
Bibliothèque nationale de
France, Performing Arts
department, inv. 4-ED-88(5)

CAT. 337
Mario Simon
Les Parfums de Rosine
Promotional fan
1915
Paper, wood and metal
Palais Galliera–Musée de
la Mode de la Ville de Paris,
inv. GAL1984.61.1

CAT. 338
Les Parfums de Rosine
Advertisement for the
perfume *Borgia*
c. 1916
Agnès Mulon

CAT. 339
Les Parfums de Rosine
Advertising catalogue
Paris, Imprimerie de
Vaugirard, 1917
Agnès Mulon

CAT. 340
Mario Simon
Les Parfums de Rosine
Poster for the perfume
Antinéa
1919
Lithograph and Indian ink
on Holland paper
Grasse, Musée international
de la Parfumerie

CAT. 341
Martine Workshop
Les Parfums de Rosine
Advertisement
c. 1920
Paris, Musée des Arts
décoratifs, UFAC Collection,
1995

CAT. 342
Martine Workshop
Les Parfums de Rosine
Promotional fan
c. 1920
Paper, wood and metal
Paris, Musée des Arts
décoratifs, UFAC Collection,
1995, inv. UF 86-04-29

CAT. 343
Les Parfums de Rosine
Scented card
c. 1920
Paris, library of the Musée des
Arts décoratifs

CAT. 344
Les Parfums de Rosine
Scented card for the perfume
Nuit de Chine
c. 1920
Paris, Musée des Arts
décoratifs

CAT. 345
Les Parfums de Rosine
Scented card for the perfume
Nuit de Chine
c. 1920
Paris, Musée des Arts
décoratifs

CAT. 346
Les Parfums de Rosine
Scented card for the perfume
Nuit de Chine
c. 1920
Agnès Mulon

CAT. 347
Les Parfums de Rosine
Scented card, for the perfume
Toute la forêt
c. 1920
Agnès Mulon

CAT. 348
Les Parfums de Rosine
Advertisement for the
perfume *Le Fruit défendu*
c. 1920
Agnès Mulon

CAT. 349
Les Parfums de Rosine
Bookmark
c. 1920
Agnès Mulon

CAT. 350
Mario Simon
Les Parfums de Rosine
Advertisement for the
perfume *Maharadjah*
1921
Bibliothèque nationale de
France, Performing Arts
department
Inv. 4-ED-88(14)

CAT. 351 [REPR. PP. 3 & 166]
Les Parfums de Rosine
Advertising catalogue
Cannes, Imprimerie Robaudy,
1923
Agnès Mulon

CAT. 352
Mario Simon
Les Parfums de Rosine
Advertisement for the
perfume *Nuit de Chine*
1923
Bibliothèque nationale de
France, Performing Arts
department, inv. 4-ED-88(7)

CAT. 353
Kh. Nijam Nulle
Les Parfums de Rosine
Poster for the perfume
Maharadjah
1927
Linocut or woodcut
Grasse, Musée international
de la Parfumerie, inv. 96441

Archive films

An artistic education

CAT. 354
Portrait of Paul Poiret
Document GP archives –
Collection Pathé

CAT. 355
Actualité féminine ('At the
Club de la Publicité, Paul
Poiret presents his "cruise"
designs')
Document GP archives –
Collection Pathé

**Dressing dancers and
actresses for the city
and the stage**

CAT. 356
Isadora Duncan dancing at
a garden party
c. 1910, silent
Choreographed and
performed by Isadora Duncan
Director unknown
Document from the
collections of the multimedia
library at the Centre national
de la danse, Association
Cinémathèque de la danse
collection

CAT. 357
Actualité féminine
('Les Ballets Nyota Inyoka,
Cortège [inspired by Thebes]')
Document GP archives –
Collection Pathé

CAT. 358
Tamara Karsavina doing
dance practice
c. 1924
Archive film edited for the
documentary *The Glory of the
Kirov* (1995)

Biblio-graphy

Primary sources

DIOR, Christian, *Christian Dior & moi*, Paris: Amiot-Dumont, 1956

GROULT, Benoîte, GROULT, Flora, *Diary in Duo* (1962), trans. Humphrey Hare, New York: Appleton-Century, 1965

GROULT, Flora, *Tout le plaisir des jours est dans leur matinée*, Paris: Plon, 1985

IRIBE, Paul, *Les Robes de Paul Poiret racontées par Paul Iribe*, Paris: Paul Poiret, 1908

LEPAPE, Georges, *Les choses de Paul Poiret vues par Georges Lepape*, Paris: Paul Poiret, 1911

OBERLÉ, Jean, *La vie d'artiste*, Paris: Éditions Denoël, 1957

POIRET, Paul, *Pan: Annuaire du luxe à Paris, an 1928*, Paris: Devambez, 1927

POIRET, Paul, VOIROL, Sébastien, ALIX, Marie, *107 recettes ou curiosités culinaires recueillies par Paul Poiret, président honoraire du club des Purs Cent, suivies de quelques pages de publicité gratuite*, Paris: H. Jonquières, 1928

POIRET, Paul, *En habillant l'époque*, Paris: Grasset, 1930

POIRET, Paul, VAN DONGEN, Kees, *Deauville*, Paris: M-P. Trémois, 1931

POIRET, Paul, *Revenez-y*, Paris: Gallimard, 1932

POIRET, Paul, *Art et Phynance*, Paris: Éditions Lutétia, 1934

SCHIAPARELLI, Elsa, *Shocking Life*, New York: Dutton, 1954

Secondary sources

General works

BACHOLLET, Raymond, BORDET, Daniel, LELIEUR, Anne-Claude, *Paul Iribe*, Paris: Éditions Denoël, 1982

BAUDOT, François, *Poiret: Fashion Memoir*, London: Thames & Hudson, 1997

BEATON, Cecil, *The Glass of Fashion*, Garden City, NY: Doubleday, 1954

BEN LAKHDAR, Khémaïs, *L'Appropriation culturelle. Histoire, domination et création: aux origines d'un pillage occidental*, Paris: Stock, 2024

CAMILLI, Anne, MARTIN-HATTEMBERG, Jean-Marie, *Le flacon en majesté: esprit d'une collection*, Paris, Clichy: Éditions Desgrandchamps, Éditions Marie B, 2020

CLOAREC, Françoise, *J'ai un tel désir. Marie Laurencin et Nicole Groult*, Paris: Stock, 2018

DAVIS, Mary E., *Classic Chic: Music, Fashion and Modernism*, Berkeley, CA & London: University of California Press, 2008

DESLANDRES, Yvonne, *Poiret: Paul Poiret, 1879–1944*, New York: Rizzoli, 1987

DESLANDRES, Yvonne, MÜLLER, Florence, *Histoire de la mode au XXe siècle*, Paris: Somogy, 1986

EVANS, Caroline, BASARAN, Betül, RADO, Mei Mei, CLARCK, Judith, ROMANO, Alexis, DEGREGORIO, William, DOROGOVA, Waleria, RAMPHAL, Christine, *An Eye for Couture: A Collector's Exploration of 20th Century Fashion*, London: Prestel, 2024

FARGUE, Léon-Paul, *Portraits de famille*, Fontfroide-le-Haut: Fata Morgana, 1987

LEPAPE, Claude, DEFERT, Thierry, *From the Ballets Russes to Vogue: The Art of Georges Lepape*, trans. Jane Brenton, London: Thames & Hudson; New York: Vendôme Press, 1984

MACKRELL, Alice, *Paul Poiret*, London: B.T. Batsford, 1990

MAYER LEFKOWITH, Christie, *The Art of Perfume: Discovering and Collecting Perfume Bottles*, London & New York: Thames & Hudson, 1994

MAYER LEFKOWITH, Christie, *Paul Poiret and his Rosine Perfumes*, New York: Stylissimo, 2007

OLIVIER, Fernande, *Picasso and His Friends* (1945), trans. Jane Miller, New York: Appleton-Century, 1965

PARKINS, ILYA, *Poiret, Dior and Schiaparelli: Fashion, Femininity and Modernity*, London & New York: Berg, 2012

SOZZANI, Carla, BUCHER, Antoine, PECORARI, Marco, *Alaïa and Poiret: Exploring Fashion Heritage*, Paris: Fondation Azzedine Alaïa, 2021

TROY, Nancy J., *Couture Culture: A Study in Modern Art and Fashion*, Cambridge, MA: MIT Press, 2003

VÖLKER, Angela, *Textiles of the Wiener Werkstätte, 1910–1932*, New York: Rizzoli, 1994

WHITE, Palmer, *Poiret*, New York: C. N. Potter; London: Studio Vista, 1973

Exhibition catalogues

La Collection particulière de M. Paul Poiret, exh. cat., Paris: Galerie Barbazanges (26 April–12 May 1923), Paris: Devambez, 1923

Poiret le magnifique, exh. cat., Paris: Musée Jacquemart-André (17 January–17 April 1974), Paris: Institut de France, 1974

Dufy–Poiret, exh. cat., Paris: Galerie Fanny Guillon-Laffaille (24 September–27 November 1998), London Neffe-Degandt (February–March 1999), Paris & London, 1998

Touches d'exotisme, XIVe–XXe siècles, exh. cat., Paris:

Musée de la Mode et du Textile (24 January 1998–late May 1999), Paris: Union Centrale des Arts Décoratifs, 1998

Raoul Dufy. Tissus et créations, exh. cat., Troyes: Musée d'Art Moderne (28 February–7 June 2015), Carcassonne: Musée des Beaux-Arts (3 July–3 October 2015), Ghent: Snoeck, 2015

ARZALLUZ, Miren, SAILLARD, Olivier, *Azzedine Alaïa, couturier collectionneur*, exh. cat., Paris: Palais Galliera (27 September 2023–21 January 2024), Paris: Paris Musées, 2023

AUCLAIR, Mathias, BARBEDETTE, Sarah, BARSACQ, Stéphane (eds.), *Bakst: des ballets russes à la haute couture*, exh. cat., Paris: Palais Garnier, Bibliothèque-Musée de l'Opéra (22 November 2016–5 March 2017), Paris: Albin Michel, BNF Éditions, Opéra National de Paris, AROP, les Amis de l'Opéra, 2016

CALAFAT, Marie-Charlotte, SAMUEL, Aurélie (eds.), *Fashion folklore. Costumes populaires et haute couture*, exh. cat., Marseille: Mucem, (12 July–6 November 2023), Paris: Gallimard, 2023

GADY, Bénédicte (ed.), *Le dessin sans réserve. Collections du musée des Arts décoratifs*, exh. cat., Paris: Musée des Arts décoratifs (planned 26 March–19 July 2020, presented 23 June 2020–31 January 2021), Paris, 2020

GALLAIS, Jean-Marie, CALAFAT, Marie-Charlotte (eds.), *Folklore: Artistes et folkloristes, une histoire croisée*, exh. cat., Metz: Centre Pompidou Metz (21 March–21 September 2020), Marseille: Mucem (20 October 2020–22 February 2021), Paris: La Découverte, 2020

GARNIER, Guillaume (ed.), *Paul Poiret et Nicole Groult. Maîtres de la Mode Art déco*, exh. cat., Paris: Palais Galliera (5 July–12 October 1986), Paris: Paris Musées, 1986

KODA, Harold, BOLTON, Andrew, *Poiret: King of Fashion*, exh. cat., New York: Metropolitan Museum of Art (9 May–5 August 2007), New Haven, CT: Yale University Press; New York: Metropolitan Museum of Art, 2007

NOEVER, Peter, DAVIGNON, Étienne, MOMMENS, Anne (eds.), *Yearning for Beauty: The Wiener Werkstätte and the Stoclet House*, exh. cat., Brussels: Palais des Beaux-Arts (17 February–28 May 2006), Vienna: MAK; Ostfildern: Hatje Cantz, 2006

PARPOIL, Catherine, COUDREC, Gregory (eds.), *Paul Poiret, couturier-parfumeur*, exh. cat., Grasse: Musée International de la Parfumerie (7 June–30 September 2013), Paris: Somogy Éditions d'Art; Grasse: Musée International de la Parfumerie, 2013

SAILLARD, Olivier, MAURIES, Patrick, LACROIX, Christian, *Christian Lacroix: Histoires de mode*, exh. cat., Paris: Musée de la Mode et du Textile (8 November 2007–20 April 2008), Paris: Les Arts Décoratifs, 2007

SCHULMANN, Didier (ed.), *Le Paris de Dufy / Dufy's Paris*, exh. cat., Paris: Musée de Montmartre (5 March–12 September 2021), Paris: In Fine Éditions d'Art, 2021

SINGER, Juliette (ed.), *Le Paris de la modernité, 1905–1925*, exh. cat., Paris: Petit Palais–Musée des Beaux-Arts de la Ville de Paris (14 November 2023–14 April 2024), Paris: Paris Musées, 2023

Academic publications

ARZATIAN, Céline G., *Mode et cinéma en France de 1896 à 1930*, doctoral thesis in Film and Audiovisual Studies, supervised by Laurent Véray, Paris: Université Sorbonne Nouvelle, 7 February 2013

LAURENT, Stéphane (ed.), *Une émergence du design: France, 20e siècle*, Paris: HiCSA, 2019

PILLIERE, Caroline, *Etude et conservation-restauration d'un costume de danse dessiné par Natalia Gontcharova à l'époque des Ballets russes, Evaluation de la photosensibilité des soies peintes*, diploma in Textile Restoration and Heritage, supervised by Cécile Argenton, Paris: Institut National du Patrimoine, 2019

Auction catalogues

La Créations en Liberté. Univers de Paul et Denise Poiret, 1905–1928 (2 vols), Piasa, Paris, 10 & 11 May 2005

Index

Page numbers in *Italics* refer to illustrations.

A

Abrams, Leon
224
Alaïa, Azzedine
15, 21, 132, 135,
194, 195, 196, 200,
201, *216*
Alix, Marie
171, *172, 173,*
225
Alméras, Henri
167, *168,* 169
Amiot, Camille
73
André, Adeline
200, 201, *213*
Andréani, Henri
223
Apollinaire, Guillaume
29, 178, 183, 189,
191, 222
Arletty (Léonie Bathiat)
223
Arnoux, Guy
178
Asquith, Emma Alice
Margaret, Countess of
Oxford and Asquith
162, 220
Asquith, Herbert Henry
162

B

Babin, Gustave
88, 175, *179*
Bach, Johann Sebastian
189, 221
Badovici, Jean
155
Bailby, Léon
162
Bakst, Léon
30, 32, 93, 221
Barbazanges, Henri Jean
177, 186, 187, 221
Barbier, George
132
Bartet, Julia
31
Bartram, Nikolai
149, 152
Baur, Harry (Henri Marie
Rodolphe)
136
Beaton, Cecil
132
Beethoven, Ludwig van
189, 221
Belperron, Suzanne
53
Ben Lakhdar, Khémaïs
77
Bernard, Paul
162
Bernard, Raymond
223
Bernhardt, Sarah
31, 132, 224
Bernheim, Michel
161, 226
Bertillon, Alphonse
37
Bertin, Rose
134
Besnard, Albert
29
Bibesco, Jeanne
162
Blareau, Richard
60-61
Bloch, René Marcel
224, 225
Bloch, Roger Julien
224, 225
Blondeau, Étienne
125

Blum, Georges
225
Boccherini, Luigi
189, 221
Boivin, Jeanne
21, 226
Boivin, René
53, 220
Boivin Sonrel, Germaine
53
Boldini, Giovanni
188
Bonafé, Pépa
161
Bongard, Germaine
21, 113, 220
Bongard, Louis
220
Bonnat, Léon
29, 175
Bonney, Thérèse
108, 109, *154,*
155, *191*
Boucher, François
131
Bouguereau, William
175
Boulet, Denise see
Poiret, Denise
Boussingault, Jean-Louis
178, *187*
Boutet de Monvel,
Bernard
221, *221,* 224
Brancusi, Constantin
139, *180*
Breerette, Geneviève
132, 136
Breslauer, Marianne
37
Breton, André
177
Buffet-Picabia, Gabriële
49, 223

C

Cain, Julien
132
Calm, Lotte
135
Camoin, Charles
184
Carolus-Duran (Charles
Auguste Émile Durant)
175
Caryathis (Élisabeth
Toulemont)
185, 223
Castelbajac, Jean-
Charles de
200, 201, *207*
Chanel, Coco (Gabrielle
Chasnel)
134
Charensol, Georges
135, 136
Chériane (Chérie-Anne
Fargue)
187
Chéruit, Louise
21, 220
Cižek, Franz
149
Clair, René
224
Clairin, Georges
175
Cocteau, Jean
53, 183, 189,
200, 225, 226
Colette (Sidonie Gabrielle
Colette)
21, 31, 162, 225
Constant, Benjamin
29
Constantini, Martiale
148

Cornu, Paul
37, 81
Corot, Camille
177
Cottet, Charles
175
Couperin, François
189, 221
Cousin, Françoise
77
Cron, Michel
60-61
Croze, Austin de
224
Curtiz, Michael
224, 225

D

Damia (Louise Marie
Damien)
178
Damita, Lili
224, 225
Daquin, Louis-Claude
221
David, Fernand
142, 224
Delaroche, Paul-Charles
34
Delarue-Mardrus, Lucie
29, 35
Delaunay, Robert
222
Delbo, Pierre
169
Delphi
38, 59, *139, 168,*
181, 225
Derain, André
15, *20,* 53, *177,*
178, *186,* 220, 222,
225
Deslandres, Yvonne
14, 105, 132
Diaghilev, Sergei
85, 93, 221
Diamant-Berger, Henri
225
Dior, Christian
15, 19, 21, 189,
191, *192,* 195, 200,
201, *211*
Domergue, Jean-Gabriel
178
Dongen, Kees van
15, 53, *152,* 178,
181, 184, 187, 222,
225
Doucet, Jacques
26, 29, 93, 134
143, 162, 175, 177,
189, 220
Drapier, Gabrielle
148, 155
Dreyfus, Alfred
220
Dufrène, Maurice
226
Dufy, Raoul
15, 30, 31, 34,
38, 73, 89, 132,
142, 145, 155, *168,*
178, *181,* 183, *186,*
189, *191,* 221, 222,
224, 225
Dullin, Charles
178
Dumas, Paul
155
Dumont, Marcel
223
Duncan, Isadora
15, 222
Dunoyer de Segonzac,
André
15, 26, 178, 221,
224, 225

E

El Glaoui, Thamis
31
Epstein, Jean
224
Erté (Romain de Tirtoff)
31, 81, 101, 222

F

Faramond, Maurice de
31, 221
Fargue, Léon-Paul
14, 24
Fath, Jacques
50, 132
Fau, Pierre
225
Fauconnet, Guy-Pierre
142, 143, 145,
155, 221, 223
Ferrare, Marthe
223
Ferry, Jules
145, 146
Feure, Georges de
131
Feyder, Jacques
224
Fiorillo, Federigo
221
Flanner, Janet
45
Fokin, Mikhail
221
Fossey, Gaston
225
Foujita, Tsuguharu
182, 225
Frondaie, Michelle
63, *227*

G

Gabriel, Ange-Jacques
221
Galland, Antoine
29
Galliano, John
14, 200, 201, *211*
Garnier, Guillaume
19, 134
Gastoldi, Giovanni
Giacomo
222
Gérard, François
29
Géry, Alice
178
Gidding, J. M.
42
Gignoux, Régis
223
Goncharova, Natalia
185, 223
Goursat, Victor
25, 256
Grange, Jacques
132
Grès, Alix
134, 195
Groult, André
53, 54, 220
Groult, Benoîte
53, 54
Groult, Flora
53, 54
Groult, Nicole
19, 21, 53, 54, 55,
55, 56, 57, 134,
220, 221
Guimard, Hector
131

H

Harald Hansen, Henny
131
Harlingue, Albert
50
Haydn, Joseph
189, 221
Hays, Blanche
49
Hoffmann, Josef
121, 135, 142,
146, 221
Horta, Victor
131
Houry, Marcelle
182, 183

I

Inyoka, Nyota
21, 223
Iribe, Paul
15, 53, 68, 72,
73, 76, 131, 132,
134, 135, 175, 178,
189, 200, 221

J

Jallat, Agnès
15, 150, 151,
Jaurès, Jean
222
Jesser, Hilda
135
Jullian, Philippe
141

K

Kahnweiler, Daniel-
Henry
178
Kandinsky, Vassily
32
Kars, Georges
187
Karsavina, Tamara
92, 93, 222
Kiss, Paul
122, 123, 125,
234
Klee, Paul
149
Köhler, Mela
135
Krull, Germaine
27

L

La Fontaine, Jean de
14, 24, 136, 162,
226
Lacroix, Christian
14, 133, 134, 137,
200, 201, 206
Lagerfeld, Karl
136, 200, 201,
203
Laguionie, Pierre
161
Lanvin, Jeanne
37, 117, 134, 195
Laparcerie, Cora
32
Largillière, Nicolas de
177
Lartigue, Jacques Henri
54, 131
Lauren, Ralph
143
Laurencin, Marie
57, 221, 222, 225
Lebel, Jacques
178

Leblanc, Georgette
224
Leclair, Jean-Marie
221
Léger, Fernand
53
Leloir, Maurice
131
Lemonnier, Élisa
146
Léon, Auguste
112
Léon, Paul
142, 224
Lepape, Georges
15, 35, 46, 77,
132, 134, 135, 136,
178, 193, 196, 221
Leroy, Isidore
155
Lesage, François
51, 132
L'Herbier, Marcel
224
Lhuer, Victor
15, 80, 81
Likarz-Strauss, Maria
135
Lipnitzki, Boris
37, 43, 128, 147,
155, 160, 184
Lisenko, Natalya
224
Lyautey, Hubert
31

M

Mackintosh, Charles
Rennie
131
Maitrepierre, Alphonse
14, 200, 201, 217
Mallet-Stevens, Robert
159, 223
Man Ray (Emmanuel
Radnitsky)
37, 48, 49, 223
Manuel, Henri
37, 88, 96, 116,
175, 179, 223
Manzana-Pissarro,
Georges (Georges Henri
Pissarro)
93
Marchal, Arlette
224
Marcovitch, Emile
160
Mardrus,
Joseph-Charles
29, 34, 162, 226
Margiela, Martin
195, 200, 201,
208
Margueritte, Victor
223
Mariaud, Robert
226
Marquet, Albert
225
Marty, André Édouard
132, 190, 226
Mary, André
222
Matisse, Amélie
53
Matisse, Henri
149, 177, 186,
225
Maurice, brothers
93
Max, Édouard de
31, 221, 223
Meisel, Steven
137
Mercanton, Louis
224

Mérode, Cléo de
(Cléopâtre-Diane de
Mérode)
132
Meyer, Adolf de
37
Millerand, Alexandre
222
Milowanoff, Sandra
224
Modigliani, Amedeo
186, 225
Monnot, brothers
73, 93, 105
Monnot, Henri
93
Morancé, Albert
155
Moreau, Luc-Albert
178
Moser, Koloman
121
Mozart, Wolfgang
Amadeus
189, 221
Mucha, Alphonse
131, 132
Müller, Florence
129
Muller, Henry
26

N

Nattier, Jean-Marc
177
Naudin, Bernard
178, 189, 221,
222, 222, 223
Nepo, Arik
50
Newton, Helmut
60-61
Nijinsky, Vaslav
221

O

O'Doye, Paul
54
Oberlé, Jean
26, 109, 189
Olivier, Fernande
178, 189
Oury, Gérard
183

P

Paquin, Jeanne
37, 69, 131
Peche, Dagobert
121, 234
Pereire, Édouard
225
Perugia, André
81, 223
Picabia, Francis
49
Picasso, Pablo
167, 177, 178,
189, 222, 225
Piguet, Robert
189, 223
Plessy, Armand du
223
Poincaré, Raymond
222
Poiret, Amable Jeanne
see Boivin, Jeanne
Poiret, Colin
21, 113, 161,
167, 222, 226,
233
Poiret, Denis Auguste
220

Poiret, Denise
15, 19, 21, 32, 35,
41, 43, 53, 59, 59,
60-61, 69, 77, 84,
85, 89, 96, 97, 100,
101, 105, 109, 132,
134, 139, 171, 175,
180, 184, 195, 197,
220, 221, 223, 224,
225
Poiret, Jeanne Louise
Germaine see Bongard,
Germaine
Poiret, Louise (born
Heinrich)
21, 171, 220
Poiret, Louise Eugénie
21, 220
Poiret, Martine
21, 113, 147, 159,
221, 233
Poiret, Pauline Marine
see Groult, Nicole
Poiret, Perrine
113, 184, 222
Poiret, Rosine
113, 167, 220,
222, 231
Popescu, Elvira
159, 25
Princess Lucien Murat
(Marie de Rohan-Chabot)
178, 223
Proust, Marcel
32
Purviance, Edna
225

Q

Quénioux, Gaston
149

R

Rambova, Natacha
223
Rameau, Jean-Philippe
189, 221
Regnard, Jean-François
178
Reutlinger, Léopold-Émile
37
Richepin, Jacques
29, 31, 32, 101,
222
Richepin, Jean
101
Richepin, Tiarko
32
Rinhart, George
43
Rimsky-Korsakov, Nikolaï
221
Rodrigue, Madeleine
224
Rockline, Vera
187
Rochas, Marcel
167, 200, 201,
212
Rochegrosse, Georges-
Antoine
29
Ronzel, Jean-Pierre
194
Rossignol, Muolle
185
Rothschild, Baron
Edmond de
178
Rothschild, Baroness
Robert de (born Gabrielle
Beer)
178
Rousseau, Henri
109

Rousselin, Gabrielle see
Drapier, Gabrielle
Ruhle, Ambroise
146
Ruty, Alice
146

S

Sachs, Maurice
15, 178
Saint George Perrot, Paul
162
Salmon, André
177, 189, 222,
223
Sardou, Victorien
31
Schaller, Maurice
167
Schaschl, Reni
135
Schiaparelli, Elsa
14, 19, 21, 37, 48,
49, 50, 51, 161, 195,
200
Schiaparelli, Giovanni
p. 49
Schulmann, Léon
224
Schumann, Robert
189, 221
Schwab, Roger
225
Segonzac, Dunoyer de
15, 26, 178, 221,
224, 225
Sérusier, Marguerite
142, 149, 221
Sérusier, Paul
32, 142
Simon, Mario
4
Spinelly, Andrée
p.21, 65, 101, 143,
168, 223
Steichen, Edward
37
Steinlen, Théophile
Alexandre
132
Süe, Louis
55, 81, 175, 178
Suréda, André
30
Survage, Léopold
53

T

Tharaud, Jean
31
Tharaud, Jérôme
31
Theyskens, Olivier
200, 201, 212
Tzara, Tristan
49

U

Utrillo, Maurice
225

V

Valentino, Rudolph
223
Van de Velde, Henry
131, 135
Van Noten, Dries
200, 201, 214
Vassilieff, Marie
169, 187
Vigoureux, Pierre
224

Vionnet, Madeleine
37, 117, 134, 195
Vlaminck, Maurice de
177, 178, 220
Vogel, Lucien
190, 196, 222,
226, 226
Voisin, Gabriel
223
Volkoff, Alexandre
224

W

Wärndorfer, Fritz
121, 146
Wendt de Kerlor,
Wilhelm de
49
Wimmer-Wisgrill, Eduard
Josef
135
Woolman Chase, Edna
45
Worth, Charles Frederick
26, 177
Worth, Gaston
171, 177, 220
Worth, Jacques
37
Worth, Jean Philippe
175, 177, 220

Z

Zamora, José de
31, 33, 81, 222
Zinkeisen, Anna
164
Zuckerkandl, Berta
121

This book was published on the occasion of the exhibition 'Paul Poiret. La mode est une fête' at the Musée des Arts décoratifs, Paris, from 25 June 2025 to 11 January 2026.

The exhibition was conceived by Les Arts Décoratifs and produced with the support of the Friends of the Musée des Arts Décoratifs and GRoW @ Annenberg.

With the support of Krystyna Campbell-Pretty and her family, as well as Hubert and Mireille Goldschmidt.

With the generous help of Christine and Stephen A. Schwarzman for the restoration of pieces from the Fashion and Textiles department of the Musée des Arts décoratifs presented in this exhibition.

With thanks to the Cinémathèque Française.

LA CINÉMATHÈQUE FRANÇAISE

Les Arts décoratifs

Lionel Sauvage
President

Camille Herody
Interim general director

Bénédicte Gady
Interim director of the Musée des Arts décoratifs and the Musée Nissim de Camondo

Yvon Figueras
Director of international development and production

Olivier Hassler
Director of communication

Nathalie Coulon
Director of patronage and development

Exhibition

Curators

Marie-Sophie Carron de la Carrière
Curator, Musée des Arts décoratifs, collection manager for Fashion and Textiles from 1800 to 1946

Assisted by
Marie-Pierre Ribère
Assistant curator, Musée des Arts décoratifs, Fashion and Textiles collection from 1800 to 1946
and Astrid Novembre,
exhibitions assistant

Production

Stéphane Perl
Head of production

Claire Berthet
Charlotte Hamel
Project managers

Anette Lenz
Art direction

Atelier Anette Lenz
Graphic design, motion design with Romain Graille, assisted by Louis Baroni

Paf atelier, Christopher Dessus
Exhibition design

Catalogue

Atelier Anette Lenz
Graphic design and layout of the original edition

Musée des Arts décoratifs

Catherine Ojalvo
Head of publishing and images

Éditions Gallimard

Nathalie Bailleux
Editorial director, illustrated books

Astrid Bargeton
Editor

Adèle Ehlinger
Editorial assistant

Natércia Pauty
Departmental assistant

Marion Bello
Proofreader

Anne Lagarrigue
Art direction

Pascal Guédin
Production controller

Béatrice Bourgerie
Fabricante

Mathilde Barrois
assisted by
Coline Briand
Coeditions

Béatrice Foti
assisted by Laetitia Copin
Press office

Acknowledgements

We are extremely grateful to all the institutions, designers, galleries, heritage funds and archives, libraries, agencies and collectors whose generous loans made this exhibition possible:

Agnès Mulon

Alphonse Maitrepierre

Avignon, Musée Angladon–Jacques Doucet Collection: Lauren Laz

Bayonne, Musée Bonnat-Helleu, Musée des Beaux-Arts: Barthélémy Etchegoyen-Glama, Hélène Ferron

Biot, Musée national Fernand Léger: Anne Dopffer

Boulogne-Billancourt, Musée des Années Trente / MA-30: Pierre-Christophe Baguet, Gabrielle Soullier

Jean-Charles de Castelbajac

Chartres, Musée des Beaux-Arts: Jean-Pierre Gorges, Grégoire Hallé

Chelles, Musée archéologique Alfred Bonno: Brice Rabaste, Christian Charamond

Alain Bras Collection

Claude Bernès Collection

Maison Vlaminck Endowment Fund Collection

Louis Vuitton Collection: Aurélie Samuel, director of the department of art, culture and heritage Coline Manesse, Bleue-Marine Massard

Private collection, courtesy Comité Jacqueline Marval, Paris: Camille Roux dit Buisson, Raphaël Roux dit Buisson

Thomas Fritsch Collection, Paris

Grasse, Fragonard Parfumeur: Agnès Costa, Charlotte Urbain, Marion Berton

Grasse, Musée international de la Parfumerie: Laure Decomble

Grenoble, Musée de Grenoble: Sébastien Gokalp

Librairie Diktats / Diktats Bookstore: Antoine Bucher, Nicolas Montagne

Musée départemental Albert-Kahn – Département des Hauts-de-Seine: Georges Siffredi, Nathalie Doury

Neuilly-sur-Seine, GP archives – Pathé Collection

New York, The Metropolitan Museum of Art: Max Hollein

Pantin, Médiathèque du Centre national de la Danse, Fonds Association Cinémathèque de la Danse: Catherine Tsekenis, Laurent Sebillotte

Paris, Bibliothèque Forney: Lucile Trunel

Paris, Bibliothèque historique de la Ville de Paris: Emmanuelle Toulet, director

Paris, Bibliothèque nationale de France, department of performance arts and department of prints and photography: Gilles Pécout, Philippe Lonné, Joël Huthwohl, Sylvie Aubenas

Paris, Centre Pompidou–Musée national d'art moderne, Centre de création industrielle: Xavier Rey

Paris, Cité de l'Architecture et du Patrimoine / Archives d'architecture contemporaine

Santiago (Chile), Fundación Museo de la Moda: Jorge Juan Yarur Bascuñan

Paris, Fondation Azzedine Alaïa

Paris, Galerie Jacques Lacoste

Paris, Galerie Roger-Viollet: Gilles Taquet, director

Paris, Cinémathèque Française: Costa-Gavras, president and Frédéric Bonnaud, general director

Paris, Mobilier National: Hervé Lemoine

Paris, Musée d'Art Moderne de Paris: Fabrice Hergott

Paris, Musée Carnavalet – Histoire de Paris: Carine Rolland, Valérie Guillaume

Paris, Musée d'Orsay: Sylvain Amic

Paris, Palais Galliera–Musée de la Mode de la Ville de Paris: Carine Rolland, Miren Arzalluz, Laurent Cotta, Sophie Grossiord, Marie-Laure Gutton

Pau, Musée des Beaux-Arts: François Bayrou, Fabien Leclerc

Quimper, Musée des Beaux-Arts: Guillaume Ambroise

Sabine Rang des Adrets

Saint-Germain-en-Laye, Musée départemental Maurice Denis: Pierre Bédier, Marie-Aline Charier

Tokyo, Miyake Design Studio

Versailles, Osmothèque, Conservatoire international des parfums: Thomas Fontaine, president

And all those who wished to remain anonymous.

Marie-Sophie Carron de la Carrière would like to express her deepest thanks to everyone who contributed to the preparation of the exhibition and the book that accompanies it:

Anna Antonova
Miren Arzalluz
Johan Berlet
Andrew Bolton
Christian Briend
Antoine Bucher
Ludovic Carpuat
Jean Cottin
Mary E. Davis
Sophie Fontanel
Olivier Gabet
Steeve Gallizia
Claudine Grammont
Sophie Grossiord
Tatiana Kaboulova
Alma Huet Lévy
Alexandra Jaffré
Sophie Krebs
Christian Lacroix
Marie-Pierre Lambelin
Laurent Le Bon
Christine Macel
Daniel Marchesseau
Sophie-Caroline de Margerie
Jacqueline Munck
Marion Neveu
Christine Peltre
Emmanuel Pernoud
Cécile Pichon-Bonin
Diane Poirier
Colombe Pringle
Éric Pujalet-Plaà
Sébastien Quéquet
Assia Quesnel
Xavier Rey
Olivier Saillard
Estelle Savoye
Jean Solanet
Geneviève Taillade
Anne Théry
Christopher Thompson
Danièle Thompson
Jean-Charles Virmaux
Michi Yamaguchi

Finally, at les Arts décoratifs, we would like to thank:

The curators, especially Bénédicte Gady, Sonia Aubès, Catherine Gouedo, Marion Neveu, Sébastien Quéquet; Amélie Gastaut, Axelle Baroin, Romain Condamine, Christelle Di Giovanni; Anne Monier, Raphaèle Billé, Marie-Lou Canovas, Mathurin Jonchères, Lisa Jousset-Avi, Ariane James-Sarazin, Sophie Motsch; Sophie Lemahieu, Éric Pujalet-Plaà; Hélène Renaudin; Mathieu Rousset-Perrier;

The library and document archives, especially Anne-Laure Charrier-Ranoux, Emmanuelle Beuvin, Karine Bomel, Laure Haberschill, Gwenhael Cavanna-Kernemp, Marie Kersebet, Mario Nlonza, Carole Pilarz, Freddy Serva, Sully Severien, Véronique Sevestre, Antony Warint, Marie Watier;

The collections department, especially Florence Bertin, Cécile Huguet-Broquet, and Giulia Nardelli; For conservation and restoration of works: Emmanuelle Garcin with the collaboration of Déborah Panaget, Nataly Herrera, Violaine Blaise, Ségolène Bonnet, Cécile Argenton, Agathe Strouk, Émilie Enard, Bathilde Grenier, Thalia Bouzid, Claire Musso, Naomi Kuperholc, and Cécilia Aguirre; For coordination and exhibitions: Anne-Gaëlle Dufour and Stéphanie Wahli with the collaboration of Lila Fournier, Garance Lapaire, Anna Rinzo, Rabia Sadiq and Myriam Teissier;

The department of international development and production, especially Claire Berthet and Charlotte Hamel;

The inventory department, especially Christophe Heer and Louise Marx;

The department of publishing and images, especially Catherine Ojalvo, Amélie Segonds, Christophe Dellière, Ève Briend and Léa Krief;

The department of communications, especially Olivier Hassler, Guillaume Del Rio, Laure Godini, Sarah Liebelin-Manfredi, Anne-Cécile Lourenço and Isabelle Mendoza;

The visitor services department, especially Marguerite Héliot;

The department of patronage and development, especially Mélite de Foucaud and Nina Vigneron;

The department of finance and administration, especially Vivianne Besombes and Christine Etting;

The department of buildings and security, especially Pascale Guigou and Gino Anoumantou;

And in the museums department, Liliia Polshcha and Xavier Montagnon.

Picture credits

Back cover
Based on a design by Anette Lenz, after Lumière NY,
Mademoiselle Spinelly dressed by Paul Poiret, 1919-1920,
gelatine-silver print. Paris, Musée des Arts décoratifs [CAT. 219, P. 65]

Opening pages
p. 1: Martine Workshop, wallpaper, c. 1912, brushed texture on
cylinder-printed ground on continuous paper. Paris, Musée des
Arts décoratifs, purchased, 2005, inv. 2005.37.14 (coloured detail)
p. 2: *Joséphine* evening dress, 1907. Paris, Musée des Arts
décoratifs (coloured detail) [CAT. 2, P. 71]
p. 3: 'Les Parfums de Rosine', advertising catalogue, 1923.
Agnès Mulon Collection (coloured detail) [CAT. 351, P. 166]
p. 4: Mario Simon, Les Parfums de Rosine, advertisement for the
perfume *La rose de Rosine*, c. 1912. Paris, Bibliothèque nationale
de France, Performing Arts department (colourised image)
[CAT. 334]
p. 5: Anonymous, photograph of a Paul Poiret design for the legal
registry, 1922, gelatin silver print. Paris, Musée des Arts décoratifs
Archives de la Seine collection, 1940 (colourised image)
p. 6: Paul Iribe, rose studies made for a fabric produced by
Bianchini-Férier for Paul Poiret, c. 1910. Paris, Musée des Arts
décoratifs (colourised image) [CAT. 171]
p. 7: Paul Poiret, woven label with logo, c. 1913, silk, satin, metallic
thread and brass. Paris, Palais Galliera–Musée de la Mode de la
Ville de Paris (colourised image)
pp. 8–9: Graphic design by Anette Lenz. Spot and stripe motif
inspired by Poiret's signature markings on his Louis Vuitton
luggage.

Closing pages
p. 246: Anonymous, Denise and Paul Poiret, before 1910, gelatine-
silver print. Sophie Rang des Adrets collection (colourised image)
pp. 254–255: Quotation from 'Paul Poiret Here to Tell of His Art',
New York Times, 21 September 1913, p. 11.
p. 256: Anonymous, *Der Bart aus Nägeln* [The Beard of Nails],
1931, gelatin silver print. Paris, Musée des Arts décoratifs
(colourised image)

Translated from the French *Paul Poiret, la mode est une fête* by
Bethany Wright

First published in the United Kingdom in 2025 by
Thames & Hudson Ltd, 6–24 Britannia Street, London WC1X 9JD

First published in the United States of America in 2025 by
Thames & Hudson Inc., 500 Fifth Avenue, New York, New York
10110

© 2025 Musée des Arts décoratifs, Paris
Original edition © 2025 Éditions Gallimard, Paris
This edition © 2025 Thames & Hudson Ltd, London

EU Authorized Representative: Interart S.A.R.L.
19 rue Charles Auray, 93500 Pantin, Paris, France
productsafety@thameshudson.co.uk
www.interart.fr

A CIP catalogue record for this book is available from the British
Library

Library of Congress Control Number 2025936053

ISBN 978-0-500-03081-3
01

Printed in Italy

'I AM AN ARTIST,

NOT
A DRESS
MAKER.'

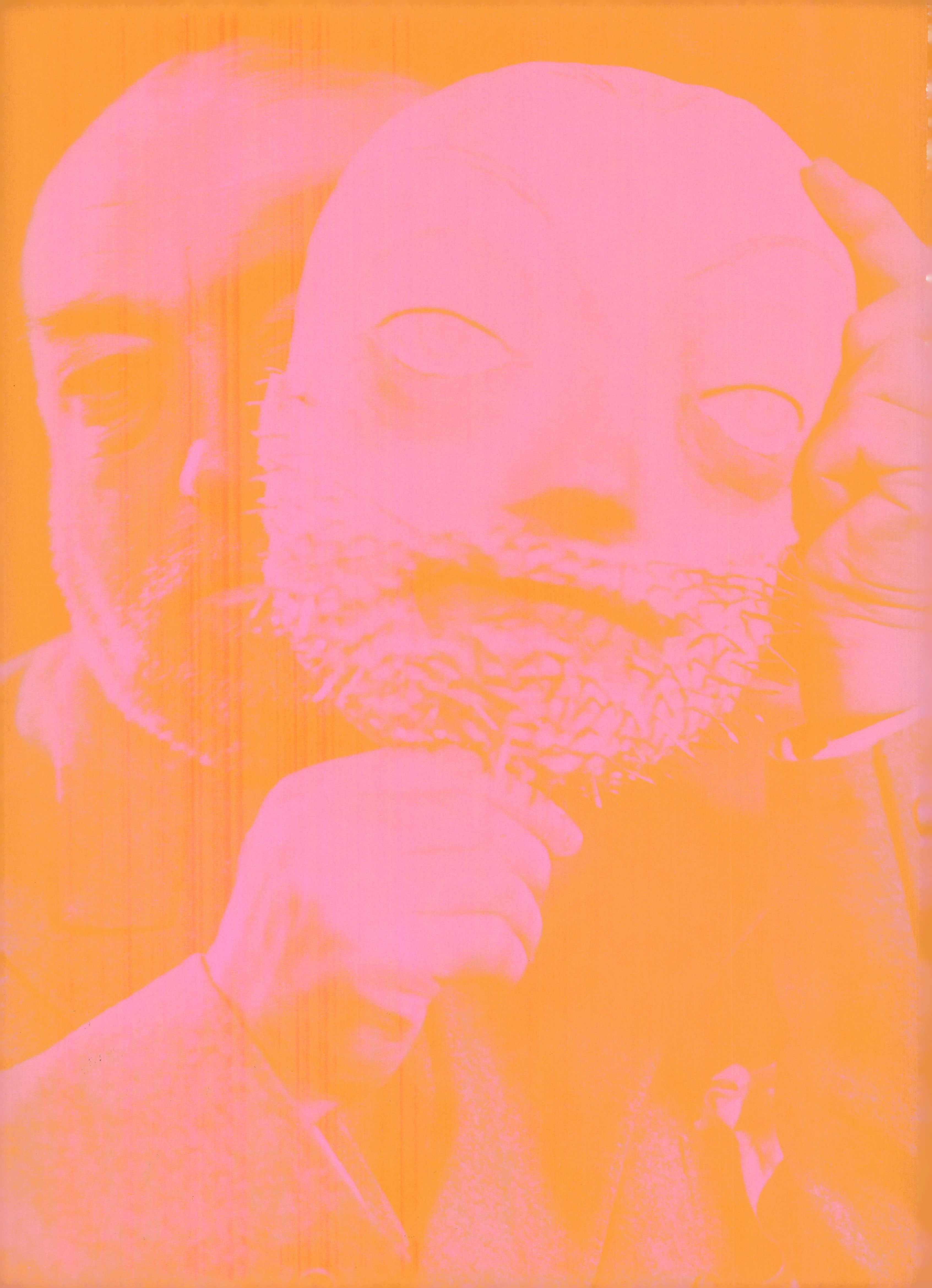